Crime, Punishment, and the Elderly

Hosoi, Tatsuno, and Pratt examine the realities, problems, and backgrounds of crimes committed by elderly people in both Japan and from international perspectives.

Japan's aging population is a commonly known issue globally, and the world looks to Japan to understand the issues that other nations may experience in the future. One such aspect is an increase in crimes committed by the elderly. According to the National Police Agency in Japan, the proportion of elders arrested for committing theft has doubled over the past 10 years. The chapters in this volume look to answer questions around the reason for elder crime, the types of crime and punishment that exists in this cohort of society, and how this increasingly large problem in society can be managed.

This book offers important insights into the societal issues and potential solutions for aging societies around the world. It will be a valuable research reference for scholars of mental health, criminology, population studies, and Asian studies.

Yoko Hosoi is Emeritus Professor of Sociology at Toyo University, Tokyo, Japan.

Bunri Tatsuno is an adjunct researcher in Criminal Justice Policy at Kokushikan University, Japan.

John Pratt is Emeritus Professor of Criminology at the Institute of Criminology, Victoria University of Wellington, New Zealand.

Routledge Studies in Asian Behavioural Sciences

Series Editor: T. Wing Lo, City University of Hong Kong

Empowering Asian Youth through Volunteering
Examples of Theory into Practice
Elaine S. C. Liu

Understanding Crime in Villages-in-the-City in China
A Social and Behavioural Approach
Zhanguo Liu and T. Wing Lo

Creativity in Chinese Contexts
Sociocultural and Dispositional Analyses
Chau-kiu Cheung and Xiaodong Yue

Grief, Bereavement and Meaning Making in Older People
Views from Rural China
Haimin Pan

Psychology in Southeast Asia
Sociocultural, Clinical, and Health Perspectives
Edited by Grant J. Rich, Jas Laile Jaafar, and David Barron

Happiness and Well-Being in Chinese Societies
Cultural Traditions and Psychological Analyses
Cheung Chau-kiu and Yue Xiaodong

Crime, Punishment, and the Elderly
Japan and Beyond
Edited by Yoko Hosoi, Bruni Tatsuno, and John Pratt

For the full list of titles in the series visit: https://www.routledge.com/Routledge-Studies-in-Asian-Behavioural-Sciences/book-series/RABS

Crime, Punishment, and the Elderly

Japan and Beyond

Edited by Yoko Hosoi, Bunri Tatsuno, and John Pratt

Routledge
Taylor & Francis Group
LONDON AND NEW YORK

First published 2024
by Routledge
4 Park Square, Milton Park, Abingdon, Oxon OX14 4RN

and by Routledge
605 Third Avenue, New York, NY 10158

Routledge is an imprint of the Taylor & Francis Group, an informa business

British Library Cataloguing-in-Publication Data
A catalogue record for this book is available from the British Library

Library of Congress Cataloging-in-Publication Data
Names: Hosoi, Yōko, 1942- editor.
Title: Crime, punishment, and the elderly : Japan and beyond / edited by Yoko Hosoi, Bunri Tatsuno, John Pratt.
Description: Abingdon, Oxon ; New York, NY : Routledge, 2024. |
Series: Routledge studies in Asian behavioural sciences | Includes bibliographical references and index. |
Identifiers: LCCN 2023042402 (print) | LCCN 2023042403 (ebook) |
ISBN 9781032669489 (hbk) | ISBN 9781032669472 (pbk) |
ISBN 9781032669519 (ebk)
Subjects: LCSH: Older offenders--Japan. | Crime--Japan.
Classification: LCC HV7113.5 .C75 2024 (print) | LCC HV7113.5 (ebook) |
DDC 364.952--dc23/eng/20231102
LC record available at https://lccn.loc.gov/2023042402
LC ebook record available at https://lccn.loc.gov/2023042403

ISBN: 9781032669489 (hbk)
ISBN: 9781032669472 (pbk)
ISBN: 9781032669519 (ebk)

DOI: 10.4324/9781032669519

Typeset in Galliard
by KnowledgeWorks Global Ltd.

Contents

Preface

For much of the modern period, particularly the post-1945 era, crime problems were centered largely around young men and their attendant conduct, attitude, and values: the 15–24 year age group was the most criminogenic cohort of the population. This meant that criminal justice resources were largely targeted at youthful misdeeds and misbehaviours – "larrikinism" in the 19th century, for example; "Jack-rolling" in the American prohibition era of the 1920s; post-1945, ethnic gangs (as featured in the movie *West Side Story*); followed by accelerating concerns about hooliganism, drug use, political protests, student demonstrations, and so on. At the same time, criminal justice systems were also preoccupied with juvenile and youth offending. Police have developed their Youth Aid systems. Various forms of juvenile justice systems have been at work from around the beginning of the 20th century. Special sanctions for juvenile and youth offenders have been introduced: borstal, detention centres, outward bound activity programmes and so on. Meanwhile, prisons have been organized around the assumption that their inmate populations will be (reasonably) healthy and mobile: hence the absence of elevators in prison design, but lengthy corridors that lead to workshops and dining areas, along with staircases to be climbed up and down on innumerable occasions, as inmates make these journeys. Indeed, by around 1980, prison was thought of in terms of being it being – increasingly – the terrain of young men (Baldock, 1980). They were likely to be competing against each other – often very violently – in the struggle for the meagre resources that prison had to offer, or to establish supremacy within the prison culture. When elderly people – that is, those aged 65+, the age of retirement in many modern societies, thereby marking an important point of differentiation in the human life course – were involved in such competitions, it was usually as victims.

In the early 21st century, however, many of these previous assumptions about crime, crime control, and punishment have had to be revised. This is because of the problem of crime committed by the elderly, although this takes on markedly different forms from society to society. In New Zealand and similar societies, this has mostly involved the discovery/revelations of historic sex crimes, usually committed by fathers or other family members, clergy, school teachers, sports trainers, and others in positions of trust or authority against children in their care and responsibility. But in Hong Kong, crimes by the elderly are more likely to involve drugs and corruption. It is in Japan, though, where crime committed by the elderly shows the greatest expansion and, remarkable though it might seem to an outsider, usually involves petty theft from supermarkets and other outlets: they steal food that is necessary for their day-to-day survival. Indeed, Japan, well known for its supposed reintegration of offenders (Braithwaite, 1989), is at the centre of this reconceptualization of crime, criminogenic groups of the population, and what should be the responses to them.

That Japan should be in this position speaks to a number of factors specific to that society: acute demographic changes, with much smaller family units on the one hand, and a growing elderly population on the other; the inadequacy of the welfare and pension systems (with big corporations the main providers) in Japan; and, rather than the reintegrative nature of this society, the way in which shame operates to exclude, more or less permanently, those who make a mistake, do something wrong, or otherwise let down their families and employers. Those in those positions then find that there is no way back into society: cut off from families, and with no private pension to support them, they are reduced to stealing from supermarkets, etc. to keep themselves going.

As these crime patterns have emerged, so they have led to significant changes in prison populations. In many modern societies, it is the 65+ age group that is the fastest growing prison cohort. As regards Australia, *Old and Inside* (2015, 15) noted that "there has been an 84% increase in older inmates across Australian prisons between 2000 and 2010. The greatest growth has been observed among the most elderly inmates (those aged over 65) whose number rose over 140%." Similarly, the Office of Inspector General of the U.S. Department of Justice (2015, 2) notes that "not only are the numbers of aging inmates increasing, they are generally increasing at a faster rate in older age groups … the number of inmates aged 65 to 69 increased by 41 percent [between 2009 and 2013]; 70 to 74 increased 51 percent; inmates aged 75 to 79 increased 43 percent; and inmates aged 80 and over increased 76 percent." The selection of the 65+ group thus allows more concentrated light to be shed on the pains of being old in prison, rather than a wider and more general study of ageing within it. Typically, this age group may now constitute between three and five per cent of the total prison population. *In Japan, those aged 65+ constitute a remarkable 15 per cent of the prison population there*.

In effect, sections of the prison, despite being designed for youthful, mobile, and potentially aggressive inmates, have to accommodate a greying group likely to have restricted mobility, dietary and health issues specific to the elderly, with a good number of them likely to die in prison. This kind of transformation in the role of the prison and the responses of its staff to such matters has led to the following media headlines around the world: "[UK] jails struggle as the number of older sex offenders soars" (Morris, 2013); "[Hong Kong] jails struggle to cope with ageing inmates" (Lam, 2018); "[New Zealand] prison plans expansion for ageing inmates" (Cowlishaw, 2013); "Elderly Inmates

Burden [US] State Prisons'" (Ollove, 2016); "America's elderly prison population boom is becoming a nightmare" (Price, 2015); "Ageing Japan: prisons cope with swelling ranks of elderly prisoners" (Takenaka and Umekawa, 2018).

This book, with Japan as the main focus, attempts to tell the story of how these changes have occurred, the kinds of lives the elderly were living before they became involved in crime, their experiences in prison, and the hopes and expectations they might have for their release.

John Pratt
Victoria University of Wellington, New Zealand

References

Baldock, J.C. (1980) 'Why the Prison Population has Grown Larger and Younger', *Howard Journal of Crime and Justice*, 19(1–3), pp. 142–155.

Braithwaite, J. (1989) *Crime, Shame and Reintegration. Cambridge*: Cambridge University Press.

Cowlishaw, S. (2013) Prison plans expansion for ageing inmates, Stuff.co.nz, 16th December, http://www.stuff.co.nz/national/crime/9520605/Prison-plans-expansion-for-ageing-inmates. Last accessed 5th October 2019.

Inspector of Custodial Services [New South Wales]. (2015) Old and inside: Managing aged offenders in custody. Sydney: NSW Department of Justice.

Lam, J. (2018) 'Jails struggle to cope with ageing inmates', *Sunday Morning Post*, June 24th, p. 1.

Morris, N. (2013) 'Jails struggle as number of older sex offenders soars', *The Independent*, 12th September, https://www.independent.co.uk/news/uk/crime/jails-struggle-as-number-of-older-sex-offenders-soars-8810096.html. Last accessed 5th October 2019.

Ollove, M. (2016) Elderly inmates burden state prisons, *The Pew Charitable Trusts*, March 17th. https://www.pewtrusts.org/en/research-and-analysis/blogs/stateline/2016/03/17/elderly-inmates-burden-state-prisons. Last accessed 5th October 2019

Price, M. (2015) America's elderly prison population boom is becoming a nightmare, MSNBC 5th June, http://www.msnbc.com/msnbc/americas-elderly-prison-population-boom-becoming-nightmare. Last accessed 5th October 2019

Takenaka, K., and Umekawa, T. (2018) Ageing Japan: prisons cope with swelling ranks of elderly inmates, *Reuters World News*, 14th March. https://www.reuters.com/article/us-japan-ageing-prisons/ageing-japan-prisons-cope-with-swelling-ranks-of-elderly-inmates-idUSKCN1GQ0AL last accessed 5th October 2019

US Department of Justice. (2015) The impact of an aging inmate population on the federal bureau of prisons. Washington, DC: US Department of Justice Evaluation and Inspections Division, pp. 15–105.

Introduction

Yoko Hosoi

Toyo University, Japan

Japan has long been known as a "safe and secure country" with a relatively low crime rate compared to other countries in the world. While the crime rate as a whole has been declining since its peak in 1998, the number of crimes committed by the elderly has been on the rise or has remained at a high level, and today, one out of every five criminal arrests is of an elderly person.

The issue of "aging society and crimes" is not recent; the Ministry of Justice in Japan has long issued warnings and has actively engaged in attempts to identify and respond to the situation. They included a special section for the subject in the 2008 White Paper on Crime to call for public attention to the need for comprehensive measures to combat the problem. Ten years have elapsed since then, and the authors have been made aware of the severity of the problem fortuitously, which was through an "inquiry from outside" rather than an "awareness from within."

0.1 What is the current issue: Indications by Western researchers

Several research papers and newspaper articles were published in 2009 by researchers and journalists in Europe and the United States regarding "elderly crimes" in Japan. These publications are broadly divided into three categories. The first addresses why elderly crimes have consistently increased to a level that exceeded the population rate and why most of those elderly criminals would re-offend repeatedly, despite the low crime rate in Japan in the first place. The second addresses the "question" of why most elderly crimes are property crimes. The elderly supported the period of rapid economic growth in Japan and were considered economically successful; the property crimes committed by this group are extremely rare in Western society and attracted intense scrutiny. The third concerns the fact that female criminals and female recidivists among the elderly have become prominent. What factors lie behind this trend? All facilities housing elderly female criminals have become extremely overpopulated and accommodating new facilities is the most immediate need.

Neither the Ministry of Justice nor the relevant academic community has addressed these three issues directly to propose solutions. They have focused

DOI: 10.4324/9781032669519-1

on how to reduce crimes and prevent recidivism. However, it seems that the real issue lies much deeper than that.

It has been more than ten years since the authors began investigating elderly crimes; initially, our focus was mainly on clarifying the "actual situation" without noting these three questions beneath the surface issues. The above-mentioned publications by Western researchers made us open our eyes. This is precisely what it means to "look at the tree and not the forest." We planned this book to re-consider the "structural aspects of Japanese society" from this "international perspective" through the theme of "elderly crimes." Though by no means sufficient to explain the whole problem regarding the issue discussed in this book, international perspectives were introduced to the studies discussed in the following chapters.

0.2 Theoretical framework of the research: Focusing on the concept of "Lifeworld"[1]

The present research is an interdisciplinary project based on sociology, social psychology, social welfare studies, and criminal policy science, whose common ground is to clarify the "lifeworld" of elderly people. Crime is an action conducted on "one's own self-responsibility," and rehabilitation from crime is also accomplished on one's own responsibility. However, a large social structure of Japanese society lies behind the choice of the elderly to commit crimes. The social structure in question has two axes; one expands horizontally, and the other moves chronologically in time. Large forces sweep over individuals along these two axes and influence their choices of specific actions. Although the lifeworld of elderly people is centered on each individual, it could be a critical energy box leading to criminal actions by constructing a "lifeworld" unique to each elderly person depending on how each of them would perceive, evaluate, and choose/discard the surrounding circumstances (the bundle of forces). They would interpret various "hardships and adversities" that surround them in their own ways to reject, sometimes adapt excessively, or react to them to live their daily lives. The process is equally and extremely essential for them as members of society, regardless of whether they are criminals or ordinary people. The purpose of this book is to depict their lifeworld from these perspectives (Figure 0.1).

0.3 Composition of the book

This book consists of four sections. The first section, titled "Considering the Society and Elderly Criminals," discusses the underlying structural characteristics and changes driving the lifeworld of the elderly from the perspective of social space developed in the timeframe of contemporary and contemporaneity. Specifically, the post-war social conditions in Japan, particularly changes within the society in the 1960s, are outlined in terms of population, household, social security, and employment to identify the issues within the welfare

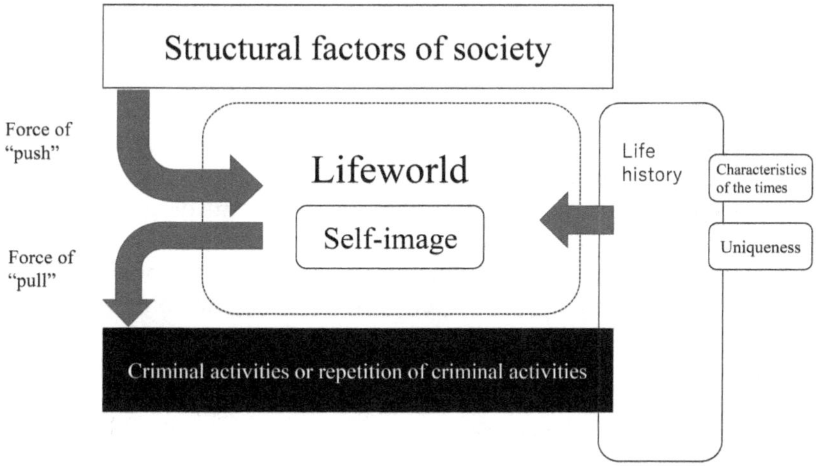

Figure 0.1 Mechanism of crimes

society (Chapter 1). In this context, the fundamental challenges faced in Western society are discussed from theoretical standpoints (Chapter 2). Next, after reviewing the current situation of elderly crimes in Japan by examining government white papers and reports of relevant research (Chapter 3), some of the studies conducted so far on elderly ex-convicts are discussed from the perspectives of judicial welfare, clinical psychology, and sociology (Chapters 4, 5, and 6).

The second section, titled "Characteristics of Elderly Criminals Based on Surveys on Elderly Inmates in Japan" (surveys conducted in 2012, 2016, and 2017), forms the core of this book. This section discloses circumstances that lead the elderly to commit crimes, not from the standpoint of society but from that of the parties involved (the elderly offenders). The real voices of the elderly can be heard and understood through several possible ways; in this section, the "lifeworld" of the elderly was clarified through three rounds of questionnaire surveys by the "Study Group on Elderly Offenders," the base organization of this book, conducted on male and female inmates incarcerated in correctional institutions throughout the country. The three rounds of surveys (the 2012 survey on 635 male and female inmates aged 65 years and above, the 2017 survey on 486 female inmates aged 40 years and above, and the 2018 survey on 377 female inmates aged 40 years and above) on a total of 1,498 inmates reveal "crime, self, and society" as described by the offenders themselves. Chapter 7 presents the outline and the results of all the three surveys. Chapters 8 to 10 focus on several themes from all the three surveys (offender typology by sex, perpetration and victimization of crime, and differences between female inmates and ordinary women) for a more in-depth analysis to understand the complete profile of the elderly criminals who were the subjects of the surveys.

The third section, titled "Trends and Issues in Elderly Crime from Around the World," illustrates the actual situation of elderly crimes in the four nations chosen by the study group for an international comparison: New Zealand, Australia, Hong Kong, and the United Kingdom. In the case of New Zealand and Australia, researchers from these countries and Japan, respectively, contributed articles on the subject, and thus the real situations and issues in both countries are discussed from both an inside and an outside perspective. Discussing the issue of "elderly crimes" from both sides enables reflecting on various aspects of society from comparative sociological viewpoints since "the problem" varies depending on the perspective. Amid the commonalities and differences, we may be able to identify the deep-rooted problems in elderly crimes and, at the same time, understand the responses of the people and the country (criminal policies) to these problems in each nation.

The fourth section, titled "A Comparative Cultural Study on Elderly Crime: Results of a Joint Questionnaire Survey in Four Countries (New Zealand, Hong Kong, Australia, and Japan)," is based on the results of questionnaire surveys conducted in the above-mentioned four nations. The issues faced by each nation are revealed based on data from different perspectives drawn from the third section, so that the common problems surfacing in the course of discussion can be examined from comparative sociological viewpoints.

0.4 Goal of the book

Japan's Ministry of Justice filed the Recidivism Prevention Project in December 2017 as a cabinet decision and formulated the Recidivism Prevention Plan the following year, taking the issues of the elderly into account and placing recidivism prevention as the most pressing matter for the crime policy of the nation. One of the significant points of the plan is the enforcement of measures for the elderly, stating that the rapid increase in the number of elderly convicts at penal institutions across the country is a matter of grave concern. However, there is a catch in the term "recidivism prevention." It is for the benefit of the criminals themselves, albeit concurrently, it has an aspect of strong social demands not to create victims and establish a safe and secure society. Sometimes, it prioritizes the elements of surveillance over the benefits of criminal rehabilitation. Consequently, there remains a concern that the measures could be implemented to prioritize the good of society instead of for the benefit of criminals. The above-mentioned Recidivism Prevention Plan sets numeric targets, such as reducing the rate to the target value within the target number of years, to be accomplished as a national policy. They are the target values for reducing recidivism risks. The criminal justice system evaluates the recidivism risk in its decisions on criminal punishments to prevent criminals from re-offending. Simultaneously, the subject of rehabilitation should be the criminals themselves; unless the criminals themselves chose to act accordingly, practical and sustainable rehabilitation would not be accomplished. "Recidivism prevention measures" and "rehabilitation support" are never the same; they are a pair of wheels that must coexist harmoniously.

The purpose of this book is not to contribute directly to the national policy of "recidivism prevention." In this book, we aim to elucidate the inevitability of people committing crimes repeatedly in their old age by investigating struggles and conflicts in the minds of elderly criminals in Japan. What would drive them to choose criminal activities? Let us hear what they have to say.

Note

1 The "lifeworld" referred to in this book is mainly based on the concept established by Alfred Schütz, who argued that the objective social world would comprise subjective meanings (Schutz, 1962/1990).

Reference

Schutz, A. (1962/1990) *Collected Papers I: The Problem of Social Reality*, Natanson, M and van Breda, H. L. (eds.) Kluwer Academic Publishers.

Section I

Considering the Society and Elderly Criminals

1 Social Circumstances Surrounding the Elderly

Twenty-Year Trends

Yoko Hosoi

Toyo University, Japan

Japan's period of high economic growth in the 1960s can be described as a time when all of Japan came together in pursuit of this common goal. Figure 1.1 provides a hint of how Japan managed to achieve such miraculous economic growth. It was a time when the working-age population spearheading the labor market was sizeable, and the elderly people who needed to be socially supported were exceedingly few. The problem of elderly crime facing us now is related to those who lived, played a central role in society, and made contributions as valuable workers. While we cannot know the extent to which they realistically thought about their post-retirement lives in that period, we can be certain that people generally assumed that the elderly would be adequately cared for at a societal level. What must have gone through their minds as they subsequently lived through the various phases of society, before finally arriving at the twilight of their lives? It goes without saying that a form of society most likely became imprinted in their consciousness over the course of sixty-five or seventy years. I would like to identify the societal forces that propelled the elderly from behind, as we consider the multilayered ways of looking at the transformation of Japanese society and examine the social conditions affecting the elderly. While we may not understand how these forces affected elderly persons and criminals at the individual level, they are at least important in terms of assessing actions (crimes) by the elderly from a macro perspective and interpreting these phenomena. We will provide an overview of changes in the composition of the population, social security schemes, the family structure, the arrival and impact of a stratified society, and the changes in local communities below. We believe that this exercise will be meaningful in explaining the quantitative and qualitative characteristics of elderly criminals, which will be discussed later.

1.1 Changes in population composition

It can be said that Japan is the fastest among developed countries to become an aging society. What other countries took 50 years or a century to achieve was accomplished by Japan in a fraction of this time. While Japan was among the lowest-ranked countries in the world until the 1980s, and more or less in

DOI: 10.4324/9781032669519-3

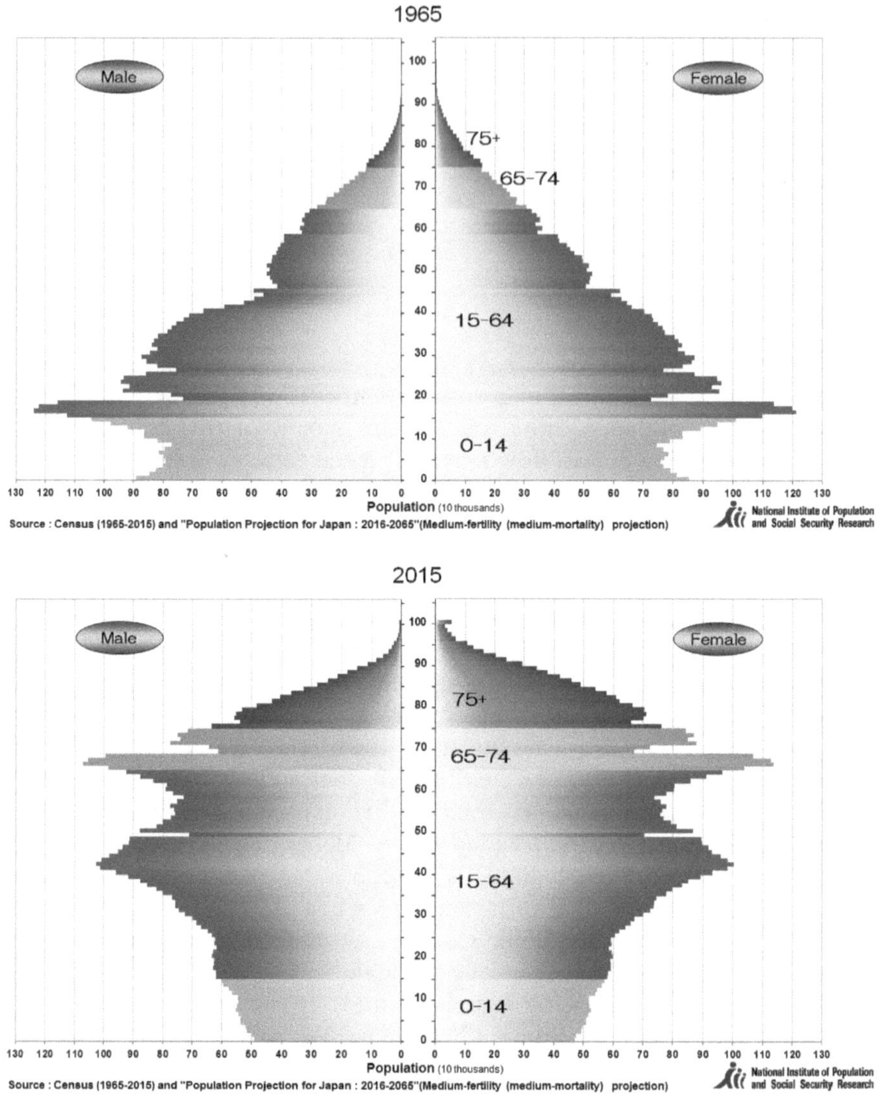

Figure 1.1 Changes in population composition.

Source: Census (1965–2015) and "Population Projection for Japan: 2016–2065" (Medium-fertility (medium-mortality) projection).

the middle of the pack during the 1990s in terms of aging, it was leading the world by 2005. It took a hundred years for the elderly in France to go from accounting for 7% of the overall population to 14%. Japan managed this in twenty-five years—in other words, a quarter of the time. One reason behind this rapid aging of Japan was the sharp decline in the birthrate in the 1950s.

Against the backdrop of rapid economic growth, there were also rapid changes in the industrial structure, and substantial changes in the form of the family, which will be discussed later in this book. All sorts of distortions occurred in a way that affected not only the framework and systems pertaining to society as a whole, but also came to affect the way lives were designed for the elderly, and the manner in which people were made aware of them, since economic progress was being made without proper preparatory programs having been put into place. The elderly began to worry that they were becoming devalued in terms of their collective weight and level of scarcity, and that they would be shunted to the edges of society. They could see that their own ranks were rapidly increasing in number, thereby causing them to go from being treated as a cared for segment of society to a surplus portion of the population. Since they played an important role in promoting the economic growth that began in the 1960s and were proud and assured of their place as the engines of society, they simply could not imagine the kind of life that might befall them decades later. Before anyone realized it, the birthrate declined at an unexpected rate, while lifespans for the elderly were increasing. The distorted state of an aging society, combined with a declining birth rate, thus emerged in Japan.

Japan's population began declining in 2008. Since then, the country has been suffering from severe levels of population decline and aging never before seen in the world. When the overall population of Japan decreases by 20 million, the emergence of Japan in a form that is unexpected will bring about great concern. On June 7, 2019, the Ministry of Health, Labour, and Welfare released its 2018 report on demographic trends, which showed that the decline in the rate of childbirth and the aging of society proceeded at serious levels.

While greater longevity had already been anticipated in the 1970s, the rapid pace at which lives are prolonged means that individuals are thrilled to be living longer and reaching their 80s or 90s. On the other hand, the elderly are becoming more insecure about their futures, as society fails to keep pace with efforts to support them, and as they have not properly planned for their own lives. One cannot help but be amazed to see how much the average lifespan of the Japanese people has increased over the course of eight decades. The gap between the average life expectancy at the time of a person's birth and when the same individual reaches old age necessitates preparation. There needs to be a process by which a person constantly reformulates his or her own life plan, and a flexible course correction on the part of society. In 1948, the average life expectancy of both men and women in the country was less than 60 years (Table 1.1). This number has risen by more than 20 years over the course of the last seven decades. In light of this factor alone, we are forced to reshape society, as the composition of Japan's population undergoes a significant transformation.

Another issue is the declining birthrate and aging of society. This viewpoint is important for thinking about life awareness among the elderly. Let us examine households, which are the basic units within which individuals live.

Table 1.1 Changes in average life expectancy

1948	*Males 55.60*	*Females 59.40*
1951	60.80	64.90
1971	70.17	75.58
2018	81.09	87.26

Source: Ministry of Health, Labour and Welfare, 2019 Vital Population Statistics.

In 1975, the majority of households with elderly members were three-generation households, and elderly members of these households often lived together with their children's families. The number of households consisting of single-person elderly individuals, or just elderly couples has increased, such that these types of households now account for the majority of households with elderly members (Figure 1.2). Underlying this change is that social security schemes have been enhanced to enable elderly individuals to live independently, without having to live together with their children. There is also the fact that children are no longer able to provide financial security for their parents' generations, as they had done previously.

1.2 Changes in social security schemes

The latter half of the 1990s coincided with a period in which Japan's social welfare underwent major shifts from an era of measures to an era of contracts.

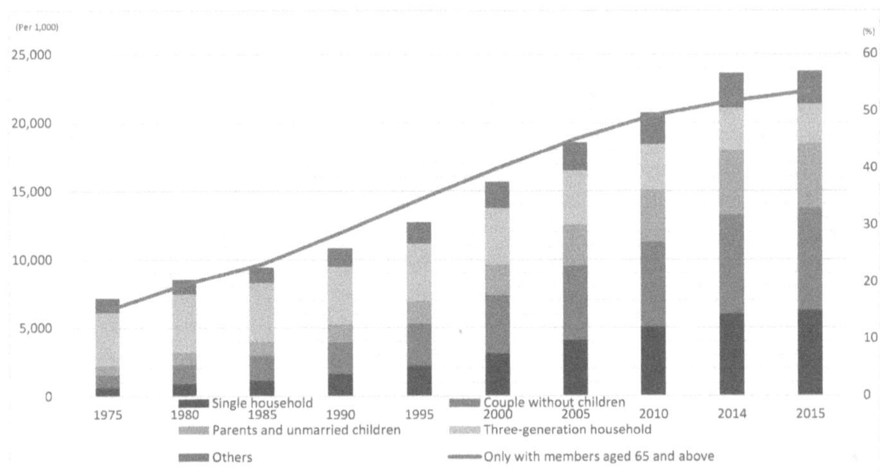

Figure 1.2 Number of households with a member aged 65 years and above, by household structure, and percentage of households accounted for by households consisting only of elderly persons.

Source: Shirahase, 2018, p 269.

Welfare in this era of measures was strongly associated with the provision of care, as a redistribution of relief by the state, to the poor and needy. Thus, care providers consisted of care-providing staff members, nurses, physicians, and other actors who could be described as carrying the nation on their collective backs. Since they were required to distribute care equally to those receiving it, they were compelled to provide it on a uniform basis. Consequently, collective care designed to suppress the individuality of each elderly person has been developed.

In 1970, society was aging (elderly people aged 65 years and above accounted for 7% of the total population). In 2010, Japan had a super-aging society (23%). This figure is expected to increase to 30% in 2024, and 39.9% in 2060. By 2060, four out of ten persons will be 65 years of age and above, five out of ten will be between 16 and 64 years of age, and only one out of ten will be 14 years of age or younger. Currently, there are 2.8 members of the working generation (between the ages of 16 and 64 years) for each elderly person, and this number is expected to decline to 1.3 by 2060. This would be akin to having elderly persons shift from riding horses to riding on their shoulders for support. While figures vary for different regions, the average number of household members in Tokyo is 1.99, which is less than two. This suggests that the terms "home" and "family" have begun to be deprived of any real meaning.

Currently, it is being said that public- and private-sector actors need to come together to promote urban development and enable people to continue to live with peace of mind, since it is difficult to realize this goal through the long-term care insurance system. In order to exceed the limits of long-term care insurance, the revitalization of the power of local communities to get people to help one another is required through active efforts on their part. People have come to resort to long-term care insurance as their first course of action if they encounter difficulties in their lives. If people become accustomed to relying on long-term care insurance services, they will come to believe that they can live without having to rely on neighbors or their local communities. By habitually using long-term care insurance, relationships built over time are disrupted. One impact of long-term care insurance is the dilution of the relationships between users of long-term care services and local residents. Long-term care insurance is a system in which services are purchased in the market, based on the concept of privatization. By incorporating the market principle of contract-based service centers, reciprocal relationships and mutual aid functions are displaced by the buying and selling of services. Not only do local welfare activities and long-term insurance become decoupled from one another, but the degeneration of local welfare services is also caused as long-term care insurance services lead to the erosion of welfare activities performed by local residents. We have seen that this gives rise to the degeneration of local organizations and their activities in this field.

While the withdrawal of local relationships of reciprocity and mutual aid functions is partly attributed to the introduction of the long-term care insurance system, this development has also been shaped by neoliberalism, which swept the world in the 1990s. A factor seen in high economic growth, Fordism (mass production and mass consumption) implanted the culture of consumption in people's views on life and values (a cultural phenomenon by which value is found more in consumption than in labor and frugality). In the 15 years since the long-term care insurance system has come into effect, people's lives in their homes and communities have been transformed. Many elements relating to long-term care that had at one time consisted of reciprocal relationships and mutual aid areas outside the market coalesced into a service product market through this system.

The third point to note is that all kinds of local events, such as bon festival dances and cherry-blossom viewing parties of the past, used to be organized by local organizations, named local governments, and neighborhood associations in most local communities. In the 1990s, however, these functions underwent significant changes, as the Japanese economy suffered a prolonged period of stagnation and decline. This was the result not only of demographic changes in the form of a declining birthrate and aging population, but also a societal transformation based on the second factor mentioned above: neoliberal globalization. This can also be attributed to the disintegration of people's connections to one another, a process that helped form individuals as consumers and resulted in the dissolution of these connections and the rise of a culture of consumption.

Long-term care insurance was made to serve as the turning point in a shift from selectivity-based welfare to universality-based welfare, which allows anyone at any place to receive services according to their needs. Benefits conferred by social welfare services, as provided in the past, through measures carried out for administrative disposition consist of social aid to supplement household functions. It was assumed that the responsibility for taking care of the elderly would naturally fall to families and households. However, if the government determined that a household required nursing care for financial reasons, an illness or impairment, the inability to take care of an elderly person during the day due to work obligations, or other circumstances affecting members of the household, nursing-care measures were undertaken. With such benefits based on the principle of selectivity, household and family income, household composition, and circumstances necessitating nursing care were investigated in detail before a decision was made.

Funding for long-term care insurance was broken down as follows: 25% from the national treasury, 12.5% from prefectural tax revenues, 12.5% from municipalities, and 50% from insurance premiums remitted by insured persons. In 2000, the total cost amounted to 3.6 trillion yen, and the average premium was approximately 3,000 yen nationwide. In 2014, the total cost amounted to 10 trillion yen, and the average premium was 5,000 yen. In fiscal year 2025, members of the baby-boomer generation will all become latter-stage elderly persons (at least 75 years of age). The Ministry of Health, Labour and Welfare expects that total costs will amount to 21 trillion yen, and that insurance premiums will be approximately 8,200 yen per person in that year.

Nationwide, average insurance premiums vary depending on the total number of long-term care insurance operators in each municipality and on other pertinent factors. Because insurance premiums are set on a progressive basis according to income level, each individual pays his or her own insurance premiums. This amount is not low, by any means, for elderly people. A low-income person cannot pay the premium set at the default level. For this income class, various proposals have been made to increase the reduction rate from 50% to 70%. At this point, it is difficult to discern what might happen in the future. The generation of currently working individuals aged between 40 and 64 years, who constitute secondary insured persons, has contributed to long-term care insurance premiums, together with health insurance premiums, accounting for 29% of the funding for the long-term care insurance system. Primary insured persons, individuals aged 65 years and above, contribute 21% of the funding to this system. In terms of the breakdown of the overall population, the expansion of the working poor—a situation partly attributable to the growth of non-regular work—has begun to make it difficult for members of the currently working generation to continue to contribute 29% of the funding for this system. Thus, conditions under which intergenerational conflicts might be sparked are developing.

A low nursing care level (up to the medium level of 1 to 2) was originally meant to correspond to individuals who were not accustomed to utilizing long-term care insurance, and who could benefit from programs for the promotion of healthy and meaningful living. Various initiatives undertaken by local governments and autonomous initiatives undertaken by local residents had been incorporated from programs designed to allow the elderly to contribute to their local communities. People's activities and initiatives to enable the elderly to continue living dynamically in the communities in which they were accustomed to living were intended to be varied and flexibly in line with each community's culture, traditions, and the customs and conditions of the residents of each community. This was essentially supported by the autonomy of local residents. Initiatives were bidirectional in that service providers and receivers were not unilaterally fixed, but could be mutually replaced according to variables of time, place, and circumstances. Providers and receivers played a key role for one another when it came to these initiatives.

Over the past fifteen-odd years, active elderly persons capable of supporting themselves have been replaced by consumers of long-term care insurance services. Areas where programs had already stagnated came to be divested, based on local welfare activities, through this development. In areas where programs had been properly developed, we witnessed a weakening of connections with people in neighboring areas that had been previously established.

It was originally believed that the incorporation of preventive care into the insurance system, which had been in doubt, would get all elderly persons to become insured persons without their opposition. The casting of a broad net to capture persons with a low nursing care level, and persons on the periphery of such a status, is necessary. Since the hoisting of such a large net has become a burden, the provision of services to persons with a low nursing care level and those on the periphery of such a status has been offloaded to municipalities. To protect ministerial interests, as they relate to the long-term care insurance system, the Ministry of Health, Labour and Welfare simply abandoned persons with a low nursing care level and persons on the periphery of such a status and designated and called upon municipalities to take over the provision of services for these persons.

Those belonging to the upper and middle classes, who could purchase nursing care services even if they happen to be a little expensive, and those living in areas largely populated by the bulk of the middle class—in other words, those who belong to segments of the population capable of helping themselves—were fine. Many individuals who live in places populated by those who have trouble leading urban lives end up outside the scope of the socialization of nursing care. These legal revisions constitute a milestone by which people of low standing and many other areas will find themselves discarded by the system.

The transfer from measures to contracts means that nursing care will be liberated from the family framework, and individuals will undergo socialization. This entails a transition from a framework under which welfare services are determined and provided on the basis of lives led by families (households) to one under which welfare services are provided in the context of contractual relationships, based on the principle of self-responsibility, for which the individual is the basic unit. Insurance benefits are provided in the event of an insurance event. Any determination as to whether an insured event has occurred is made through a review of the certification of the needed long-term care in each case. During this process, an individual's family and household situations are irrelevant. Certification is based on the situation pertaining to the party or individual in question, such that service is provided only to the party or individual in question at all times.

1.3 The arrival of a society of disparities

In 1989 (the first year of the Heisei period), the bubble economy was in full swing, the Nikkei Average stood at a record high level of 38,915 yen, and there were far more than two job openings for every university graduate applicant, which meant that the job market for would-be workers was booming. At the beginning of the Heisei period, disparity did not exist in society as a whole, and most people described Japanese society as a middle-class society. Young people would have observed their own parents' generation and could accordingly predict the course of their own future. They might have assumed that their salaries would rise with each passing year and could forecast the future, albeit with some dissatisfaction. While young people 30 years ago cannot be said to have lacked any insecurity about their present circumstances, it can be said that they believed that they could see how their lives would unfold over the course of the next three decades. However, from around the end of the 1990s, disparities emerged, first among the young, and later spread throughout all cohorts in society. In the fiscal year 1998, the real economic growth rate was negative at 1.5%, and the impact of the collapse of the bubble economy in the first half of the decade spread in all directions. Around this time, people became aware of concerns about the future and disparities in society. The latter half of the 1990s saw the Asian financial crisis, the collapse of one large corporation after another, and the early stages of the crumbling myth of lifetime employment. An awareness of the fact that young people's future was unstable and replete with risks took root. Beginning in the latter half of the 1990s, non-regular employment patterns such as permanent part-time work suddenly increased. If you were a recent graduate who could not secure a position as a regular company employee, or were someone who found a part-time job temporarily, or who otherwise found non-regular employment because you could not find a job suitable for your educational background or a position you wanted, it would have been difficult to become a regular company employee later. Such people were compelled to imagine a rather uncertain future and would likely have given up on their own future or chosen to forgo thinking about it in any specific manner. When you are unable to picture where you might be in ten years' time, any dream of getting married or having a family slips away from your grasp. Terms such as winner and loser were used. This issue of disparity first spread among the young and gradually seeped into other age brackets. This was in part attributable to the fact that certain Japanese employment practices applied to those at the center of society and that they were, in a certain sense, protected accordingly.

However, it is true that we failed to visualize this issue of disparity initially, since middle-aged and elderly persons were placed under the large umbrella of Japanese society through Japanese employment practices. While it became a problem for young people initially, the roots of this problem were seen to be much deeper after the collapse of the bubble economy in the late 1990s. In other words, not all young people were directly affected in the wake of the bubble bursting. It can be said that their parents' generation—as the generation immediately preceding their own—contained seeds of disparity for their children's generation.

In his book *Framework of Japanese Society*, Eiji Oguma theorized, early on, that there was a dual-tiered structure for Japanese society. A scheme of classification pitting one category—workers with regular employment—against another—workers with non-regular employment, self-employed workers, and family workers—had long been regarded as a matter of course in the context of Japanese employment practices. It served as an important way to ensure Japan's continuity. While disparity and inequality were not outwardly recognized, since they were subsumed within society, the latter category was skillfully harnessed to provide a reservoir of labor at all times, even as it was shaped by government policies. Meanwhile, the positioning and stability of the former category continued to be somewhat openly maintained in society. This framework sustained high rates of economic growth in Japan through

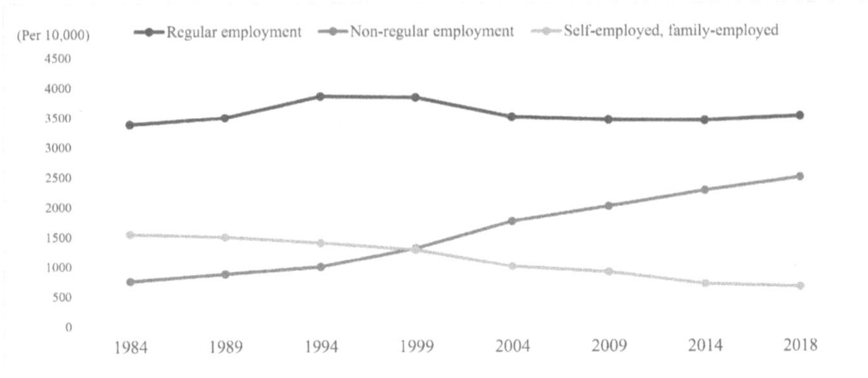

Figure 1.3 Changes by employment status.

Source: Oguma, 2019, p. 46.

Japanese employment practices and protected the living standards of many workers. Many elderly individuals today are part of this framework and have spent many years living according to this.

This framework has been meaningful in stabilizing the lives of people. After all, as heads of their respective families, workers were able to continue supporting their families. However, negative aspects gradually emerged with respect to these two points. The first was the existence of self-employed and family workers in the latter category. As shown in Figure 1.3, the thirty-four-year period between 1984 and 2018 saw both favorable economic and recessionary conditions. The number of self-employed and family workers began to decline in 1997, whereas the number of non-regular workers increased. This was not simply something that could be chalked up to an issue of how people worked. The manner in which local communities and families existed was substantially affected. The power of communities and families waned on a relative basis, and the way in which life for individual units was sustained was restructured.

The second negative aspect is the impact of hierarchy within the latter category on the next generation. As mentioned in Oguma's book, the children of workers belonging to the latter category are forced to undergo negative experiences when obtaining school education, participating in the market, and leading a married life. Consequently, the social foundation for young people to support the elderly (the children of the elderly) has weakened. It has been pointed out that Japan is a relatively equal society compared to Western society. Certainly, the mantra of a total middle-class society was played up during the 1990s, and disparities (primarily in terms of wages) narrowed in a numerical sense. However, regular employees remained regular employees over the course of almost their entire lives, and many of their children maintained their societal status as regular employees. In contrast, non-regular employees, who are self-employed workers or family workers in rural areas, tend to be bound to their status as non-regular employees. They suffer real instances of prejudice that are worse than the formal examples, and the negative links associated with non-regular employees are passed down to the next generation. It is not possible to ignore the fact that this, in turn, places the elderly in a bind, as far as their lives go. Pensions and other examples of social security, family ties to children, and the roles played by self-employed persons in local communities must be described as constituting social capital that is highly important for countering a declining birthrate and the aging of society. However, it cannot be ignored that they have incurred massive negative consequences. Even though it is understood that security cannot be enjoyed in old age with only a public pension, one tends to believe that it is possible to access minimum standards of living. There is a sense that everything will be all right, as such matters come within the purview of what the State does for its citizens. On the contrary, it is possible that the desire on the part of people to be convinced that this is true caused them to give ongoing mandates to the Liberal Democratic Party to govern over the years. Unlike an employee pension plan in which company employees are enrolled, the national pension system, which is a scheme for self-employed persons and others in a similar situation, cannot be described as capable of providing peace of mind for a hundred years by maintaining an income substitution rate of 50%. This is because, if you were enrolled only in the national pension system, you would be unable to receive more than the full amount of approximately 65,000 yen a month (approximately 780,000 yen a year), even if you had continuously paid insurance premiums for four decades. This would not cover all the basic living costs a normal person would incur. Unless you save a suitable amount in anticipation of old age, the reality is that you are highly likely to end up having to depend on welfare payments. You must not forget that persons in this predicament currently number more than 15 million. There are four conceivable patterns by which one can deal with social security: (i) turn to the side that exploits without having any need whatsoever to worry about your old age; (ii) continue to work hard, endeavor to support themselves, and continue to be exploited; (iii) concede and turn to the side being protected (which will result in being exploited by those who are working hard); and (iv) abandon this country (since you will end up forfeiting any claims to what you have already paid into the system; this would mean that you would only have been exploited up to the time of choosing to no longer deal with social security). If government guidelines set the income substitution rate (pension amount as a percentage of the wage income earned by members of the working generation) at 50% or more, and it is estimated that the income substitution rate will fall below 50%, a review of the current framework of public pension finances is mandated by law.

Apart from the unexpected widening of disparities stemming from the duality of employees' pension plans and the national pension system, it should be noted that the security and stability enjoyed by regular employees are mirrored by the anxiety and instability experienced by non-regular employees.

1.4 Two miscalculations pertaining to a Japanese-type welfare society

The groundwork for Japan's postwar social security system was laid in the 1960s. According to Shirahase, this process reflects two miscalculations. One consists of the rapid change in population, and the other consists of significant changes in families upon which the systems in Japan have been predicated. In 1961, a national universal health insurance program and a universal pension program were established. At that time, however, nobody imagined that a quarter of the population would comprise elderly persons only a quarter of a century later. The change in the population structure of Japan is notable for having been very rapid, which reflects the fact that industrialization in Japan began late but progressed at an immense speed. With respect to the population, the birthrate declined rapidly in the 1950s. This occurred alongside an increase in life expectancy, such that the rapid aging of the population began in the 1980s. The fact that such changes were so rapid meant that there was no room to accommodate them. In one sense, today's programs cannot avoid having to catch up in response to conditions.

Another miscalculation involves the existence of family. For many years, the form of a typical family had been fixed. Amid high economic growth, a strong gender-based division of labor system meant that families were supported by the wages earned by fathers. Thanks to the sort of job security that allowed fathers to believe that they could continue working until retirement under the lifetime employment system, children were raised and could study at universities in many single-income households where a man was the primary breadwinner. Such job security was also intertwined with the seniority system at work, which further improved future prospects. In addition, these employment systems were underpinned by a strong gender-based division of the labor system. A gender philosophy existed that sustained this system.

The declining birthrate in recent years might be a form of backlash against the design of Japanese programs, infused with gender-based roles that both men and women were intended to fulfill.

In terms of Japanese-style welfare, the Liberal Democratic Party of Japan published its Guidelines Concerning Measures for Enhancing the Foundation of the Family in 1979; these guidelines set a clear gender-based division of labor for this foundation and declared that domestic responsibilities to be fulfilled by women were a primary concern with the aim of building a Japanese-style welfare society. In the 1978 White Paper on Health and Welfare, income security for the elderly and the development of a home environment to allow elderly persons to make the most of a system in which people live together with elderly parents—seen as unique to Japan, and as a latent asset within the context of welfare—were sought. Since that White Paper, the number of lifelong unmarried people who will not form their own families has increased. In 2015, the lifetime non-marriage rate was 23.4% for men and 14.1% for women (as determined by Professor Shirahase, based on the national census report; National Institute of Population and Social Security Research, 2018). The family structure established in the 1960s to underpin the postwar system of social security in Japan underwent significant changes, in conjunction with rapid changes affecting the population structure, such that circumstances under which we can no longer expect to see similar functions have arisen. The family form, which should be described as a prerequisite for operating this system, has changed substantially.

I believe that the realization of a sustainable society in the future will be influenced by how quickly and flexibly we can respond to these two miscalculations that we did not account for when we envisioned a post-war social security system.

References

Arita, S., et al. (eds.) (2021) *Jinsei Kouki no Kaisou Kouzou* [*Hierarchy of Aging Society with Low Birthrate vol.3: Hierarchy in the Twilight Years in Life*], Tokyo, University of Tokyo Press.

Cabinet Office. (2017) *Annual Report on the Aging Society: 2017 (Summary)*, Tokyo, Cabinet Office. https://www8.cao.go.jp/kourei/english/annualreport/2017/2017pdf_e.html.

Hashimoto, K. (2018) *Shin Nihon no Kaikyu-shakai* [*New Class Society in Japan*], Tokyo, Kodansha.

Kasuga, K., et al. (eds.) (2011) *Shakai no Sekyurithi wan ani wo Mamoru noka: Shoshitsu suru Shakai/Kojin* [*What Social Security Protects: Disappearing Society/Individual*], Tokyo, Gakubunsha.

Kato, M., Yuzawa, Y., and Shimuzu, S. (eds.) (1979) *Rounen-ki: Yutakana Jinsei no Hakken* [*Old Age: Discovering the Richness of Life*], Tokyo, Yuhikaku Publishing.

Mizuno, H. (2015) *Kaigo Hoken to kaiso-ka/kakusa-ka suru Koreisha: Hito wa Ikitekita yonishika Shinenainoka* [*Long Term Care Insurance Dealing with Advancing Stratified and Inequality among Elderly People: Why the Ending of One's Life is Determined by Circumstances of One's Life?*], Tokyo, Akashi Shoten.

Oguma, E. (2019) *Nihon wo Shihai suru Shakai no Kanshuu* [*Social Conventions Governing Japan*], Tokyo, Kodansha.

Okuda, T., et al. (2016) *Seikatsu Konkyusha Heno Bansougata Shien: Keizaitekikonkyu to Shakaiteki Koritsu Ni Taiou Suru Totarusapoto* [*Accompanying Support for the Needy: Total Support for Economic Deprivation and Social Isolation*], Tokyo, Akashi Shoten.

Shirahase, S. (ed.) (2018) *Korekarano Nihon no Jinkou to Shakai* [*Population and Society in Japan in the Future*], Tokyo, University of Tokyo Press.

Taromaru, H. (2016) *Kohki Kindai to Kachi Ishiki no Hen-you: Nihonjin no Ishiki 1973–2008* [*Late Modernity and the Transformation of Value Consciousness: Japanese Consciousness 1973–2008*], Tokyo, University of Tokyo Press.

Todd, E. (2021) *Roujin Shihai Kokka: Nihon no Kiki* [*Nation Ruled by the Elderly: Crisis of Japan*], Tokyo, Bungeishunju.

Uemura, Y. (2015) *Fukushi no Ajia: Kokusaihikaku kara Seisakukousou he* [*Welfare in Asia: From International Comparisons to Policy Concepts*], Nagoya, Nagoya University Press.

2 Study of Social Exclusion and Inclusion in a Post-Welfare State Society

From C. Gilligan's Perspective of "Care"

Tetsu Harayama

Toyo University, Japan

2.1 The problem of aging and social reintegration

A few years ago, while on a business trip to Paris, I encountered an incident that I consider symbolic for the present study. As I was walking down the subway aisle, a woman in front of me was almost robbed of her bag by an elderly man, who tried to snatch it by the handle. Fortunately, the woman was safe and so was the bag because she could hold on to it. What surprised me was the subsequent course of events; the elderly man who tried to rob the woman did not attempt to escape. He stood still, raising his hands with his back against the wall of the subway aisle. The woman saw it and walked away without reporting the incident to the police. Neither did the bystanders around him, who just left the scene indifferently, as if disgusted.

I wondered: Did he repeatedly commit similar attempts and reach his old age without rehabilitating himself to society? Could he walk away every time, or did he ever serve a prison sentence? What happened to his family or friends? Have they all left him? He made no attempt to escape: Did he prefer to be arrested by the police? Was the prospect of rehabilitation into society very difficult for him? Looking back now, I cannot help but wonder about these countless speculations.

The woman and the bystanders were indifferent to him, probably because they were too busy with their own matters to get involved. I had my own job appointment to keep, and I had no time to get distracted by the incident.

The aforementioned incident may, in a sense, serve as a warning about how challenging it could be for those who have committed crimes to reintegrate into society in the subsequent trajectory of their lives. If this trajectory is a long one for a criminal offender, he could reach old age before he receives the necessary rehabilitation to rejoin society. The episode may also suggest that these infractions would lead to isolation, as the offender would be excluded not only from a conventional life, such as with his family, friends, and other types of acquaintances but would also receive nothing from bystanders in the town but indifferent attitudes if he repeats his infractions.

DOI: 10.4324/9781032669519-4

Even if we set aside the issue of livelihood protection support, the conventional social security systems in welfare states have disregarded the reintegration of criminal offenders into society or their inclusion into society. The discussion in this chapter begins with a review of the link to others in association with the concept of "care," which was established in the book by C. Gilligan, *In a Different Voice*, which is related to the idea of a "society of care" based on supportive relationships that would inclusively support vulnerable individuals in a post-welfare state society. Next, the possibility of the above supportive relationships beyond family connection will be discussed as a new supportive measure for individuals in the post-welfare state society. In the course of these discussions, the present study attempts to demonstrate that the chain-trajectory of sanctions, rehabilitation, and pardon would be connected to personal "recognition (reconnaissance)" through "care," as Paul Ricoeur notes in his work.

2.2 From the dilemma of moral norms to the relationship of support

2.2.1 "A different voice" in C. Gilligan's discussion

C. Gilligan criticized L. Kohlberg's standpoint on moral and ego issues based on J. Piaget's Developmental Psychology. To gauge a child's moral development during puberty, Kohlberg asks 11-year-old children about the logic of resolving conflicts between several moral codes. The moral dilemma presented to children asked them to decide if Heinz, a guy without the means to purchase drugs, should steal them to save the life of his sick wife. A boy named Jake says that Heinz should steal the drugs. It is a dilemma between the value of property and life, and "a human life is worth more than money" (Gilligan, 1982, p. 26).

According to Kohlberg, Jake's thoughts on a logical calculation of morality are generated by independent judgment; it goes beyond the level of fulfillment of self-centered desires, reaching the concept of shared conventions, namely, the concept of fairness based on social consensus.

Against Jake, Amy, a girl of the same age, presents a somewhat different logic. "I don't think Heinz should steal drugs; there must be other ways. If he can borrow money, let's say, a loan, right? He must not steal drugs. Also, his wife must not die."

When asked why medicine should not be stolen, she answered that she thought the act of theft would affect the relationship between Heinz and his wife, not because she worried about the matters of property and laws.

"If he steals drugs, he could save his wife's life, but in that case, he would go to jail, and his wife's condition would deteriorate again. That is why they need to talk to each other and think about other ways to make money" (ibid., pp. 26–28).

For Amy, there are no calculations focused on people; there is a narrative of relationships over time in this dilemma. Amy thinks that the wife would continue to need her husband and that the husband would also be interested in his wife continuously. Moreover, Amy is considering keeping a good relationship with drug dealers rather than ripping it apart (ibid., p. 28).

Amy's logic is "a different voice" for Gilligan. Starting with criticism of Kohlberg, she also investigated the decision-making process of abortion through interviews with 29 women aged 15 to 33.

Among the several cases presented by Gilligan, there is one regarding a 25-year-old woman named Sarah, who described her experience of self-destruction in a relationship with her lover who did not agree to have a baby. It was challenging for her; however, she accepted the situation as the "truth" and tried to figure out how to come to terms with it. Eventually, she started to describe the experience as a "lucky" one for herself (ibid., p. 117).

J. Tronto contends that any discussion of morality that emphasizes relationships, like in the example above, contains a critique of male-oriented morality. Jake's argument is based on morality as a convention. Tronto argues that morality is associated with politics as a power relationship in the first place. Were women excluded from politics able to create their "Voice" for morality? Here, morality is "universal," and individual circumstances are not considered. In addition, if women's activities are limited to private spaces and they are less involved in the public domain, their "voice" should be weighed.

Tronto calls this restriction of women's voices over gender as moral boundaries and argues that giving the "voice" beyond this boundary is a matter of ethics of "care" as a relationship among people because the action is derived from considerations for others (Tronto, 1993).

2.2.2 *The ethics of "care"*

According to F. Brugère, the modern age is characterized by the emergence and rise of individuals. It can be categorized into the first, second, and third modern ages in historical development. In the first modern age, individuals relied on private ownership. In other words, "possession" is not only owning property but also the possession of self (the fundamental possession of humans as individual beings), which was revealed by John Locke, a philosopher in the Age of Enlightenment. That is, "people cannot be the owners of themselves unless they own properties. Political citizenship followed this constraint." The second modern age corresponds to the welfare state or the social state, and by that, "the individual was registered in the system of collective protection of the social security system." Therefore, "every person came to be considered a brotherhood, and by depersonalizing again an individual who had previously achieved economic success through the individualization of market competition, he restored the universal value of the individual" (Brugère, 2013, pp. 46–47).

However, F. Brugère asserts that the second modern age is at a deadlock. In other words, following the discussions of R. Castel, he divides the differentiation into "positive individualism" and "negative individualism" (Castel, 2011).

"In 'positive individualism,' the realization of oneself is possible in a framework that allows one's values to be approved, to build one's self, and to flourish oneself. In French society, when the realization of individualism in this manner becomes challenging, various problems emerge, such as exclusion, unemployment, social instability, super-aging, withdrawal, social disadvantages (handicaps), and mental disabilities" (Brugère, 2013, p. 47).

Therefore, the concept of the modern age by "support" (*soutien*) and the ethics of "care" is presented as the third modern age. Its central practice is to "accompany" vulnerable people, which Brugère argues to be close to G. Esping-Andersen's Nordic model (Brugère, 2013, pp. 49–51; Brugère, 2011; Esping-Andersen and Palier, 2008).

> The concept of 'support' is represented as the third modern age, in which a society of recognition beyond the relationship between love and friendship, and beyond the rights of law, is to be developed. The development of the human subject is considered in this society and based on the collective framework, that is, a framework of solidarity and empathy that would bring harmony with competitive relationships.
>
> Brugère (2013, pp. 57–58)

If we consider the typology of the modern age in this manner, Jake's response to the moral dilemma in C. Gilligan's criticism of Kohlberg will be positioned in the first modern age, and Amy's response will be positioned in the second to third modern ages. Moreover, Gilligan's moral discussion of abortion is located in the third modern age, as seen in the case of Sara, in which the focus is placed on the interpersonal relationship concerning the problem of the individual's approval as a subject (see Table 2.1).

2.3 From the second modern age to the third

2.3.1 Beyond familialism

The practice of the ethics of care that embraces vulnerability is nothing but the formation of a supportive relationship with individuals. However, can the small world of a traditional family and a regional community before the modern age find meaning in the third modern age?

Table 2.1 The three modern ages

	Individuals by private ownership	*Welfare state by social ownership*	*Modern Age by support*
First modern age	+	–	–
Second modern age	+	+	–
Third modern age	+	+	+

When P. Bourdieu investigated lower-class workers in Algeria during the War of Independence in 1960, he attributed the poverty of workers to the habitus of individuals who were not suitable for the social system of capitalism. That poverty was caused by the exclusion of the small world that relies on mutual assistance in the family-oriented community considering it as irrational in the expanding world of capitalism.

Lower-class workers in Algeria eke out a living by finding day-labor jobs. Even when some of them do not find day-labor jobs, someone else in the community will, and community members can survive by sharing the wages. If so, you do not have to work every day. You do not have to rationally plan your living time or think about your future; they believe the same day will continue (Bourdieu, 1977). Because such a small mutual aid community has minimal contact with outside societies, it cannot be considered a supportive relationship in the third modern age.

According to G. Esping-Andersen, the relative poverty rate in 2000 for the elderly was less than 5% in Sweden, whereas it was 10% in Italy and Spain. Here, he points out the issue that Italy and Spain, the countries of familialism with a high rate of intergenerational cohabitation, exhibit a high relative poverty rate for the elderly (Esping-Andersen and Palier, 2008, pp. 112–117). However, in the international comparison of poverty rates, socially excluded populations may exist in the portion that is not included in the samples of the government survey. Simultaneously, Japan is in a group with a higher relative poverty rate of 16% compared to the Organisation for Economic Co-operation and Development (OECD) countries based on a median income of 50% or less. Moreover, the poverty rate is even higher at 18% for the elderly aged 65 and above according to the Poverty Rate Survey conducted in 2012 by Ministry of Health, Labour and Welfare. The world of familialism does not support elderly citizens as individual subjects, and if the elderly are shut away in their small world, they are not different from the lower-class workers in Algeria.

If a welfare state can be sustained, G. Esping-Andersen's "revolution" should be exemplified in the financial perspective of social security by a society where women can participate in vocational activities with men. Nevertheless, it should also be noted that if the realization of a two-income family becomes advantageous, a new problem of inequality arises.

"The more time a family member has and the number of years they work for life, the more financially they will be able to cope with their longer retirements, and a stable family from the couple's income will retire stably even after they turn 65. However, the increase in single-income households, divorces, and unmarried singles would increase the risk of poverty as they age" (ibid., p. 127).

2.3.2 Social ownership

The first modern age had already been criticized, probably at the end of the 19th century in the field of sociology, when a conception of the second modern age began to emerge. For instance, É. Durkheim proposed a welfare state he named "socialism" (*le socialisme*) in his discussion regarding government policy-making as follows:

> "A nation has a duty to take care of the well-being of society. To compare society's health with that of the human body, the balance of tension, or the right balance between parts, is essential for good health. In that sense, it is harmful to a society when its wealth is scarce in one place and rich in the other; the nation must therefore prevent such extreme inequality in wealth."
>
> Durkheim (1970, pp. 174–175)

In his study of suicide, É. Durkheim focused on population and relationships, and suicide was statistically proven to contradict the strength of the social connection.

"Suicide occurs three times more in singles than in married couples, and twice more in married couples without children than those with children. Moreover, the number of suicide cases in these married couples is inversely proportional to the number of their children. The more you have in your mind to care for others than yourself, the more you can overcome the temptation of suicide" (Durkheim, 1963, p. 58).

Divorce released women from a patriarchal rule or traditional families of paternalism, and thus, it had no impact on women's suicide, even if it affected men's suicide. As Durkheim himself acknowledged, the divorce request was usually filed by the wife against the husband who lost the job to sustain the family (60% of divorces and 83% of separations were requested by wives). In other words, supportive relationships between individuals should be generated beyond the deconstruction of the patriarchal family. In that sense, is it possible that its deconstruction has not been completed yet, and thus, the "exit" on the part of women has resulted from it?

2.4 Vulnerability and inclusion

2.4.1 Open support connections

From the perspective of economic sociology, A. O. Hirschman discusses the construction of relationships in modern ages in association not only with loyalty but also with the exit from it and the voice (Hirschman, 1970). In contrast, C. Gilligan maintains that the supportive relationship for the inclusion of vulnerable people should not be discussed in terms of the exit from a group or the change of their affiliated groups; she argues that the ability to "voice" out to make changes in relationships in the group should be essential.

> Hirschman's discussion on loyalty has brought about a correction on the general view arguing the 'exit' will make changes. He presented loyalty to the exit, yet, at the same time, he underestimated the issue of connection in the relationship. (…) This paradigm in problem-solving based on an assumption of independence of individuals and competition among

> them would obscure the reality of interdependence among individuals and mask the possibilities for their cooperation.
>
> Gilligan (1986, p. 284)

In adolescence, one would try to integrate a new image of the self with a new relationship experience and reform one's social bonds, including relationships with parents. It is also a reformation of the relationship on the parents' side. Gilligan's argument was to present reformation in relationships instead of the exit from the relationship in Hirschman's argument. Therefore, not only the exit from groups/relationships but also "a different voice" to reform groups/relationships should increase its significance.

2.4.2 Deviant career

The practice of pre-modern society of imposing criminal offenders' responsibilities collectively on their family group across generations has rarely been observed in modern society. Persistent labeling through generations, which can be called retaliation, is a concept that contradicts Gilligan's idea of supportive relationships open to community members in terms of social reintegration.

Concurrently, H. S. Becker points out that in modern society, labeling criminals, even if on an individual level, would impose separation and isolation of the labeled from normal society.

Becker indicates that the labeling of deviations is determined by absolute preference over other position attributes in society.

"The status of deviant (though depending on the type of deviance) is dominant over other statuses. If one should receive the status of a deviant as a result of breaking a rule, the identification imposed by the status is more significant than those implied by other positions" (Becker, 1963, pp. 33–34).

Here, the exclusion of those who committed crimes from a conventional society would result in the isolation of these offenders.

Therefore, the trajectory of social reintegration requires a supportive relationship realized in the third modern age. This particular supportive relationship should be an open relationship that would not be limited by family connections. According to Durkheim's argument, the social security system of the welfare state in the second modern age relied on the occupational group, which was also a male-oriented intermediate group. If the supportive relationship in the third modern age should be formulated in reference to Durkheim's discussion of the intermediate group = occupational group in the second modern age, it can be organized as depicted in Table 2.2.

Table 2.2 Intermediate groups

	Family group	*Occupational group*	*Support relationships*
First modern age	+	–	–
Second modern age	+	+	–
Third modern age	+	+	+

2.5 Social inclusion of deviant individuals

P. Ricoeur discusses justice in terms of the succession of sanction, rehabilitation, and pardon from the perspective of personal "recognition (reconnaissance)" between the criminal and the victim. He argues that, following sanctions by the law, it is necessary to construct the rehabilitation against social exclusion and the pardon for the social inclusion of deviants (Ricoeur, 1995, pp. 193–208) (Table 2.3).

Is it possible to envision a post-welfare state society from the conventional social security-based welfare state by including and caring for vulnerable individuals in supportive relationships? In conclusion, I would like to mention the change in justice, along with the possibility of "recognition (reconnaissance)" of vulnerable individuals in the field of social work. Gilligan's proposition of care for others should become significant, particularly in the rehabilitation and pardon of deviants in the judicial system. P. Rosanvallon, who has discussed the importance of civil society since the welfare state, argues that the issue of the positions of judges and social workers approaching should be the topic of discussion in the judicial system, which is as follows:

> Today, we are facing a total transformation of the relationship between individuals and social systems on a gigantic scale. The judicial system, for instance, is in the same transformation movement. In other words, the criminal justice system is also in a time of total transformation as it gradually shifts its scope from criminal behavior to criminal character. At the same time, criminal justice is taking on the role of a guardian. It is increasingly urged to go beyond its legal character to sentence on the deviant's personality itself instead of behavior. The judge becomes a therapist for the social bond. He manages the convict's self-discipline (i.e., probation measures), intervenes in basic relationships with spouses and children (i.e., guardianship, educational assistance, and divorce incidental measures), and governs emotions; sometimes, the word 'social response' replaces the word 'punishment.'
>
> Rosanvallon (1995, pp. 213–214)

However, Rosanvallon also points out the "duality" in the abovementioned practice; it is not only the "recognition (*reconnaissance*)" of vulnerable individuals but also the practice with a risk of becoming a new form of "management of subject (*magistratures du sujet*)," which he suspects that "the practice

Table 2.3 Inclusion of deviants

	Sanction	*Rehabilitation*	*Pardon*
First modern age	+	–	–
Second modern age	+	+	–
Third modern age	+	+	+

may be merely holding hands again with various forms of paternalism before" (ibid., p. 214).

Therefore, it is essential to formulate supportive relationships multifacetedly for others by including not only the role played by the judge but also those played by families and various volunteers.

References

Becker, H.S. (1963) *Outsiders, Studies in the Sociology of Deviance*, New York, Free Press of Glencoe.

Bourdieu, P. ([1977] 1993) *Algérie 60, structure économiques et structures temporelles* [*Habitat of Capitalism, Contradictions in Algeria*]. Translated by Harayama, T., and Fujiwara Shoten, Paris, Les Éditions de Minuit.

Brugère, F. (2011) *L'Éthique du "care"* [*The Ethics of Care*], Paris, Collection QUE SAIS-JE, PUF.

Brugère, F. (2013) *La poliique de l'individu* [*The Politics of the Individuals*], Paris, Éditions du Seuil.

Castel, R. (2011) *L'ambiguité de la promotion de l'individu* [*Ambiguity of the Promotion of Individual*]. Refaire société, Paris, Éditions du Seuil.

Durkheim, E. ([1970]1987) *La science spciale et l'action* [*Social Science and Action*], Paris, Presses Universitaires de France.

Durkheim, E. ([1963]1992) *L'éducation morale* [*Moral Education*], Paris, Presses Universitaires de France.

Esping-Andersen, G., and Palier, B. (2018) *Trois leçons sur l'État-providence* [*Three Lessons of Welfare-State*], Paris, Éditions du Seuil.

Gilligan, C. ([1982]1993) *In a Different Voice: Psychological Theory and Women's Development*, Cambridge, Massachusetts, Harvard University Press.

Gilligan, C. (1986) 'Exit-Voice Dilemmas in Adolescent Development'. In Foxley, A., MacPherson, M.S. and O'Donnell, G. (eds.) *Development, Democracy and the Art of Trespassing: Essays in Honor of Albert O. Hirschman*, Notre Dame, Indiana, University of Notre Dame Press, pp. 283–300.

Hirschman, A.O. (1970) *Exit, Voice, and Loyalty: Responses to Decline in Firms, Organizations, and States*, Cambridge, Harvard University Press.

Ricoeur, P. (1995) *Sanction, réhabilitation, pardon* [*Sanction, Rehabilitation, Pardon*], Paris, Éditions Esprit.

Rosanvallon, P. (1995) *La nouvelle question sociale: Repenser l'État-providence* [*The New Social Question: Rethinking the Welfare State*], Paris, Éditions du Seuil.

Tronto, J.C. (1993) *Moral Boundaries: A Political Argument for an Ethic of Care*, New York, Routledge.

3 The Actual Situation of Crimes by the Elderly in Japan

Based on Crime Statistics, the Ministry of Justice's Research Report, and Special Investigations

Yoko Hosoi

Toyo University, Japan

3.1 Overview of crime statistics

If we examine the changes in the breakdown of people arrested for criminal offenses by age bracket (over the last 20 years) on an overall basis and for women, we can observe that the elderly (aged 65 and above), at 4.2%, accounted for the lowest percentage of people arrested for criminal offenses among all age brackets in 1998. However, at 21.5%, they accounted for the highest percentage among all age brackets in 2017. Whereas percentage figures corresponding to those of ages between 65 and 69 years of age rose from 2.1% in 1998 to 6.8% in 2017, percentage figures corresponding to those 70 years of age and above rose dramatically, from 2.1% in 1998 to 14.7% in 2017.

If we consider the breakdown of women arrested for criminal offenses by age bracket, we can observe that the elderly, at 6.4%, account for the lowest percentage of those arrested, next to those between the ages of 30 and 39 years in 1998. In 2017, however, they accounted for the highest percentage of those detained, at 34.3%, such that the elderly had come to account for about one out of every three women arrested for criminal offenses. Even among women, we can observe that, while percentage figures for those between 65 and 69 years of age increased from 2.9% in 1998 to 8.7%, percentage figures for those aged 70 years and older increased sharply from 3.5% in 1998 to 25.7% in 2017 (Figures 3.1 and 3.2).

Changes in the number and characteristics of crimes committed by elderly male individuals (1989–2018)

i The number of people aged 65 years and above arrested for general criminal offenses (per 100,000 people) has risen and has continued to increase across almost all types of crimes; this trend will continue to hold true at a high level (Figure 3.3).

  Overall, the number of criminal offenses committed peaked in 2004 and has subsequently declined. However, violent crimes alone have increased, therefore it can be stated that this society has become one that is being overrun by small acts of violence.

DOI: 10.4324/9781032669519-5

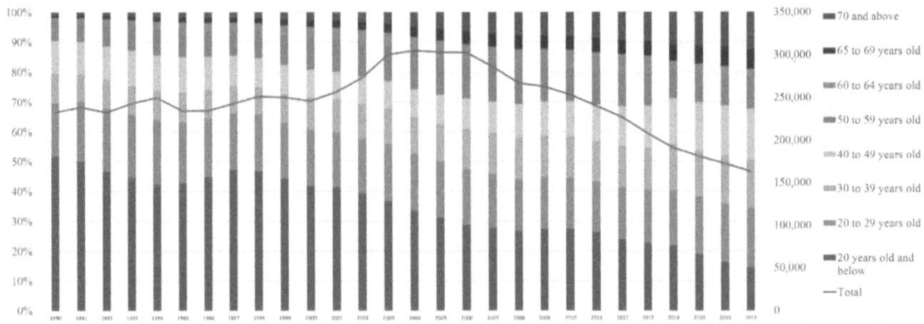

Figure 3.1 Breakdown of people arrested for criminal offenses by age bracket (male).

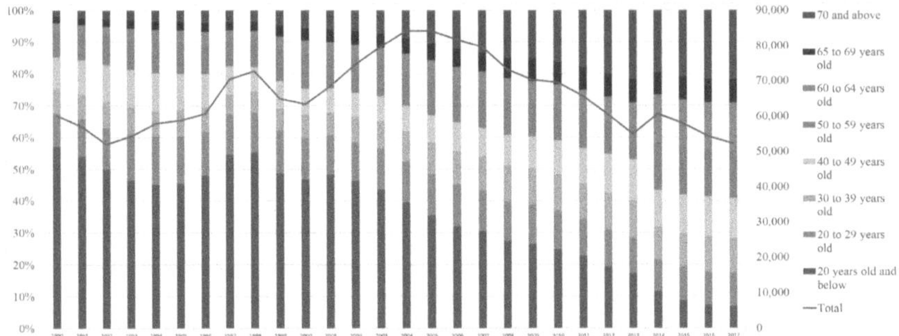

Figure 3.2 Breakdown of people arrested for criminal offenses by age bracket (female).

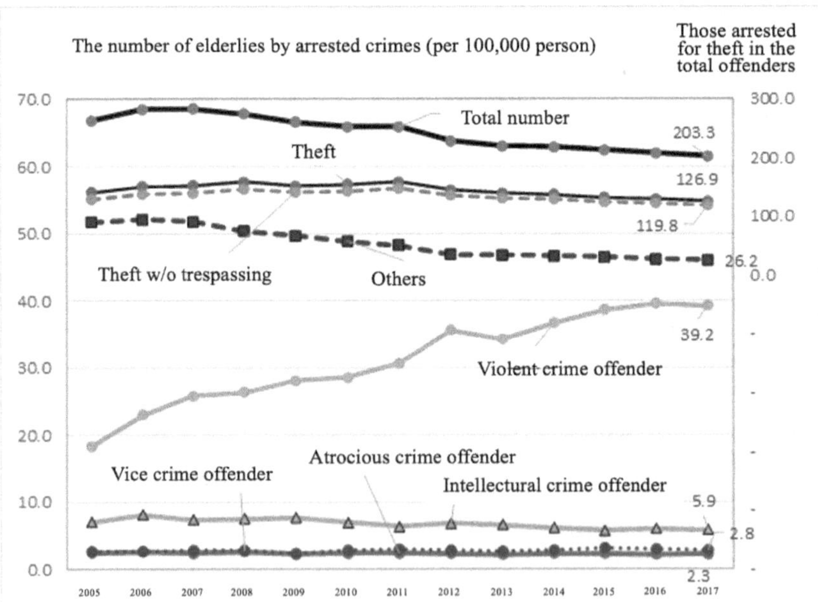

Figure 3.3 Changes in the number of elderly people arrested for criminal offenses (per 100,000 persons).

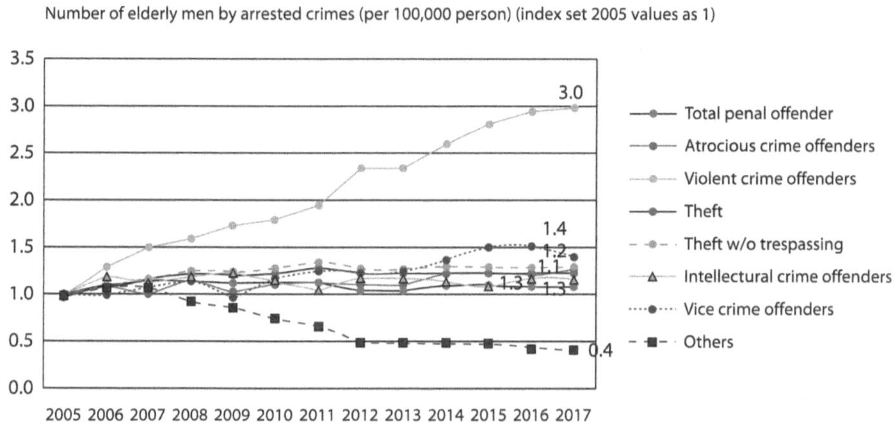

Figure 3.4 Changes in the number of arrested elderly men.

ii Different types of crimes correspond to different rising trends. Figure 3.4 reveals the rising trends according to the index. While the rising trend for violent crimes is notable, no significant increase or decrease can be observed in criminal offenses as a whole. In addition, the number of people arrested for non-criminal offenses has been decreasing.

iii Figure 3.5 outlines changes in the number of inmates. While numbers are trending downwards, figures not only for theft but also offenses involving illicit drug use are rising.

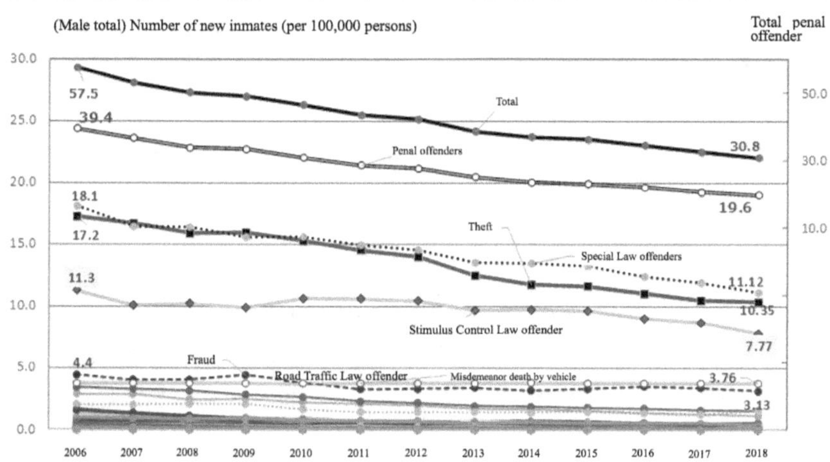

Figure 3.5 Changes in the number of new male inmates (in proportion to the population).

iv Number of arrested people and the proportion of the population they represent (per 100,000 people)

The number of elderly women peaked in 2012 (16,503), remained high thereafter, and stood at 16,297 in 2015, which is a 22.7% increase compared to 2005. In particular, the number of women aged 70 years and above was 12,094, which is a 39.7% increase compared to 2005. This was a four-fold increase when compared to 1996. Elderly women accounted for the lowest percentage of people arrested for criminal offenses among all age brackets, which was 6.7% in 1996. However, it accounted for the highest percentage among all age brackets at 33.1% in 2015, which meant that elderly women now account for about one in three women arrested for criminal offenses. While the proportion of population figures has decreased since peaking in 2012, the magnitude of the reduction in this figure for women aged 70 years and above is the lowest among all age brackets.

v Characteristics by type of crime

While much of the increase in elderly female criminals involves cases of theft, no rising trend for offenses involving stimulants can be observed (Figure 3.6).

vi The absolute index values for arrested people by crime type was low and revealed no significant trend with respect to any increase in the number of arrested elderly women.

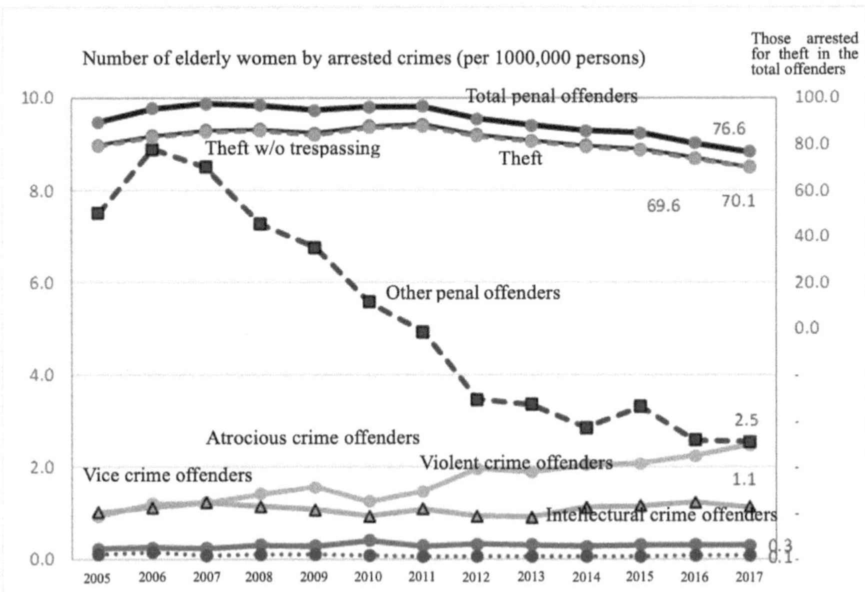

Figure 3.6 Changes in the number of arrested elderly women (in proportion to the population).

3.2 Picture of elderly criminals according to a special investigation conducted by the Ministry of Justice (2013–2015)

The Ministry of Justice focused on three types of crimes (thefts, injury-causing assaults, and homicide) and conducted an investigation into not only the pertinent contexts and factors of these crimes but also the awareness of perpetrators on the assumption that we needed to paint an accurate picture of criminals to focus on the rising rates by which elderly criminals re-enter prison shortly after they are released and know the circumstances by which elderly criminals re-commit crimes. This investigation was conducted based on the records of decisions made in criminal cases and other relevant materials. (With respect to this investigation, see Kako Takeshita's Aging and Dealing with Elderly Criminals [Crime and Punishment] 221, pp. 49–61, for information on the special investigative matters stated in the 2018 White Paper on Crime (Research and Training Institute of the Ministry of Justice, 2018) as well as the summary and interpretation of this investigation.) This investigation was compiled through retained documents on 354 perpetrators of theft (elderly people aged 65 years and above who were convicted in courts nationwide during June 2011 on theft charges), 97 perpetrators of injury-causing assaults or violent acts (elderly people whose cases were accepted by the Tokyo District Public Prosecutors Office or the Tokyo District Public Prosecutors Office in 2016 and who were either convicted or subjected to a summary order), and 82 perpetrators of homicide (elderly people who received a guilty verdict at courts nationwide during 2016 on charges inclusive of homicide and whose guilty verdict had been decided at the time of this investigation).

Figure 3.7 looks at the breakdown of people arrested for criminal offenses by the name of the offense in 2017. Among the elderly, theft and, in particular,

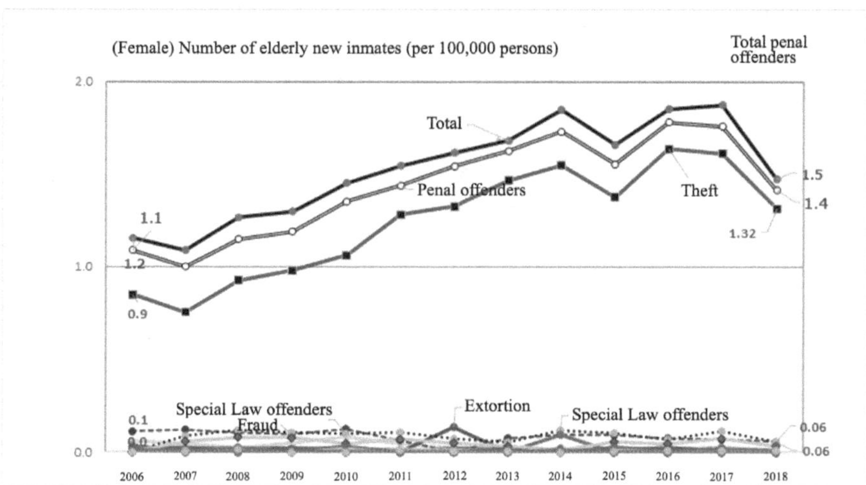

Figure 3.7 Changes in the number of new female inmates (in proportion to the population).

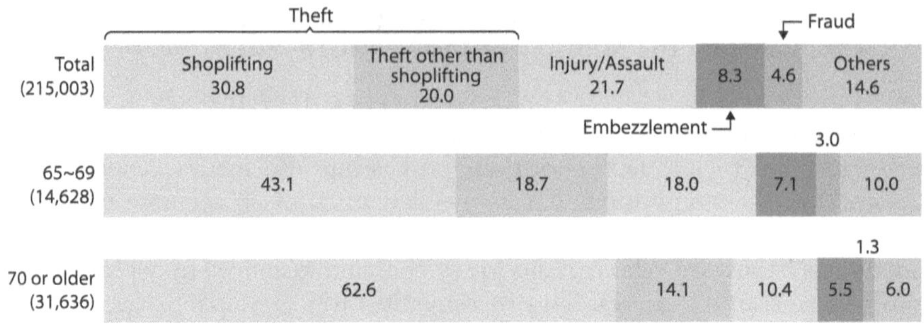

Notes: 1. The figures are based on the age at the time of offense.
2. "Embezzlement" includes embezzlement of lost property.
3. The figures in parentheses indicate the actual numbers of persons.
Source: Criminal Statistics of the National Police Agency

Figure 3.8 Breakdown of people arrested for criminal offenses by the name of the offense.

shoplifting, accounted for a significant percentage of criminal offenses. As shown in Figure 3.8, shoplifting accounted for approximately 60% of crimes committed by elderly people aged 70 years and above, followed by injury-causing assaults and violent acts.

3.2.1 Perpetrators of theft

An investigation was conducted based on the records of criminal decisions and other documents concerning 354 elderly people whose convictions for theft had been determined. Shoplifting accounted for 85% of the sample size. With respect to the pattern of perpetration, foodstuffs accounted for approximately 70% of items stolen, and items worth less than 3,000 yen accounted for approximately 70% of items stolen. In particular, items worth less than 1,000 yen accounted for 40% of the items stolen. Victimized stores were typically hit by people visiting as customers in 60% of the cases. In other words, elderly perpetrators characteristically shoplift low-value foodstuffs at stores they normally frequent for shopping purposes. When we examine their financial situation, we can note that approximately 90% of elderly shoplifters had a stable income, approximately 60% received a pension, and approximately half had savings and other assets. A little less than 90% of elderly shoplifters had no liabilities, such that they could hardly be described as being financially destitute compared to non-elderly perpetrators of shoplifting. When we examine whether elderly perpetrators lived with anyone else, we can observe that approximately half of the elderly male shoplifters and approximately 70% of the elderly female shoplifters lived with someone else, meaning that few shoplifters lived alone. When we examine motive, "living in poverty" describes a few elderly shoplifters—less than 30% of men and between 10 and 19% of women. Why do the elderly sometimes engage in shoplifting? A little over 50% of men and approximately 80% of women indicated that they do so to "save money." It is possible that the resistance that people feel towards engaging in shoplifting has weakened.

Next, when we examine criminal records and the state of recidivism for theft, we see that more than half the elderly male perpetrators had been previously convicted and had been given prison sentences. Prior convictions with at least one fine corresponded to 80% of elderly male perpetrators. Prior convictions with at least one fine corresponded to approximately 60% of female elderly perpetrators. More than 30% of female elderly perpetrators had no prior convictions but had previously engaged in multiple acts of theft. It was revealed that elderly shoplifters had been punished multiple times in the past.

When we consider the age of elderly perpetrators of shoplifting at the time of their first arrest, we see that approximately 20% of elderly male perpetrators had been arrested by the time they were 20. After the age of 50, the ratio of detained people was relatively higher. However, it is only past the age of 60 that people arrested for the first-time account for half of the elderly perpetrators. One-fourth of elderly men were arrested for the first time after the age of 65. In contrast, the number of elderly women arrested for the first time increased all at once between the ages of 62 and 63. This number rises to match the corresponding number associated with men at this point and thereafter continues to increase. In other words, while women are late bloomers, they are willing to dip their toes into the world of crime in their twilight years (Figure 3.9).

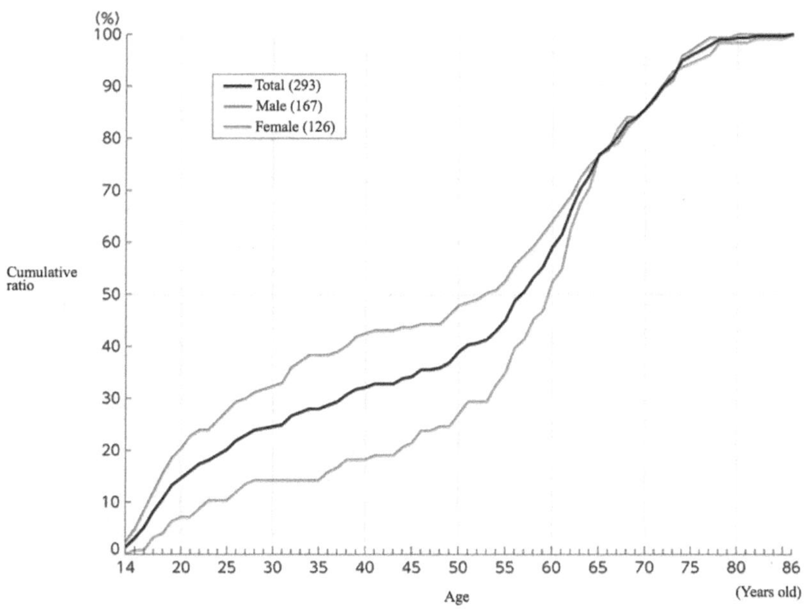

Figure 3.9 Age of elderly perpetrators of shoplifting at the time of the first arrest.

Looking at the trials held for elderly perpetrators of shoplifting, we see that approximately half of the perpetrators were fined. Among those who had been fined previously, approximately 60% of the men and approximately 40% of the women found themselves being fined again. With respect to recidivism, 18.6% of elderly male perpetrators of shoplifting who had been fined and 34.2% of elderly female perpetrators of shoplifting who had been fined went on to re-offend within two years of their initial conviction in court. The above data informs us that many elderly perpetrators of shoplifting, regardless of sex, were arrested for the first time in or after their fifties and subsequently re-offended within a short period of time and received punishment accordingly. Thus, four conclusions can be drawn. The first conclusion is that people in need, who comprise a certain segment of elderly men, might need to be connected to welfare support through the provision of integration support and special adjustments. The second is the possibility that resistance to the idea of shoplifting is lowered for those who are arrested in or after their fifties when their punishments for minor crimes are lax, their indictments are suspended, fines are imposed, or other examples of progressive dispositions are carried out such that such individuals are not subjected to correctional or probationary treatment. The third is the fact that, as we observed earlier under "motive," feelings of insecurity about the future can sometimes outweigh any sense of short-term difficulties and even the burden of being arrested and receiving the associated punishment. The fourth conclusion indicates that while it is conceivable that the living conditions are relatively good for elderly women, we need to understand why one in three re-offends within two years. In the subsequent sections, with an investigation of the inmates, we wish to clearly identify the factors that account for the crime.

3.2.2 Perpetrators of injury-causing assaults and violent acts

As with perpetrators of theft, an investigation of 97 convicted elderly people (including those on whom summary orders were imposed) was conducted in 2016, based on records of criminal decisions and other such documents. Violent acts and injury-causing assaults accounted for 68.0% and 32.0% of violent crimes committed by perpetrators of violent acts, respectively. With respect to the pattern of perpetration, these offenses typically lacked any element of premeditation, and deadly weapons were used in approximately only 10% of cases. With respect to motive and context, "fly into a rage" was indicated more than any other option by approximately 80% of the individuals surveyed, and 20% indicated "resentment and dissatisfaction." These numbers reveal that violence tended to be carried out impulsively in this cohort. In addition, elderly people or minors (under the age of 18 years) accounted for approximately 20% of the victims of these crimes.

More than half of the elderly people surveyed had a prior criminal record. Those who had committed a similar type of offense in the past accounted for one-third of all the surveyed people. It was ascertained that those who had committed a similar type of offense in the past were likely to have consumed alcoholic drinks when committing their crimes. Many of these individuals also felt that they were more justified in their actions than those who had never committed a similar type of offense.

According to the trials, approximately 80% of elderly perpetrators of injury-causing assaults and violent acts were fined; therefore, only a small percentage of these offenders received enforcement or probationary treatment. Moreover, approximately 40% of elderly perpetrators of injury-causing assaults and violent acts who had committed a similar type of offense in the past lived alone, were unemployed, and did not interact with family members or acquaintances.

3.2.3 Perpetrators of homicide

This investigation of 82 elderly individuals was based on court records and other documents. Elderly perpetrators of homicides are notable for the greater likelihood that the perpetrator and victim are related to one another than is the case with non-elderly perpetrators, records indicating that the perpetrator and victim are related to one another in approximately 70% of all cases. This rate is even higher when the elderly perpetrator of homicide is a woman, thus indicating that 13 out of 14 female perpetrators were related to their victims (eight were children of the perpetrators and five were the spouses of the perpetrators). If we look at their prior history, approximately 10% of these individuals have been previously imprisoned. Approximately 70% of the elderly perpetrators of murder received a prison sentence, which was lower than it was for non-elderly perpetrators of murder (approximately 90%).

The murderers of family members, who accounted for the majority of the elderly perpetrators of murder, can be divided into those whose victims were spouses and those whose victims were their children. The rate associated with the killing of the perpetrator's child is high for female perpetrators. For approximately 90% of perpetrators who killed their children, their victims were found to have been suffering from some sort of mental or physical impairment. For one-third of the perpetrators who killed their spouses, the victims required nursing care or were bedridden. For approximately 30% of such perpetrators, their victims had dementia.

From the above information, we can create an image of the elderly perpetrators of murder. The victim might have suffered from a mental illness like the perpetrator's child. Although there may have been problems at home, the perpetrator may have been dealing with issues for which he or she could not seek advice from others. They may have acted out of desperation and could have been pessimistic about the future. In some cases, the perpetrator may have been driven to murder to counteract acts of violence or verbal abuse by the victim. Even in cases where the spouse was a victim, the victim may have suffered from a physical or mental disorder and required nursing care. Given these circumstances, the perpetrator may be pessimistic about the future and act out of desperation. Many perpetrators have committed murder while attempting to deal with such issues. In light of such circumstances, trials involving the murder of family members, even where the crime in question has actually been committed, are characterized by the fact that a stay of execution is issued in approximately 30% of all cases.

3.3 Recidivism on the part of elderly criminals

As already observed, crimes committed by the elderly have not increased since peaking in 2007. However, there is no doubt that they remained high. One factor responsible for this trend is that a significant number of elderly criminals re-offend within a relatively short period after being freed from prison. In other words, the relative rate of recidivism is increasing.

In this connection, the Ministry of Justice conducted several special investigations concerning recidivism to learn about the actual conditions and enable the consideration of countermeasures. We can ascertain the circumstances surrounding recidivism by referring to the research concerning crimes committed by the elderly and people with mental disabilities and their treatment, a report issued by the Research and Training Institute of the Ministry of Justice (Research and Training Institute of the Ministry of Justice, 2017).

The Comprehensive Measures for the Prevention of Recidivism, which was formulated at a conference of cabinet ministers responsible for anticrime measures held in July 2015, sets forth the provision of mobility and support measures for the elderly and persons with disabilities as a set of priority measures for the prevention of recidivism, and indicates the necessity of making special adjustments and otherwise establishing links with healthcare and welfare providers.

This report was compiled in 2016 as the basic material for this purpose. It helped to ascertain the state of measures for the treatment and provision of support for societal reintegration in the context of prosecution, correctional matters, and rehabilitation, as well as the attributes associated with the trends and the state of recidivism by the elderly people released from prison, as determined by the results of special investigations into such people. In addition, it clarified the characteristics of those for whom special adjustments were deemed reasonable.

3.3.1 Actual conditions with respect to the treatment in the context of prosecution, correctional matters, and rehabilitation

With respect to the number of people indicted on criminal charges, people with a previous record accounted for between 47 and 53% of people under 65 years of age, albeit between 63 and 72% of the elderly, consistently beginning in 1996. In 2015, this number stood at 67.1% among the elderly. With respect to "women" indicted on criminal charges, people with a previous record accounted for approximately 20% of people under 65 years of age until 2008, which rose to about 30% thereafter. On the other hand, elderly women with a previous record accounted for a record low of 37.4% of all elderly women indicted on criminal charges in 2007. This figure subsequently rose and reached 52.0% in 2015.

With respect to correctional matters, the number of men under the age of 65 readmitted to prison among the prison population has been continuously decreasing since peaking in 2006. The same figure for elderly men continued to increase from 1996 to 2009 and thereafter remained high. The readmission rate for individuals under the age of 65 continued to grow, beginning in 2004 and reaching 59.5% in 2015. In contrast, the rate for the elderly, at between 71% and 83%, was at a substantially higher level than for those under the age of 65 and was at 73.0% in 2015. For women, the number of readmitted individuals rose for both those under the age of 65 and the elderly; the number of readmitted women increased by 2.1 times and 6.5 times, respectively, for those under the age of 65 and the elderly between 1996 and 2015. As with elderly men, the readmission rate for elderly women was substantially higher than that for those under the age of 65; after hitting its lowest point over the last two decades in 2006 (40.7%), it hovered between 45 and 55%, and came in at 48.6% in 2015. Overall, the number of readmitted elderly people has remained at around the 1,600 mark since 2012. In recent years, the readmission rate has stayed at around 70% and was 69.6% in 2015 (Figure 3.10).

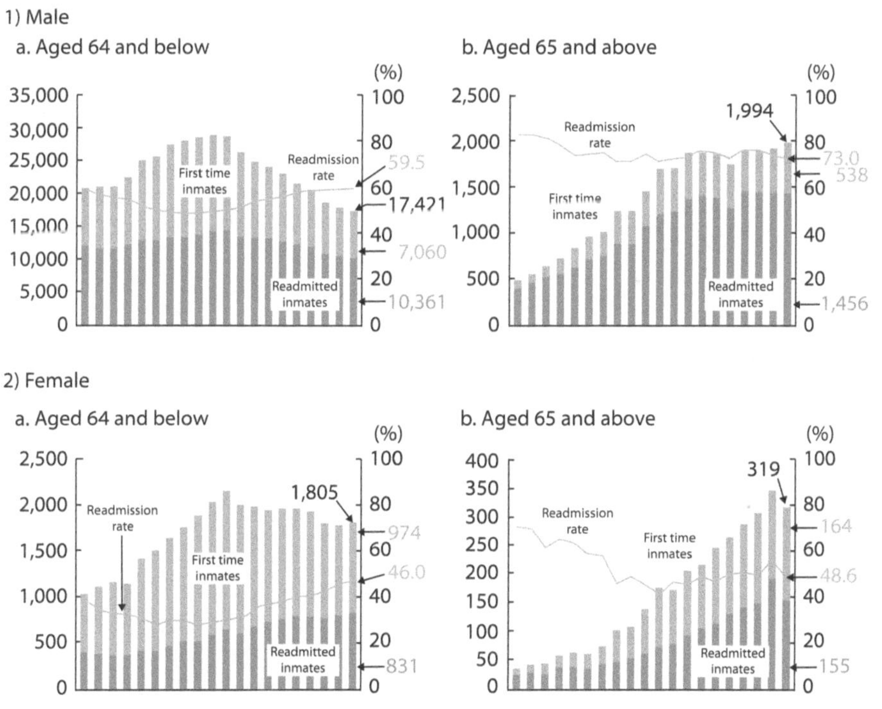

Note 1 Source: Documents of the Judicial System Department of the Minister's Secretariat of the Ministry of Internal Affairs and Communications.
2 According to the age of admittance.

Figure 3.10 Changes in the number of people readmitted to prison within the prison population and by the readmission rate (by sex).

The readmission rate within five years of the release of an inmate from prison in 2011 was consistently higher for elderly people released upon serving their full terms than for elderly parolees, as was the case for people under the age of 65 years. The readmission rate for elderly women was such that there was little difference between those who had been released upon serving their full terms and parolees. The readmission rate for men in general was consistently lower for those who had been released upon serving their full term than for parolees. Among elderly women, the readmission rate within five years for parolees was 36.9%, which was more or less the same as it was for those who had been released upon serving their full terms. This was higher than that for those who were under the age of 65 as well as for the overall population of the inmates (Figure 3.11).

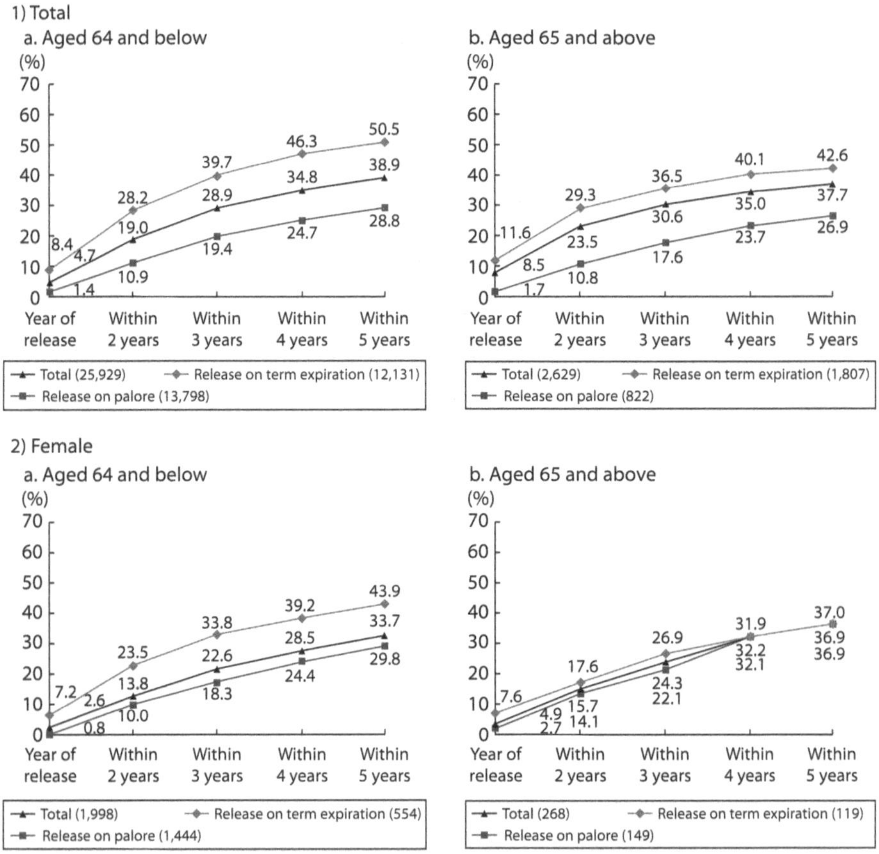

Note 1 Source: Documents of the Judical System Department of the Minister's Secretariat of the Ministry of Justice
2 Those who re-admitted for the crime on which they served in the previous improsonment and released either on prison term expiration or palore were counted here.
3 The 5 year re-admission rate indicates the rate of inmates who were released in 2011 and readimitted to prison in each year from 2011 to 2015.
4 Inmates were grouped according to the age at the time of their previous release from prison. Ages at the previous release of the re-admitted inmates were estimated from the age of their re-admittance and the year of their previous release.

Figure 3.11 Re-admission rate for released inmates within five years by grounds for release (overall population of inmates, female).

When we examine elderly people readmitted to prison in 2015, who re-offended less than a year after their release according to the place to which they returned after they were released, we see that "family member or relative" was rated the lowest while "other" was rated the highest. In particular, the percentages of people who re-offended in less than three months were such that "other" rated significantly higher than did "family member or relative" or "acquaintance, employer, relief, rehabilitation facility, etc." Similar trends were observed for elderly women. In other words, connections to blood relatives, local communities, and society are weakened as individuals re-offend within short periods of time. As such individuals end up finding other places to which they go after they are released, it can be claimed that it becomes easier to be led to commit further crimes. Measures are required to help people break out of this vicious cycle. Similar trends were also observed in elderly women.

When we consider parolees and people under probation with the execution of their sentence suspended, from 2006 to 2015 with respect to probation, we see that the number of elderly parolees increased by 2.1 times, and the number of people with a prior conviction increased by 2.3 times. The rate of elderly parolees with a previous conviction was approximately around 80% and stood at 89.4% in 2015.

3.3.2 Actual situation with respect to measures for the reintegration of elderly criminals into society

In the past, prosecutors investigated cases and participated in trial activities while working to reduce recidivism and other criminal policy perspectives. The Concept of Prosecution, which was formulated in September 2011, stated that "efforts should be made to make an active collaboration with the police, other investigative organs, as well as enforcement, probationary, and other relevant entities to contribute to the purpose of criminal policy, such as in terms of the prevention of crime and the rehabilitation of those who commit crime." In addition to providing the conventional exit support (job-related support and support for securing housing as provided to people released from prison or otherwise from a correctional facility), prosecutors' efforts came to be directed toward the provision of entry support (support provided to those who have not been subjected to detention in a correctional facility). To prepare for these new initiatives, the Supreme Public Prosecutors' Office adopted the Criminal Policy Expert Committee (2012) and the Criminal Policy Promotion Office (2016), while the regional public prosecutors' offices adopted the Placement of Staff Members in Charge and the Employment and Use of Expert Staff Members (social workers) beginning in 2013. As for concrete initiatives, coordination with welfare and medical organizations was undertaken, and some accompanying support was provided to relevant organizations. Prosecutors began to work closely with probation offices and community living establishment centers to collaborate with external organizations.

Let us examine what the Social Rehabilitation Support Office of the Tokyo District Public Prosecutors' Office has been doing since 2013 to ascertain the state of specific actions that have been taken.

The Tokyo District Public Prosecutors' Office, through its preparatory office, established the Social Rehabilitation Support Office in 2013 to support the smooth reintegration of elderly criminals into society after their release from prison and to prevent them from re-offending. Figure 3.12 shows the operation flow of the particular office. The suspects and defendants for whom this office was established consist of those who are not being sent to prison, and those who are believed to be at high risk of re-offending if they are released without assistance, because they are elderly, struggling with poverty, or dealing with other issues that make it difficult for them to reintegrate into society on their own. The Social Rehabilitation Support Office, which is manned by three support workers, is consulted by prosecutors regarding suspects and defendants believed to be in need of welfare support because of their advanced age or other factors, conducts investigations into case records, and frequently meets with public prosecutors as well as the parties in cases, identifies the issues at hand, and transfers individuals to offices in charge of providing urgent aftercare for discharged offenders. Consequently, the welfare offices carry out the steps required for involuntary admission, file demand trials, and otherwise appropriately undertake various measures. 66.5% of all cases processed result in the transfer of elderly people to a welfare office, which is a higher figure than for any other outcome.

Thus, prosecution initiatives focused on social reintegration to prevent elderly suspects and defendants from re-offending have been rapidly rolled out nationwide over the last four or five years. In carrying out these initiatives, the consent of suspects and defendants, to whom support for social reintegration is to be provided, is needed. An investigation into the handling of cases for which consent cannot be obtained should be conducted.

Next, let us examine the correctional facilities and how rehabilitation is handled. In particular, let us consider special adjustments, special treatment, and general adjustments. While some individuals released from prison comprise those who are released without having secured an appropriate support system, thus placing them in a difficult position for successful reintegration into society despite the fact that they lack relatives, require welfare support, and find it challenging to live independently because of their age, others benefit from special adjustments made for their sake. Specifically, the Ministry of Justice and the Ministry of Health, Labour, and Welfare joined forces in April 2009 to establish Local Life Support Centers that were to be operated for the benefit of certain individuals. The eligibility criteria included the following factors: (i) had to be an elderly individual, (ii) had an absence of housing upon release, (iii) deemed as a result of old age to require various welfare services to lead a healthy life subsequent to release, and (iv) requested to be treated as someone

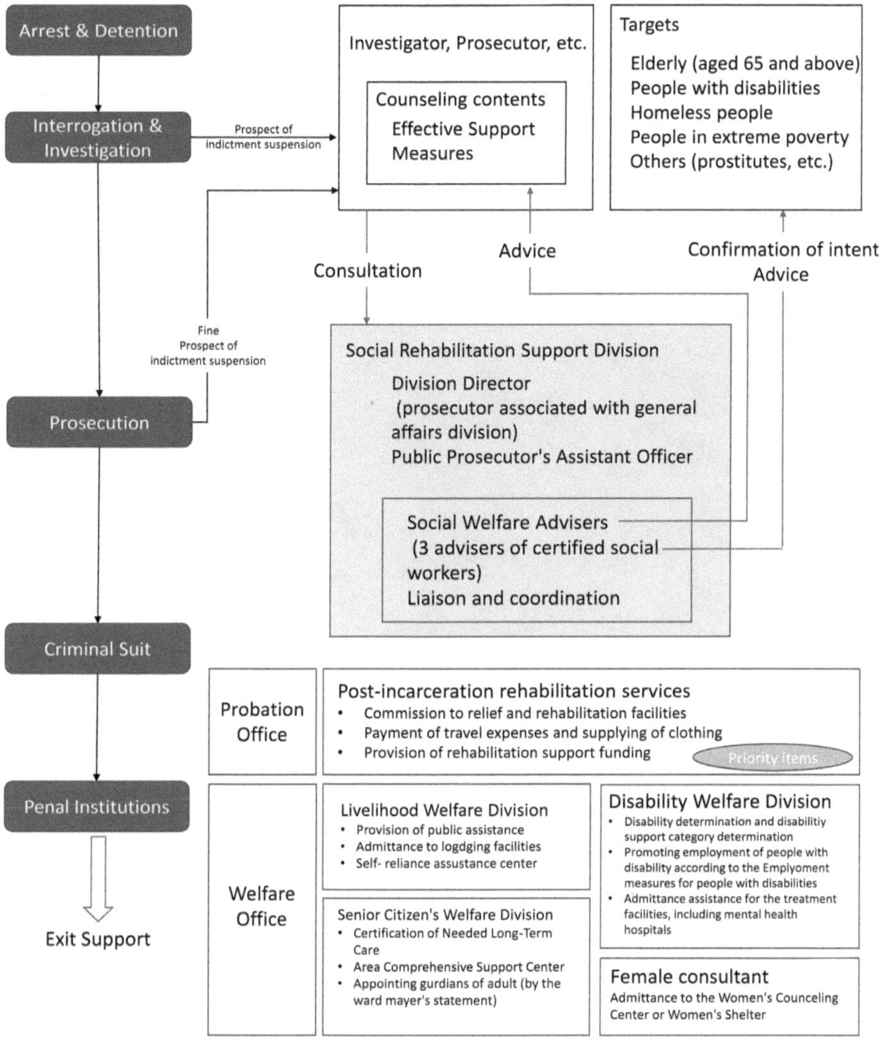

Note: Organized from data of the Social Rehabilitation Support Division, Tokyo District Prosecutor's Office

Figure 3.12 Operations of the Social Rehabilitation Support Office of the Tokyo District Public Prosecutors Office.

for whom special adjustments should be made. Let us now examine how these initiatives are being implemented. The number of people taking advantage of these initiatives has increased between the fiscal years 2011 and 2015 and stood at 389 people in the fiscal year 2015.

References

Research and Training Institute of the Ministry of Justice. (2017) *Research Department Report 56: Research on Crimes Committed by Elderly or Mentally Disordered Persons and Their Treatment*, https://www.moj.go.jp/content/001254604.pdf.

Research and Training Institute of the Ministry of Justice. (2018) *White Paper on Crime 2018: Advancing Population Aging and Crime*. https://hakusyo1.moj.go.jp/en/67/nfm/mokuji.html.

4 Reintegrating Elderly Criminals into the Society

From the Standpoint of Judicial Welfare

Kayo Konagai

Nagano University, Japan

4.1 Introduction

Crime is a type of antisocial activity that requires the ability to assess circumstantial conditions and take necessary actions to accomplish a given purpose. In that sense, the elderly and the increase in their violent crimes might be the result of the rise in the number of active elderly individuals in the present society (Cabinet Office, 2017). At the same time, the fact that most of these crimes consist of shoplifting (Ministry of Justice, 2022)suggests that such crimes are carried out to satisfy life-related needs and wants. This can be attributed to the high relative poverty rate among the elderly (Ministry of Internal Affairs and Communications, 2017).

Based on the findings obtained through interviews with elderly criminals, this chapter discusses the rehabilitation process of elderly criminals and the ways of their reintegration into society. In this chapter, the author focuses on the elderly criminals as autonomous human beings, not as vulnerable people in need of full care. Thus, this chapter explores how to reintegrate them into society through a social security system to support them with the necessary care while respecting their independence as much as possible.

4.2 Rehabilitation process of elderly ex-criminals observed in the interview-based survey

Over three fiscal years, from 2014 to 2016, the author and Prof. Yuzuru Kawabe conducted a series of approximately 90-minute-long semi-structured interview sessions with 100 former criminals to ascertain the contributing factors for their rehabilitation and the required social support framework.[1] The process of rehabilitation and social reintegration of 13 elderly ex-criminals interviewed by the author are examined in this section.

4.2.1 Outline and typification of cases

All 13 participants were men aged 65 years and above at the time of the interview. Ages at which they committed crimes, however, ranged from

DOI: 10.4324/9781032669519-6

55 to 73 years. The duration from their release from incarceration to the time of interview sessions also ranged from two to nine years, during which none reoffended. Those who had spent at least two years without reoffending were defined as "rehabilitated" in this survey.

After their release from penal institutions, all participants entered "rehabilitation aid facilities"[2] and stayed there for several to six months in preparation for a normal life in the community. Rehabilitation aid facilities accept criminals with broken family ties due to their criminal history. Broken family ties should be one of the essential factors that characterize the need for rehabilitation support for these elderly ex-criminals.

Characteristics of interview participants are as follows:

- Age distribution at the time of the crime: 1 committed the crime at 55 years, 3 at 60 years, 3 at 61 years, 1 at 64 years, 1 at 65 years, 1 at 68 years, 1 at 70 years, 1 at 71 years, and 1 at 73 years.
- Age distribution at the time of the interview: 1 was 65 years old, 1 was 66 years old, 3 were 67 years old, 1 was 68 years old, 1 was 72 years old, 3 were 75 years old, 2 were 76 years old, and 1 was 77 years old.
- The most recent criminal offences: one case of robbery, seven cases of theft (among which three were shoplifting), one case of fraud, one case of "dine and dash," and three cases of violation of the stimulant drug control law.
- Employment status at the time of the crime: 10 were unemployed, 1 was a construction worker, 1 was a home helper, and 1 was a criminal organization member.

These 13 participants can be divided into the following 3 groups according to the factors behind their crimes:

i Crime committed due to the hardships of life stemming from the failure to obtain social welfare support for their disabilities (with minor severity): two participants.
ii Crime committed due to the hardships of life stemming from unemployment: eight participants (of which one participant lost his job due to his reckless lifestyle).
iii Drug addiction: three participants.

4.2.2 "Human Life Composition Model"

In this section, the author would like to propose that human life is composed of the following four elements: life-related infrastructure (i.e., community/organization one belongs to, residence, and source of income), identity (i.e., coherent conception on oneself), human capital (i.e., the capacity, knowledge, and skills that support one's life), and social capital (i.e., the human relations and social resources in the community). The terms presented in parentheses constitute the definitions used in this chapter.

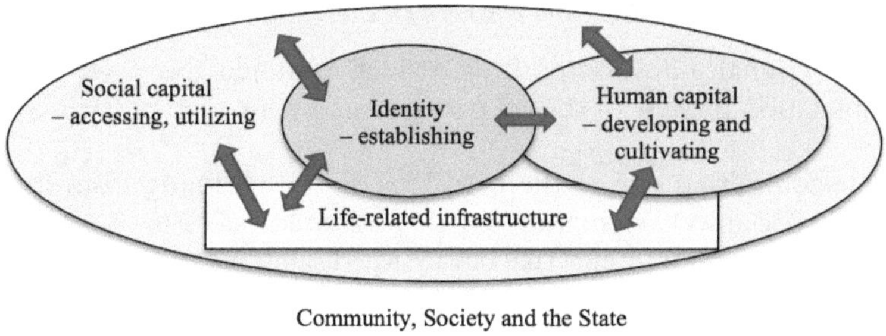

Figure 4.1 "Human Life Composition Model".

These elements are related to one another, as shown in Figure 4.1. An individual's human capital is formed upon his/her life-related infrastructure, and he/she uses social capital to lead his/her social life. The elements of life-related infrastructure, human capital, and social capital are integrated to establish the element of identity, and these four elements interact with one another. When each element is firmly rooted in a sound interaction, a synergistic effect is brought about to enrich one's quality of life. In contrast, if these elements are fragile, a negative chain effect will occur, resulting in problematic behaviors and chaotic life, such as withdrawal, suicide, and criminal activities.

Let us now consider the mechanism of crime in accordance with this figure. If an individual's life-related infrastructure is fragile, harnessing his/her potential human capital could be challenging and could lead to a troubled life. His/her connection with the community/society could also be insufficient, and effective utilization of social capital to resolve various problems in life would be nearly impossible. Consequently, he/she falls into a vicious cycle in which he/she cannot establish his/her identity. He/she will then attempt to resolve any difficulties he/she faces with a shortsighted approach, through crime, which will become his/her behavioral pattern because the quick and easy satisfaction of his/her desires through crime will grant him/her with the false sense of a stable life. Even though each element could be affected by the age, personality, and living situation of the person concerned, this model of behavior mechanism might apply to any criminal behavior, regardless of the criminal's age and gender.

In that sense, the direction of rehabilitation and reintegration of criminals should be steered toward enriching the connotation of each of the four elements to make them firm and consolidate the connections among these elements. In other words, the process of rehabilitation is the process of improving one's life-related infrastructure to establish a foundation for the individual's life, so that they can develop and cultivate their potential human capital by harnessing their social capital. This, in turn, enables restoring their diffused identity and their leading a self-sufficient and wholesome life. The author's conceived model of rehabilitation should be considered valid based on the discussion so far.

4.2.3 The reality of rehabilitation observed in case examinations

Using the "Human Life Composition Model" outlined above, let us examine the rehabilitation process of the 13 participants by the type of their crimes.

i "Crime committed due to the hardships of life stemming from the failure to obtain social welfare support for their disabilities."

Those with minor intellectual or physical disabilities and in need of welfare support fell under this category. Although they could manage to make ends meet until they reached their middle age under the protection of family and employers, they were deprived of this protection after the death of key family members or the economic recession. They could not receive social welfare support partially because their disability was too minor to qualify for such support. Eventually, they turned to the quick solution entailed in criminal behavior (such as shoplifting, habitual theft, and "dining and dashing") in response to the hardships of life due to unemployment.

Looking at the criminal factors in accordance with the "Human Life Composition Model," their life-related infrastructure was fragile because of unemployment, their human capital to lead an autonomous, independent life was inadequate because of their disability; and their social capital to utilize support from the private sector and public services (welfare support programs for people with disabilities and public assistance) was lacking due to their social isolation. Thus, they became unable to sustain their lives. Consequently, their identity was established on a negative self-conception, whereby they viewed themselves as "inferior and incompetent beings rejected by others and the community." With nothing to lose, they began to engage in crime as a way of life.

How did these individuals become rehabilitated? Let us trace their rehabilitation process by organizing the information obtained through interviews according to the "Human Life Composition Model."

The two individuals were connected to public welfare services through the criminal justice procedure. The length of time without reoffending ranged from four to nine years. They were released from penal institutions and reintegrated into society before the implementation of the "Promotion Project for Settlement in Local Communities" (Ministry of Health, Labour and Welfare, 2023) which is discussed later. Nevertheless, they received similar support that is offered through the above-mentioned project by the staff of "the rehabilitation aid facility," where they were sent through the probation office after their court rulings (with a suspended sentence with probation) or release from prison.

After leaving "the rehabilitation aid facility," the two individuals were promptly forwarded to "relief facilities," so that they could rebuild their lives. Here, let us describe their life structure at the time of the interview survey, focusing on their commonalities:

- Life-related infrastructure: Restored by their admission to the "relief facilities" and successful application and approval of welfare benefits or pensions for their disabilities.

- Human capital: Won others' trust, had gratitude for those who provided them with care and support, had an eagerness to repay such support, and developed self-control and self-sufficiency (the ability to recognize and be satisfied with what is good in oneself and one's own life).
- Social capital: Established the relationships with staff members of "the rehabilitation aid facilities" and "the relief facilities" and obtained support provided by the welfare offices in the municipality.
- Identity: Established positive self-conception, for instance, considering oneself as "a person who has successfully secured a stable life and desisted from crime" or "a person capable of engaging calmly in self-reflection without comparing oneself to others."

The structures of their lives were restored, as described above. They all unanimously mentioned that they no longer had anxiety about their present lives, and they wished to maintain what they enjoyed at that time.

ii "Crime committed due to the hardships of life stemming from unemployment."

The eight individuals who belonged to this category suffered hardships due to unemployment. Instead of rebuilding their lives through lawful, realistic means, such as selling off property or using public services, these individuals succumbed to despair, indulged in alcohol abuse, and ruined their lives by repeatedly engaging in property-related crimes and fraud.

On examining criminal factors according to this model, their life-related infrastructure broke down because of unemployment or a reckless lifestyle. In terms of human capital, the lack of insight into the self or problem-solving skills among them should be noted, despite their relatively high levels of educational background (of these eight individuals, three graduated from university, one graduated from high school, and three graduated from junior high school). Their lives also collapsed without access to social capital represented by acquaintances or public services (such as public consultation services on public assistance or loan repayments). These individuals developed a negative identity characterized by a feeling that they were failures in life.

Consolidating information obtained through this interview in accordance with the "Human Life Composition Model," their rehabilitation process can be described as follows.

These eight individuals were compelled to isolate themselves from a chaotic life through criminal justice proceedings. They came to lead wholesome lives owing to living by the rules stipulated by penal institutions or rehabilitation aid facilities, and then having to confront themselves through this process. In this way, they reset their psychological state/mindset as well as their lifestyle, gained a renewed sense of diligence, and restored their lives while saving money during their stay at "the rehabilitation aid facilities."

The life structures of all eight individuals can be described with a focus on the following common points:

- Life-related infrastructure: Stabilized by securing stable earnings and housing. Out of these 8 individuals, 5 were aged 70 years and above, and although they all worked to earn money, only 2 of these 5 were fully independent financially. Their minimum living costs were either covered by employment earnings, a combination of employment earnings and supplementary welfare benefits, or a combination of employment earnings and pension payments. These individuals lived in rented housing, the costs of which were affordable.
- Human capital: Developed diligence (if they were emotionally stable), the ability to produce results at work by thinking intelligently, and self-sufficiency (i.e., the ability to recognize and be satisfied with what is good in oneself and one's own life).
- Social capital: Established relationships with the staff of "the rehabilitation aid facilities" and employers; social relationships were limited to this scope except for one individual, who was a restaurant owner who committed fraud when he lived a reckless life. He maintained relationships with neighbors and political party colleagues.
- Identity: Established positive self-conception, for instance, "a person who demonstrates his skills and capacity through work, and a person whose work is valued by others," "a person who has recovered his self-respect," and "a person who leads a high-quality life (regardless of the amount he earns)."

Their lives were restored, as described above. Each of them declared their intent to maintain their then-current lifestyle, which they worked hard to achieve by standing on their own two feet.

iii "Drug addiction" group

Three individuals who were convicted for stimulant-related offences fell under this category. Since stimulants are highly addictive, recidivism occurs based on brain-level dependence,[3] despite the intent or personality of the individual. It might have started as a casual indulgence derived from their unhealthy, frivolous attitude toward life, underscored by a weakness of character attributed to their life history; drugs were used to compensate for such weakness of character. This survey verified that the risk of drug possession increases among those with weakness of character if they live in an area where drugs can be easily obtained.

If we consolidate the relevant criminal factors in accordance with the "Human Life Composition Model," their life-related infrastructure broke down through financial difficulties caused by excessive spending on drugs or by a slowdown at work brought about by the use of drugs. With respect to human capital, qualifications previously held were lost because of the use of drugs. Since relationships with sound, healthy people were also destroyed as a result of drug addiction, these individuals also came to be deprived of social capital, through isolation. Consequently, these individuals suffered from a negative identity, being isolated from society because of drug addiction and being perceived as a feeble person who could not live without drugs. They repeatedly engaged in drug use, as they became increasingly dissociated from reality.

Let us examine the rehabilitation process of these individuals, consolidating the matters learned through these interviews in accordance with the "Human Life Composition Model."

All three individuals were liberated from drugs through imprisonment, during which their physical and mental health recovered. After comparing the risks of diminished physical capacity due to aging and the loss of human relations with the benefits of drug use, they firmly decided to stay away from drugs at the time of their release. By entering "the rehabilitation aid facility," they completely cut their former ties to drug-related associates and chose to rebuild their lives by securing new social connections through employment. They also tried to improve their personalities by working and supporting themselves through self-help activities for drug addicts or religious activities.

Let us now describe their life structures at the time of the interviews, focusing on their commonalities as follows:

- Life-related infrastructure: Cut former ties to drug-related associates and rebuilt their lives by securing new social connections. All of these individuals were in their late 60s and were working. Only one of them was financially independent, whereas the other two lived either on a combination of welfare benefits and supplementary employment earnings, or employment earnings and pension payments. They lived in rented or public housing in the municipality, which was affordable.
- Human capital: Recovered from drug addiction. Their previous intellectual capacity and diligence re-emerged after drugs were eliminated from their lives. With the foundation of self-confidence accomplished by rejecting drugs, these individuals shifted away from a shallow character to a positive character and maintained a level of self-sufficiency (i.e., the ability to recognize and be satisfied with what is good in oneself and one's own life).
- Social capital: Established relationships with the staff of "the rehabilitation aid facility" and employers; mutual support relationships with colleagues at the churches or "rehabilitation aid facilities."
- Identity: Established positive self-conception, for instance, as "a person who accepts oneself as who he is, including his weaknesses," "a person who lives a moral life," "a person who demonstrates his skills and capacity through work," and "a person who makes contributions to society by helping other drug addicts to restore their lives."

The life structures of these three former drug addicts were restored, as described above. All indicated that they wished to maintain their then-current lives.

4.2.4 Findings of these case studies

Regardless of the crime path typology, including mental ability, the following matters were shared across all cases:

- Eleven individuals indicated that their sentence was either correct or light for the nature of their crime. Although two individuals said their sentences were relatively heavy, they did not express dissatisfaction with the criminal justice proceedings. These responses reflect their trust in the criminal justice system, which might be the first step toward trusting society.
- Their involvement with the criminal justice system offered them the opportunity to reset their chaotic lives. A life with limited freedom in correctional institutions enabled them to confront the problematic nature of their lifestyle and helped foster self-awareness. Compelling these individuals to lead a well-regulated life helped them recover their physical and mental health and rediscover their underlying positive attributes.
- The spiritual awakening through aging and improved discretion helped them motivate themselves to gain greater self-awareness and rehabilitate themselves. Given their advanced age, they desired to lead stable and peaceful lives in their twilight years.
- During imprisonment, each acknowledged the fact that he had perpetrated a crime and accepted who he was, warts and all.
- At the time, these individuals returned to society with a desire to become rehabilitated, and they received greater amounts of support from probation services and local welfare services. Their levels of motivation and efforts to engage in realistic rebuilding of their lives were reinforced by receiving support from these services.
- These individuals learned that rehabilitation consists of leading normal lives and doing what they can do steadily while avoiding recidivistic tendencies.
- Even after being liberated from the criminal justice system, these individuals have maintained connections with those who supported them in the penal institutions and rehabilitation support facilities. Indeed, they realized that proactive efforts on their own part to interact with others were vital in acquiring human relationships.

Thus, it was verified that these 13 elderly ex-criminals restored themselves as persons leading normal lives by obtaining the sort of discretion that comes with age and through their involvement with the criminal justice system. It was also verified from these cognitive and behavioral changes observed in them that trust in the criminal justice system, and ultimately, in society, was established in them.

4.3 How to see elderly criminals

In 2009, the Japanese Ministry of Health, Labour and Welfare established a project to support and promote stable community living for the elderly and disabled criminals. In commencing with this project, a Health and Labor Sciences

Research team (Primary Researcher : Mr. Yoshiaki Tajima) revealed that many elderly criminals have welfare needs[4] and proposed that if proper welfare support were provided to meet their needs, fewer of them would commit crimes (Tajima, 2009). In fact, this project encourages many elderly criminals to be smoothly connected to community welfare services from the criminal justice system, resulting in a significant reduction of recidivism, according to a report at a national conference of the implementing body (Japan Council of Regional Sustained Community Life Support Centers, 2014).[5]

It has been verified that this project has been effective in providing elderly criminals with welfare support. It is understood that reoffending cannot be effectively prevented if the necessary welfare support for needy criminals is not provided. Criminal justice interventions and welfare support should go together to prevent crimes. However, when we consider the prognostic well-being of elderly criminals, the author is skeptical of them simply being socially vulnerable people in a literal sense.[6] For instance, in a survey conducted by the Tokyo government (Research Committee of Experts on Shoplifting, 2016; Konagai, 2017; Usui, 2018) on shoplifting suspects, the respondents were not necessarily those who were described as particularly deprived owing to their old age in general. While they might have had problems recognizing the real world and relationships, they still possessed sufficient capacity to engage in activities in society. Crime is a kind of social phenomenon that cannot be executed without a certain degree of autonomy regarding situational judgment and physical dynamism. For this reason, elderly criminals should be regarded as human beings more capable and resourceful than socially vulnerable people.

4.4 Policy on the reintegration of elderly criminals and perpetrators into society

4.4.1 How criminal justice deals with criminal liability for actions

Society's response to someone who commits a crime is determined by the individual's liability. In the case of an elderly suspect, criminal liability is assigned, in order to maintain law and order, if the judge determines that the suspect in question is competent enough to be held liable for his/her action and if the case is too malicious to be ignored. The perpetrator is then found guilty of the crime.

If a criminal is regarded as proactive or autonomous (agency), he/she must be held criminally liable according to the culpability of his/her act and the magnitude of the liability. This can also be seen as the recognition of the offender's potential for possible recovery through his/her own initiative. The process of criminal justice is not restricted to holding the offender criminally liable for his/her crime. It also constitutes an opportunity to make him/her aware of his/her social responsibilities and to confront himself/herself internally. This applies regardless of age, such that the realization of one's responsibility in this respect is just the other side of the coin with which the dignity of human beings is maintained. Thus, we should avoid forcibly diverting elderly criminals toward other measures, assuming they are socially vulnerable. Instead, we should have them undergo proceedings corresponding to the proper magnitude of their crimes and the damages they cause.

For this purpose, however, appropriate criminal justice proceedings, respect for an individual's dignity in such proceedings, and fair and proper dispositions and rulings are vital (Yoshikai, 2018). If these conditions are met, the individual can accept the contents of the judgment and the process by which it is reached. Trust in the criminal justice proceedings and criminal justice professionals enables a criminal to confront his/her own issues. This is true even when elderly persons are concerned, as confirmed by the 13 individuals surveyed.

4.4.2 Intervention process by the sentence executing organizations

Since a criminal is stuck in a loop of criminal mechanisms in terms of cognition and behavior, intervention to eliminate recidivism risk by breaking down these mechanisms is essential.[7] Penal institutions and probation offices assume this responsibility. Since abiding by the law is the major prerequisite underlying social reintegration, an intervention that restricts an individual's autonomy will still contribute to the well-being of the individual if it is done according to a proper method, and intervention results in a reduction of the risk of recidivism. Interventions at penal institutions differ from the type of care that might be contractually provided in a social welfare context in that it is undertaken on a forced basis, as a part of criminal punishment, and it is of integral importance that the individual accepts the purpose and method of intervention, and consequently, that the person regards it as an opportunity for rehabilitation.

4.4.3 Support for reintegration into society

Interventions at sentence executing organizations are conducted by dealing with the subjects' "criminal aspects" according to the above-mentioned methods as well as through an approach based on a strength-based model to promote the development of the subjects' humanity to support them in rehabilitation and reintegration into society. First, interventions are made to help individuals acquire an appropriate and proper awareness of themselves and the current status of society. If their awareness of society and themselves is adequately established, realistic and practical support for their social participation will be possible. A comprehensive person-centered approach focused on building a "purpose in life' for the subject should be appropriate as an ideal form of support for his reintegration into society.

Since the criminality of individuals remains intact and criminal punishments continue to be imposed even with this process, offender-treatment organizations will serve as the main institutions in charge and collaborate with relevant organizations and specialists in the community.

4.4.4 Flow to connect individuals to the care systems in the community

The appropriate opportunity to connect an individual to the comprehensive community care system and local welfare services arises when he/she is discharged from the criminal justice system. In other words, the appropriate opportunity arises when "entry support" is provided at the time the individual is diverted to an alternative disposition from criminal justice proceedings and when "exit support" is provided at the time the disposition of criminal justice is completed to allow him/her to return to his/her community.

In recent years, multi-agency collaboration has flourished in Japan's fields of criminal justice and community welfare. In order to provide comprehensive care and support for the elderly and disabled criminals with complex problems, various cooperation schemes are proactively pursued among practitioners working in relevant fields and organizations, including criminal justice, local government, community welfare, medical and nursing care as well as public health. It is a welcome trend, yet, at the same time, there is still room for improvement in information sharing and collaboration practices to provide the elderly and disabled criminals with comprehensive support by taking every aspect of their lives and relationships into account. In several European countries, experts from the relevant organizations collaborate closely by sharing relevant data (even assessment forms regarding the individual risks and needs of the subjects) on a real-time basis (Konagai, 2018b). In collaboration among experts from various organizations with different purposes and operational practices, establishing a checks-and-balance system for operational procedures/decision making is vital. The forms of multi-agency collaboration have been evolving in some of these world-leading European nations from a framework of points into lines.[8]

The "entry support" practice in Japan is currently provided by welfare support specialists, psychology/probation officers of the Ministry of Justice and non-governmental psychologists based on commissions with judicial community personnel, namely, the judge, prosecutor, or attorney. Since multiple specialists are involved in the practice, securing the validity and reliability of the assessment regarding various relevant perspectives is essential, including the issues and needs of the subjects and the contents of supervision/support that should be implemented in the course of criminal treatment. It is also vital to establish a systematic approach in the "entry support" practice to formulate proper rehabilitation plans, systematically accumulate experiences of pre-sentencing investigations, and further develop the whole practice. Since offenders' assessments, treatment, and support are undertaken bi-directionally, investigations pertaining to "entry support" should ideally be systemized.

At the same time, the "exit support" practice requires proper assessment regarding the subjects' needs, a precise distinction of roles among relevant specialists, and collaboration based on differences among specialists' expertise, which should allow a synergy effect to be realized in the multi-agency collaboration.

4.4.5 Form of integration and re-participation of elderly criminals into society

As mentioned above, there are significant differences among elderly people in various aspects, including health conditions, cognitive/physical functions, social skills, relationships, and levels of financial strength (Cabinet Office, 2017). Their desire for and forms of social participation vary, such as in terms of full-time employment, part-time employment, volunteer work, hobbies, and day service participation. In short, providing practical support focusing on their needs (building a purpose in life) is essential to accomplish proper social participation support that is suitable for each individual.

To this end, each community must offer various options to accommodate the differences among individuals. Various ways of social participation are conceivable, including not just working at regular for-profit companies, but also working for a social solidarity economy through a non-profit organization or social firm and engaging social activities.

As for the social participation support targeting elderly people and those with cognitive impairment, it is essential to confirm their specialties and expertise and figure out a way to integrate their traits into a collaboration with the activities of healthy people. For instance, a work-sharing activity could be an excellent support practice where a single job is divided among multiple elderly persons.[9]

As mentioned above, elderly people often need assistance from others to offset their age-oriented limitations in their social participation; nevertheless, they should be regarded as members of the society who contribute to society according to their abilities instead of mere unilateral care recipients. The awareness of recognizing them as contributing assets to society elevates the dignity and self-respect of elderly people as well as the cohesiveness of local communities.

At the same time, not all elderly people with jobs can earn enough income to sustain their lives; therefore, life security measures to cover income shortfalls are vital. Thus, the involvement of local governments is essential.

4.5 Conclusion

In this chapter, elderly criminals and perpetrators are recognized as people with proactive and autonomous agency, and the ideal approach to reintegrate them into society has been discussed. By recognizing them as autonomous beings, the matters explored here can also be applied to the participation of elderly persons in society in general. Moreover, the resources and social capital belonging to the community would accumulate over time through community initiatives to support the elderly comprehensively from the perspectives of health, psychology, and social activities, which, in turn, would contribute to enhancing the local life welfare support for community members belonging to every age group.

Notes

1 This survey was conducted as part of a Grant-in-Aid for Scientific Research, Basic Research (C) "Research on issues in supporting the reintegration of offenders into the community, and in partnership with community welfare organizations" (project number: 26380784).
2 Rehabilitation aid facilities are the halfway houses operated by private-sectors, whose operations are primarily financed by commission fees from the Ministry of Justice. Room and boarding are provided free of charge for a certain period to persons who have been released from criminal incarceration but have nowhere to go due to their broken family ties. The mission of these facilities is to support efforts by residents to prepare for their reintegration into society, for instance, by helping residents save independent funds during their stay.
3 From the interview for Dr. Toshihiko Matsumoto on Drug Addiction" carried on HP of the Japanese Society of Psychology and Neurology, https://www.jspn.or.jp/modules/forpublic/index.php?content_id=30, accessed on 29 March 2022.
4 The difficulties affecting elderly criminals have been reported in detail by Yoshiaki Tajima and others (2009).
5 That the rate of re-imprisonment has been significantly reduced was reported in a survey report issued at a conference of the National Community Living Establishment Support Center (2014).
6 It is the author's position and was argued by Kayo Konagai (2018a) that elderly persons are not synonymous with "socially vulnerable persons," as this term is used in the fields of social welfare and social policy even if they are mired in a state of misfortune, as described in a socioeconomic sense.
7 "Mechanisms leading to crime" and interventions for breaking these mechanisms down are explored in detail in another paper (Konagai 2018a).
8 To the extent that the author has explored multi-agencies collaboration over many years, the Safe House in the Netherlands, the Family Justice Center in Belgium, and the Young Offending Team in the United Kingdom have matured in terms of the comprehensiveness and depth of collaborations. Each consists of a body that was developed at a local governmental level. The British example is a scheme set up under the youth justice system.
9 Work performed by the elderly as a reason for living and work sharing by multiple elderly persons are discussed by Tetsuo Tsuji in a special feature published in the Nihon Keizai Shinbun (2017), as listed in the references.

References

Cabinet Office. (2017) *White Paper on an Aging Society.* https://www8.cao.go.jp/kourei/english/annualreport/2017/2017pdf_e.html

Japan Council of Regional Sustained Community Life Support Centers. (2014) *Survey Tracing The Readmission of Individuals to Correctional Facilities in Connection with Support Provided by Prefectural Sustained Community Life Support Centers.*

Konagai, K. (2017) *Report on The Social Inclusion of Elderly Persons Who Shoplift, The Formation of Communities, and Shoplifting by The Elderly: Exploring The Actual Conditions of and Factors Behind Shoplifting by The Elderly*, Tokyo, Government of Metropolitan Tokyo, pp. 136–152.

Konagai, K. (2018a) 'Reintegrating Persons Who Have Committed Crimes Back into The Community: Issues and Prospects Concerning Ties Between the Justice System and Welfare', *Social Welfare Research Journal*, 131, pp. 22–29.

Konagai, K. (2018b) 'Recidivism Prevention Plan in the Netherlands - Multi-agency "Entrance Support" and "Exit Support" Mechanisms', *Crime and Punishment*, 56(1), pp. 68–79

Ministry of Health, Labour and Welfare. (2023) *Support for community life settlement for those released from correctional institutions who need welfare support due to old age or disabilities (Community Life Settlement Promotion Scheme).* https://www.mhlw.go.jp/stf/seisakunitsuite/bunya/hukushi_kaigo/seikatsuhogo/kyouseishisetsu/index.html, accessed on 8 November 2023

Ministry of Internal Affairs and Communications. (2017) *Statistical Topics No. 103: The Elderly in Japan as Seen with The Help of Statistics (65 Years of Age or Older) – In Connection with Respect-For-The-Aged Day.*

Ministry of Justice (2022) 'White Paper on Crime 2022, English version', Section 1 Trends in Offenses, Chapter 8 Offenses by the Elderly.

Research Committee of Experts on Shoplifting. (2016) *Report on Shoplifting by The Elderly: Exploring The Actual Conditions of and Factors Behind Shoplifting by The Elderly*, Tokyo, Government of Metropolitan Tokyo.

Tajima, Y. (2009) Research on Community Life Support for Disabled Persons Who Have Committed Crimes, 2008 Health and Labor Science Research, report presented at a conference for the presentation of the results of general research on healthcare and welfare for persons with disabilities, Japanese Society for the Rehabilitation of Persons with Disabilities, 2009.

Usui, I. (2018) 'Results of a Survey on Shoplifting by The Elderly – Conference Report and The Response of The Metropolitan Tokyo Government. A Report Presented at a Conference Symposium in 2017 by the Japanese Society of Law and Forensic Social Services', *Law and Forensic Social Services Journal*, 17.

Yoshikai, T. (2018) 'Measures to Prevent Recidivism in Association with Suspensions Of Indictments', *The Horitsu Jiho*, 90(4), pp. 30–35.

5 Rehabilitation Process of Elderly Ex-criminals

Analysis of Interview Sessions with Elderly Ex-criminals Who Received Support at Relief and Rehabilitation Facilities

Yuzuru Kawabe

Surugadai University, Japan

The present chapter aims to elucidate the rehabilitation process by analyzing findings obtained from interview sessions with ten elderly ex-criminals who have desisted from crime.

5.1 Interviewee

In this study, those aged 65 years and above were defined as elderly persons, and desistance from crime was defined as being released from a penal institution such as prison, jail, or detention center, having passed four or more years without recidivism, and maintaining good social adjustment.

The interview session participants were ten elderly ex-criminals from 67 to 77 years of age (mean age 71.3 years), consisting of five men and five women. All of them reintegrated into society from penal institutions via relief and rehabilitation facilities.

The sample size is small and biased in that all had gone through a relief and rehabilitation facility upon release from a penal institution. Therefore, they are not representative of elderly criminals. However, given that there are cases of recidivists who also received support provided by relief and rehabilitation facilities but eventually reoffended, certain meaningful insights into the rehabilitation process should be obtained from the analysis of interviews with these ex-criminals.

The criminal convictions of the ten respondents were diverse; five of them received a deferred prosecution or suspended sentence but did not serve the prison sentence, while the other five served their time in correctional institutions, among them the one most committed to prison served 19 times. The most recent crimes included theft (7), murder (2), and dine and dash (1). Four were homeless at the time of their most recent offense. All of them had previously had a stable livelihood but had become homeless due to unemployment or divorce.

DOI: 10.4324/9781032669519-7

Other notable characteristics are that none were associated with gang organizations, nor did any have a history of drug abuse. They are also a biased sample in this respect.

There are two types of elderly criminals: those who have committed crimes at an older age, and those who have repeatedly been sentenced to prison and have reached old age. Each type has different characteristics. In addition, gender, health, intelligence, education, and various other factors influence the rehabilitation process. However, in this study, the interview content was analyzed qualitatively without prejudice, excluding any presumptions based on participants' attributes. Suppose there is a difference in the factors contributing to desistance from crime between criminals whose first crime was committed at old age and those who committed criminal offenses repeatedly. In this case, the results of the interview analysis were divided into these two groups.

There is also no guarantee that what was said is objective. However, knowing the subjective memories and perceptions of rehabilitated ex-criminals is useful for exploring internal factors.

5.2 Interview methods

Interviews were conducted between July 2015 and March 2017 in one-on-one sessions with the participant and author in a private setting, without witnesses. Subjects were informed of the purpose of this study and confidentiality in writing and orally at the beginning of the interviews, and written consent was obtained. Each participant received an honorarium of JPY 2, 000.

Interview duration ranged from 60 min to 2 h and 40 min (mean, 1 h, and 35 min). The interviews were semi-structured. Most of the narratives were about the process of criminalization and rehabilitation, accompanied by episodes of upbringing and life history.

5.3 Analysis of interviews

Interview analysis was conducted according to the KJ method (Kawakita, J. 1969), a qualitative analysis method.

Spoken content was divided into smaller units and coded using the KJ method. Similar units were then put into smaller groups, and the process of integrating similarities among these smaller groups and further grouping according to the degree of similarity into larger groups was repeated until theoretical saturation was reached.

The larger groups were arranged in chronological order. The max grouping then became a narrative about the criminalization process, including descriptions of upbringing circumstances and narratives about the process of leaving crime after the most recent arrest and detention. Both the criminalization and rehabilitation processes can be categorized into three phases for each group in a total of six phases, each of which includes the same three themes as follows: (A) a narrative about the "living condition," (B) a narrative about the

Table 5.1 Overview of interview contents

Phase	*(A)Living condition*	*(B)Relationship*	*(C)Identity*
I	Breakup of family life	Loss of family relationships	Upset of prosocial identity
II	Breakup of social life	Loss of social relationships	Diffusion of prosocial identity
III	Criminalization	Loss of interpersonal relationships / oneself	Identity Diffusion
IV	Arrest and Detention	Rediscovery of interpersonal relationships / oneself	Reconsideration of identity
V	Entry into relief and rehabilitation facility	Reconstruction of social relationships	Reconstruction of prosocial identity
VI	Social self-reliance	Reorientation of identity	Reintegration of identity

"relationship" between oneself and one's surroundings, and (C) a narrative about "identity (how one is)." The themes of (A), (B), and (C) in each phase consisted of narratives that could be categorized into several groups, as shown in Table 5.1.

Details of the analysis results are presented in Table 5.2.

The most noteworthy point in these results probably lies in the fact that the content of the narratives about upbringing and the process of criminalization is essentially symmetrical with the narratives about the process of rehabilitation from crime. In other words, the hypothesis regarding the process of criminalization and rehabilitation is established from these results. Examining it from the perspective of relationships with others, the process of criminalization should be defined as an extension of a series of successive events from the loss of family and social relationships to the loss of oneself, while rehabilitation is the reverse process of criminalization, starting from the rediscovery of interpersonal relationships, reconstruction of social relationships, and reorientation of oneself in social relationships.

Rediscovering interpersonal relationships promotes awareness of the lost self and arouses the desire to recover the self as a social being. Those who have desisted from crimes have probably gone through the process of acquiring a new identity and sense of values as they have restored human and social relationships with others surrounding them, including rehabilitation facility staff, workplace supervisors, and colleagues. This is the process of living as an individual. The results also strongly suggest that the deepening of relationship restoration and reacquisition of identity proceed interactively and simultaneously.

Although none of the participants here achieved recovery of family relationships, their success in desistance from crimes was accomplished by establishing human and attachment relationships with "significant others" equivalent to family members.

Table 5.2 Results of interview analysis

Max group (Phase)		*Large group (Theme)*	*Middle group*	*Small group*	*Typical narratives*
Process of criminalization	I	A-I Breakup of family life	Financial stringency	Gambling addiction	I spent all the money I earned in horse racing/pachinko.
				Excessive drinking & extravagance	I drank everyday even though I had no money.
				Debt	I borrowed money from loan sharks/relatives.
				Unemployment	As I got older, no one would hire me anymore.
				Disease	I broke because of the payment of medical bills.
		B-I Loss of family relationships	Relationship failure	Discord	My wife and I came to be on bad terms when she found out that I borrowed money without telling her.
				Unfaithfulness	I cheated on my wife/ husband, and my family fell apart.
			Discontinuation of communication with the original family	Trouble	Once they settled my debt, they cut me off.
				Estrangement	I lost touch with my home and siblings since my parent died.
		C-I Upset of prosocial identity	Loss of consciousness of his role in family or work	Upset of family identity	Looking back now, I'd done nothing for my family as a parent or a husband.
				Upset of professional identity	No work I see as "My work" came to me anymore.
	II	A-II Breakup of social life	Financial collapse	Hardships of life	I could no longer pay my rent.
				Unable to pay	I could no longer pay my debt from loan sharks.
		B-II Loss of social relationships	Family disruption	Divorce	My debt was found out, got divorced, and I left the house.
				Separation	I had to sell my house to settle the debts and lived separately from my family.
			Loss of work	Bankruptcy	I lost a contract, folded my company, and become a day laborer.
				Dismissal	I got fired because I couldn't focus on my work and kept making mistakes.
			Loss of place to stay	Homeless	I was no longer able to pay the rent, so I was evicted from my apartment and became homeless.
			Social isolation	Social withdrawal	I didn't see my friends/ neighbors anymore.

(*Continued*)

Table 5.2 (Continued)

Max group (Phase)		*Large group (Theme)*	*Middle group*	*Small group*	*Typical narratives*
		C-II Diffusion of prosocial identity	Loss of meaning of his existence	loss of purpose	I didn't know why I kept on living
				loss of willpower	I didn't feel like doing anything.
Process of rehabilitation	III	A-III Criminalization	Momentary life	Living only for the moment	I no longer thought about my future.
				Desperation	I was desperate.
		B-III Loss of interpersonal relationships/ oneself	Mental confusion	Mental instability	I became mentally unstable.
				Inability to think	I couldn't think of anything.
		C-III Identity diffusion	Loss of value standards	Normless state	I thought that I'd do anything because things couldn't get any worse.
				Lack of vision	I didn't care if it was right or wrong. All I could think of was food.
				Loss of the gaze of others	I no longer care how others would see me./I no longer felt embarrassed.
	IV	A-IV Arrest and Detention	Recognition of turning points	Freedom from anxiety about crime	When I got arrested, I felt relieved./What would have happened if I was not arrested.
				Feelings of self-punishment	I thought that I had to be punished because I had committed a crime.
		B-IV Rediscovery of interpersonal relationships/ oneself	Approach from supporters	Recognition of the presence of people Who accept	It was nice to feel that someone cared about me.
				Recognition of the presence of supporters	Mr./Ms. X was very accommodating and encouraged me to apply to enter the facility.
			Responses to supporters	Feelings of gratitude	I was grateful for their concern./ I felt that I had to redeem myself for them.
		C-IV Reconsideration of identity	Reflection on self in past	Questioning the present state of self	I knew I couldn't go on like this.
				Positive recognition by others	I was happy to be told that I was not the kind of person who would come to prison.
				Recovery of social self	I thought I might still be able to start over again.

(*Continued*)

Table 5.2 (Continued)

Max group (Phase)		*Large group (Theme)*	*Middle group*	*Small group*	*Typical narratives*
	V	A-V Entry into relief and rehabilitation facility	Gratitude for entrance into rehabilitation aid facility	Gratitude for the place to stay	I was happy to have address, because job hunting would be very difficult without address.
			Acquisition of basic lifestyle habits	Acquisition of rhythm of life	I have developed a regular lifestyle.
				Savings	I learned to save/spend money on a budget.
			Gratitude for guidance	Gratitude for employment guidance	They took care of me to find a job and I was able to become positive.
				Gratitude for daily living	I'm grateful for strict guidance/Thanks to it, I no longer lead a loose life.
				Gratitude for welfare procedures	I'm glad that they helped me to go through the public assistance application. I could not have done it myself.
			Gratitude for emotional relationships	Gratitude for consideration	I was really grateful that they cared about me a lot
			Feeling debt of gratitude	Relationship retention	Thanks to Mr./Ms. X./I can't betray Mr./ Ms. X
		B-V Reconstruction of social relationships	Acquisition of social skills	Acquisition of consulting skills	I am now able to visit public offices./ I am now able to consult my issues at public offices for myself.
				Acquisition of interpersonal skills	I am now able to talk politely./ Be patient.
			Experiences of social relationships	Experience of consultation	A Public Employment Security Office was helpful. I found out that I could find a job if I looked for one.
				Experience of working	It was interesting/fulfilling when I worked.
				Experience of building new relationships	Everyone at work was good to me. I was worried at first, but able to get along with the other members.
		C-V Reconstruction of prosocial identity	Restoration of self-esteem	Positive evaluation by work	I was happy to be thanked by my boss and others. I could become confident in my work.
				Utilization of skills	I was able to do a job where I could put my skills in good use, and it gave me a sense of pride.
				Sense of fulfillment	I was just happy to be able to work every day.

(*Continued*)

Table 5.2 (Continued)

Max group (Phase)		*Large group (Theme)*	*Middle group*	*Small group*	*Typical narratives*
	VI	A-VI Social self-reliance	Daily life fulfillment	Maintaining regular habits	Every day I will get up at 6 o'clock and do xx in the morning.
				Boasting of thrift	Shopping is done at half price after xx o'clock. I often do shopping at flea market.
				Using social service	I use free services for elderly as much as possible.
			Positive social responses	Maintain working life	I don't skip a day of work. (All participants mentioned similar comments.)
				Acquisition reliance in work	They value me because I do more than what I am supposed to do in my job.
				Positive responses in community life	They thanked me because I clean the neighborhood/ weed the grass.
			Active & independent behavior	Job search by self	I looked for work on my own. I registered myself at local silver human resource center.
				Moving	I applied for and won an apartment room provided by the Urban Renaissance Agency. I moved to a place closer to my workplace.
		B-VI Reorientation of self in social relationships	Retention in workspace & community	Retention in the workplace	Boss wants me to work as long as I'm healthy.
				Satisfaction	It's nice to feel needed.
			Maintaining of feeling debt of gratitude	Maintaining relationships with facilities	I make a call to the facility on the day Mr./Ms. X on duty.
				Gratitude for workplace	I'm just grateful to be allowed to work.
				giving back to society	I do volunteer work in the community. I do something for free when asked by my neighbors.
			Trust in & use of consulting institutions	Active consulting	If I have a problem, I will consult it with Mr./Ms. X/public office.
				High consulting skill	I use public help desk at city office available for free.
		C-VI Reintegration of identity	Acceptance of his own life	Acceptance of self	I am fully satisfied with the present. I am fine just the way I am now. I have no avarice.
				Endogenesis of the new value of life	The best thing is to be able to live without bothering anyone.

5.4 Life of elderly ex-criminals

5.4.1 Criminalization process

Many researchers and practitioners have pointed out that the loss of relationships, along with the destruction of livelihoods, was at the core of the criminalization process of the participants in this study.

Loss of relationships and financial ruin are crises that may occur to the elderly in general, and their criminalization should be viewed as a result of being unable to overcome those crises due to their inadequate or severely-weakened relational and economic foundations. Nevertheless, the interview sessions in this study indicate that the leading causes of their financial failure were squandering and dissipation and that the loss of relationships was also a "consequence of their deeds." Their lack of knowledge and skills in accessing the social welfare system could be another cause of their criminalization.

This is inferred from the fact that older people and those with chronic diseases receive social welfare support and stabilize their lives after going through relief and rehabilitation facilities.

5.4.2 Rehabilitation process

The process of rehabilitation of elderly ex-criminals is very similar at several points to the various studies on the rehabilitation process of non-elderly ex-criminals in terms of the process of relationship restoration, which occurs as if to reverse the process of relationship loss and the process of acquisition of a new identity and a new set of values.

As pointed out in previous studies, "relationship" and "identity" are key concepts in the rehabilitation of criminals in general. When comparing the non-elderly ex-criminals with elderly ex-criminals, the latter are different from the former in the following ways: 1) they do not show a positive attitude to expand the variety of social re-participation; 2) although they want to be productive, they only do what they are capable of and do not pursue any social value beyond that, nor do they aim to contribute to society; and 3) though they have a sense of control over their own lives, the scope of the control is emphasized more on adapting themselves to the surrounding living environments and less on proactively working on their environment.

Significant issues regarding the rehabilitation process of criminal offenders, in general, are typically indicated in the cases of interview session participants of this study. Once a livelihood is secured, the remaining issues for their reintegration into society can be narrowed down to the two core issues of restoration of "relationship" and "identity," the required levels of which are set within their means. In that sense, the rehabilitation of elderly criminals is more dependent on their economic and social welfare than that of criminals of other age groups.

Few people in the general public would get involved with ex-criminals knowing that they have a criminal record, and even fewer would see them as capable of living a decent life and conveying such a message to them. In that sense, it is significant to rekindle their awareness of relationships during the judicial process or the incarceration period in a penal institution. The elderly rehabilitated ex-criminals analyzed here experienced awareness of their relationship and self when they met understanding and supportive people during their arrest and detention. This experience of awareness was solidified through guidance at the relief and rehabilitation facility, and the process of its amplification in their lives after they became self-reliant was observed in the analysis.

The turning point from the process of criminalization to that of desistance from crime can be found in the "encounter" in the penal institution. Although the efforts of those involved in rehabilitation support could often end in vain, the chances of desistance from crime would likely be significantly reduced without such efforts at the relevant facilities.

5.4.3 Characteristics of guidance in relief and rehabilitation facilities

Next, how the study participants reviewed the guidance they received in the relief and rehabilitation facilities was discussed. As shown in Table 5.2, many participants stated that they were "grateful for strict guidance" in terms of lifestyle, and they also recognized and appreciated that they received very specific, positive, and valuable guidance regarding employment, finding housing, and access to social services such as social welfare. In other words, there are many references to "what was done for me." In contrast, none of them mentioned that they were asked to reflect on or confront their past selves. Although some of them might face such confrontations, none were mentioned in the interview.

However, all the participants in this interview were able to speak candidly about their lives leading up to their crimes, and in that sense, they were able to confront their past selves. This suggests that confrontation with the past is spontaneous or natural. If there was guidance, it was probably given by directing them to confront themselves only when they were ready to do so.

In addition, it is noteworthy that the guidance narratives they received were almost always followed by comments related to emotional relationships, including "I was really grateful that they cared a lot about me"; "I was happy when they encouraged me"; and "Mr. and Mrs. X are like father and mother to me" (as a matter of fact, they are only a few years older than the participant). These narratives strongly demonstrate that the most important thing for those who had lost all relationships with the people around them was their emotional ties, for which they felt very grateful. We call this an attachment relationship. It is highly possible that this emotional bond is the source of motivation for the rehabilitation and deterrence of recidivism. This is indicated by the fact that most participants expressed their gratitude to the relief and rehabilitation facility staff by personal names, as seen in their comments such as, "Thanks to Mr./Ms. X," or "I can't betray Mr./Ms. X."

Among the guidance in relief and rehabilitation facilities described by these ex-criminals, the most effective was to repeatedly reach out to them by showing care or talking to them constantly to build an emotional connection and to use this connection as a foundation for providing hands-on guidance to supplement the social skills they lacked. The goal is to make them aware of what they need to do "here and now," instead of what they have done in the past, and to encourage them to do what needs to be done one at a time. In the course of the guidance, the subjects will gain confidence that they can do so and increase their trust in the guidance and staff. It was confirmed again that relationship building is the most fundamental condition for advancing guidance.

5.4.4 Identity issues

The final goal of the desistance from crime process was to help the subjects modify their antisocial or asocial identities into prosocial identities or to support them in constructing prosocial identities.

Building a good relationship with one's surroundings is also an indispensable factor in modifying or constructing one's identity. This is because the self cannot be recognized or constructed through pure introspection alone; it can be constructed, modified, and maintained through relationships with others in the process of inference based on the approval and reaction of others. Regarding the construction of a prosocial identity, one needs to be seen as a prosocial person by those around him or her and given the reputation of being viewed as such. In these interviews, many participants often mentioned that relevant support personnel, including the relief and rehabilitation facility staff, constantly reached out to them to make them aware of their "decent and doable selves" and to encourage and reinforce their prosocial behaviors. The prosocial identity constructed in this manner should be recognized by the people around them in their life of self-reliance, and the process of its further solidification through positive evaluation by others can be observed in these narratives.

There are two identity-related challenges faced by elderly ex-criminals. One is the modification of their identities, from those of criminals to those of ordinary citizens. Another challenge is identity modification from that of active "working adults" in society to that of the elderly.

According to Erikson, the psychological task at the final stage in life is "ego integrity," the acceptance of our life cycle, and the fact that our life is our responsibility. It is not an easy task for us to reach this state of mind; yet, all interview participants provided narratives suggesting that they might have reached it. Some of these narratives include, "I am fully satisfied with the present," "I am fine just the way I am now," "I have no avarice," "While I can work, I will work. If I become unable to work, that is it, then," "I am happy about an everyday trifle," The best thing is to be able to live without bothering anyone," and "I have finished a procedure for the donation of my body after death."

It is not absolute poverty or deprivation, but relative poverty that leads to crimes. The livelihoods of the interview participants were at minimum levels, not impoverished but never luxurious, and it was natural for them to feel relative poverty; however, none mentioned relative poverty or dissatisfaction. When asked if they ever felt dissatisfied, only one participant mentioned distrust of politics, while the other nine said they were not dissatisfied with their current lives. On the contrary, what they expressed in response to the question was joy in being able to work every day, being appreciated by others through their work, and living without everyday worries. These narratives suggest a shift in their attitudes from evaluating their current situation in comparison with others to appreciating their current situation based on absolute values internalized within themselves. In other words, they discovered their true purpose in life and true selves. In that sense, they may be close to the state of "ego integrity" and "the acceptance of their life cycle."

6 Duplication of Social Poverty

Elderly Criminals and Homeless People

Kaoru Watanabe

Toyo University, Japan

The increase in the number of elderly criminals has become a social issue in Japanese society in the 21st century. This chapter discusses cases of homeless people as typical examples of insufficient social support for elderly criminals. Those having unstable employment/residential status are defined as homeless people, and the scope of this study is limited to those who live on the street and have criminal experiences. This study aims to illustrate the relationship between homeless experiences and criminal activities.

A common concept indicating the issues observed among homeless, elderly people with criminal histories is social exclusion, which should also be described as a lack of participation in society (Iwata, 2008). Social exclusion is a loss of the "cardinal point" in life and the dynamic process of disruption of social participation associated with said loss.

The existence of homeless people with criminal experiences has been noticed empirically from interviews conducted by homeless support organizations (Mashiko et al., 2012:7). Regional homeless support organizations also provide rehabilitative support for ex-criminals in society (Akiyama, 2012a, 2012b), helping ex-convicts with a homeless status. In that sense, ex-convicts with difficulties in life can be viewed as subjects of support in homeless support activities (Furukawa, 2015; Maruyama, 2018).

6.1 Post-modernity and selective relationship that becomes the mainstream in society

Since the 1990s, people in post-industrial society have become increasingly free from connections or bonds with groups represented by families, workplaces, or communities, and each individual has acquired the freedom to select the nature of the relationships they have with others, as well as the degree of responsibility that accompanies their freedom. In this post-modern society, we are free from conventional gender roles or hierarchical relationships and face the necessity to design our own lives by acquiring relationships to enjoy the relationship itself, i.e., a "pure relationship" (Giddens, 1992/1995).

When such selective relationships become mainstream in society, we become free from family bonds, and our connection to the local community

DOI: 10.4324/9781032669519-8

fades, resulting in the loss of inclusion in workplace groups (Ishida, 2018). As individualism progresses, life course support by the nation's social security system becomes the core issue for social policy. When the progress of individualism and social security system reformation occur simultaneously, risk management becomes an individual responsibility, and the insufficient progress of individualism generates isolation. This is the result of detachment from traditional social frameworks and benefits once provided by families or corporations, which causes the loss of various forms of support once provided by traditional society, while support from families or corporations remains insufficient (Nihei, 2011). That is to say, changes in social inclusion methods in traditional societies have caused social exclusion.

The Japanese social security system was designed based on the premises of the workplace and family. Specifically, it was intended to benefit individuals in connection with the workplace or family, and those who have lost their connection with workplaces or families are not the subject of the system. Securing a residence (and resident registration) represents the "cardinal point" of stable relationships, and support from local communities consists of the social security system. Upon loss of connection with the workplace or family, elderly citizens without informal support will eventually use the Public Assistance System, which mandates securing a residence. Without a residence, homeless people cannot receive benefits from the Public Assistance System due to their extreme poverty of being unable to secure a place to live; the contradictory situation of their being poor without a home made them unable to receive benefits from the system, a situation that continued until the 2000s.

Social exclusion leads to poverty and isolation. The underlying issues of social structural discrimination are centered on the problem of the exclusion of elderly citizens (Ishida, 2011:102). If elderly citizens do not have families providing emotional support, support from friends, acquaintances, and communities becomes essential. In that sense, if their social participation at the place of the "cardinal point" is viewed as the realization of social inclusion, the issue of how to provide them with such a "place to belong" would be vital. Families, communities, and workplaces (being employed) represent channels of social participation; when participation through families and communities is impossible for them, they can achieve self-independence and participation through labor at workplaces. However, if we depend on a single relationship, we will lose the only "place to belong" when we lose the relationship. Therefore, the challenges are to provide a "place to belong" to those without one and to increase the number of places to which they could potentially belong.

6.2 Social poverty: Homeless people and elderly crimes

The background factors for the increase in the prevalence of elderly criminals include issues of social isolation and financial difficulties. Social capital is a useful resource for suppressing the increase in elderly crime (Hosoi, 2012). However, a study indicated that the lack of sufficient social connection among elderly criminals (e.g., without housemates or someone to consult with) is a primary factor of elderly crime, along with financial difficulties; the study also showed that elderly citizens who commit crimes owing to financial difficulties or social isolation often face prison sentences without a stay of execution because many of them cannot satisfy the necessary criteria for the judicial proceeding (Hamai, 2011:105). Many elderly criminals are loners isolated from communities and the social welfare administration. Thus, preventing the social isolation of elderly citizens should be an effective measure to prevent elderly crimes (Research and Training Institute of the Ministry of Justice, 2007; Oota, 2008, 2009).

The 2006 arson case at JR Shimonoseki Station is a symbolic crime that illustrates the connection between homeless people and criminal activities in Japan (Okuda, 2010). This particular arson case was committed by an elderly ex-criminal who had been released from a correctional institution after serving his full sentence, immediately after which he set the prehab warehouse of JR Shimonoseki Station on fire. In this case, the penitentiary system had to play the role of a safety net for the man, who could not receive appropriate support to deal with financial difficulties and isolation. The case attracted attention for the uniqueness of ex-convict's second offence. Further, it should be noted that the support provided for the social rehabilitation was so insufficient that the offender could not even secure employment and a residence for himself, thus causing him to lose the social connection that is acquired with these elements[1].

Let us summarize the challenges posed to homeless people with criminal experience, as illustrated by this arson case. First, we should consider the need to secure a domicile that serves as the "cardinal point" after release from a correctional institution. Building sound human relationships through daily living would be difficult for those without a home. It would also be challenging for them to receive the benefits of social capital available in the region where they live if they have no domicile. The address registered as the domicile of a person is his/her "cardinal point" to receive benefits from the social security system; he/she has to secure a residential address to use the system, including the public assistance system.

Preliminary support is available for those who are scheduled to be released from correctional institutions to orient themselves on how to use social security services, and support centers for settlement into community life have been established. However, these support centers do not provide sufficient informal support.

Second, we should note the ambiguity of the bonds in the community of day laborers (homeless community) that provides a place for outdoor sleep (environment). A homeless community offers mutual support and a unique shared culture among those who live at the bottom of the social strata (Aoki, 2000). Informal relationships acquired through homeless life influence both inhabitation and detachment from the situation of homelessness (Watanabe, 2010). It is a fellowship of mutual support which simultaneously carries the potential risk of creating a network of recidivism; in other words, it represents the dark side of social capital.

The utter loneliness of a person rejecting the mutual support provided for concerned individuals would further deepen their isolation from the community, as well as from support connections. Thus, it is challenging for homeless people to acquire connections through community formation to voice their need for support (Watanabe, 2010). Whether peer support among the concerned individuals could play a preventive role against the recidivism of homeless people with criminal experience is a challenging issue.

6.3 Two types of support for elderly criminals: Judicial and welfare system collaboration

Securing a residence and employment to establish an ordinary life in the community after release from a correctional institute is a challenging task left to a person for his/her own responsibility. The necessity of proper support through social work, from a social welfare standpoint, has been voiced from a criminal policy perspective. In response to this situation, the Ministry of Health, Labour and Welfare initiated the Support Project for Settlement into Community Life and established the Support Center for Settlement into Community Life in 2009. By 2011, these centers had been established in all prefectures. The support service provided for elderly criminals by these centers commences while the beneficiaries are still serving their sentences, and these support centers are allocated certified social workers to provide them social welfare support so that the beneficiaries can receive the necessary assistance after being released from the correctional institutes. However, the support project is currently focused on providing assistance in using various governmental services, such as securing domiciles or social welfare service application assistance, and efforts to establish social connections for service beneficiaries are far from sufficient (Furukawa, 2015).

As discussed above, challenges arose from the perspectives of judicial and welfare system collaboration. In response to these challenges, institutional support programs were established for each judicial and welfare system that introduce the concepts of livelihood support and aftercare through judicial and welfare system cooperation and collaboration. At the same time, such a trend reveals the difference of ideas in terms of necessary support between correctional standpoints and welfare support viewpoints, thus raising issues in coordination due to these differences. A newly emerging image of those requiring support represents the victimized image of elderly criminals, thereby creating weakened individuals requiring judicial and social work support, as well as a sense of disorientation from a judicial standpoint toward the given image.

From the standpoint of social welfare and social work, elderly criminals are viewed not only as criminal offenders but also as elderly citizens in need of social welfare support. They have committed crimes to deal with life-threatening situations incurred by extreme poverty resulting from inadequate social security systems and their sluggish response to social problems. Thus, correctional institutes play the role of last resort and serve as a safety net for them.

Therefore, securing residence and providing "places to belong" by using the social welfare system should be mandatory for the welfare support system for these elderly citizens.

The difference in viewpoints on elderly criminals discussed thus far has been pointed out as the difference in viewpoints between social welfare practitioners and criminal justice personnel (Furukawa, 2016). Furukawa argued that "Simply put, sharing essential issues in criminal sociology, such as restorative justice, with newly participating practitioners is quite challenging, even if we emphasize the practical perception of social welfare, which indicates that both criminal justice and social welfare are social services based on human rights. Viewpoints should differ regarding the perspective on victims, with whom criminal justice has carefully dealt with a delicate balance, or on elderly criminals as social victims whose criminal activities are minor and unavoidable" (Furukawa, 2016:102).

The current situation surrounding the issue of elderly criminals requires cooperation between judicial and welfare systems, and concerns have also been voiced from social welfare support perspectives (Kinoshita, 2018). Kinoshita pointed out concerns regarding the legalization of social services, although he appreciated the cooperation between judicial and welfare systems to a certain extent. He argued that the progress of such cooperation would lead to the enhancement of the internalization of paternalism that social work encompasses, which he feared would result in a disturbance of the welfare system's identity and the loss of an independent viewpoint. He further asserted that collaboration between judicial and welfare systems would go hand in hand to overcome the challenges of welfare eligibility (Kinoshita, 2018:127), and that the involvement of relevant parties in preventing recidivism should be prioritized, emphasizing that social work does not have a recidivism prevention function. He also noted a problem here, cautioning that collaboration between judicial and welfare systems may create social intolerance through mutual monitoring among private organizations, communities, and volunteers, rather than contributing to society.

6.4 Life history and social rehabilitation of elderly criminals: A case study

The user data of a temporary accommodation facility for homeless people in Kawasaki City in the Tokyo metropolitan area called Aiseiryou[2] were analyzed as a case study of elderly criminals with homeless experiences. Among 220 individuals with strong willingness for self-independence and employment who used the facility between 2006 and 2007, eight men ranging from 50–75 years of age were selected to observe and extract the characteristics and experiences of elderly criminals. The data obtained by the examination are unique in that they help us understand the specific process of those with criminal experiences that leads to a homeless life. In addition to elderly people aged 65 years and above, the data include those in their 50s as a preliminary group of elderly criminals who are expected to eventually lose family assistance and their domiciles as they grow old.

The profiles of each case are as follows.

- Mr. A (in his 50s, unmarried; final academic background: middle school): He has multiple imprisonment records and has spent most of his life in correctional institutes. When he was released from prison, he lived a homeless life working occasional day labor jobs and used a social welfare facility for a while but was repeatedly imprisoned due to committing subsequent crimes. He has an issue of alcohol addiction but is unaware of it. The patient has no family support.
- Mr. B (in his 60s, married; final academic background: high school graduate): Although he committed theft in his youth, he tried to run his own business while frequently changing jobs and spent a relatively stable life with his family. After the divorce, he "made off" with money from his workplace at that time and began to live on the streets. He later found his way out of street life, but was arrested for theft. Despite support from colleagues in his workplace at that time, the court found him impenitent of his crime and sentenced him to imprisonment without suspension. After his release, he began to work as a home helper in a daycare business for hostels; currently, he lives in a group home sponsored by a homeless support organization.
- Mr. C (in his 70s, unmarried; final academic background: middle school): He has lived in Kawasaki since leaving his home on a remote island to rely on his relatives' support. Currently, he has lost his connection with his home, and his only informal connection is a bond with the homeless community. He had previously lived in a group home receiving public assistance, but was arrested for an assault at the group home. After his release from the detention center, he could return to the social welfare facility and now lives on the street.
- Mr. D (in his 60s, married; final academic background: high school graduate): He served a sentence as a result of an assault case and used a rehabilitation facility in Kawasaki after his release from prison. His life after leaving the rehabilitation center has been unstable, and he is living on the street working occasional day labor jobs. He still has connections with his family. This particular case is a typical example of the issue of how to continuously support people like him after they leave rehabilitation facilities.
- Mr. E (in his 60s, unmarried; final academic background: middle school graduate): His criminal experiences during his youth affected his later life. He became a day laborer after his release from a juvenile correctional institute and correctional institutes; he lost his connection with his family, although he had a sibling. When he used welfare facilities, he occasionally worked as a day laborer and collected aluminum cans for petty cash while living on the street; he needed support by using the public assistance system as he grew older.
- Mr. F (in his 50s, divorced; final academic background: high school graduate): He had a manufacturing job after graduating from high school, but

came to live on the street after losing his job. He committed the crime of assault in another region over a dispute concerning his street life. He came to Kawasaki after his release from prison, looking for a job and receives informal support of daily supplies or jobs from fellow homeless people who had originally lived in the area where he currently stays for shelter. He has a registration record of the governmental pension system, suggesting that he once had a stable life foundation in the past. He probably became involved in criminal activities after living on the street.

- Mr. G (in his 50s, married; final academic background: middle school graduate): He had spent a stable life as a self-employment worker in the construction industry since his youth. His livelihood, however, became unstable after his divorce, and he eventually lived on the street, during which time he was arrested for theft. When he used a group home, he worked in the informal sector (e.g., collecting aluminum cans). It is a concern that his homeless condition may continue if the decrease in job opportunities escalates.
- Mr. H (in his 50s, married; final academic background: high school graduate): He worked as a self-employed construction worker, went out of business, and was sentenced to imprisonment. After his release from prison, he lived on the streets. He lost almost all of his social connections from the loss of his business and the assault incident; his weak connection with his ex-wife is the only connection left for him.

The eight cases above are categorized into the following three types.

1 Those who go back and forth between the penitentiary and welfare systems (Mr. A and C)

In this type, the penitentiary system plays the role of a social safety net for those who go back and forth between the penitentiary and welfare systems because of the loss of connection with family or community. Social connections, except for workplace connections, are lost, and the public service is the last connection that remains for them; it is a case in which they need support for community life but are unable to receive such support.

2 Those who became homeless due to their criminal actions (Mr. B, D, E, and H).

This is a type of homelessness triggered by crime. At the time of the crime, the offenders had established a residence or had some other stability in their life. They had a history of social insurance coverage and stable employment. In addition, Mr. B and D used a rehabilitation center after their release from prison and were able to receive support after their release. They also had work-related qualifications and the potential to be employed. Those categorized as this type are more likely to reintegrate into society because they had a stable life, job qualifications, and social connections prior to committing the crime.

3 Those who committed crimes due to poverty (Mr. F and G)

This type committed crimes because of trouble in their daily lives. The instability in their lives was evident at the time of committing the crime, suggesting a connection between their financial difficulties and criminal behavior. It is also possible that they live a life in close proximity to violence or theft, as their crimes seem to be triggered by troubles in homeless or group home life.

6.5 Conclusions

Homeless people and elderly criminals are typical examples of social exclusion, as both share a common experience of social isolation and deprivation. The temporary shelter users discussed in this case study emerged as people with difficulties obtaining institutional support, where both types of support (residence and employment) are inadequate. Support for rehabilitation to help criminals reenter society should include support for employment and support for providing a domicile, but their advanced age makes it difficult for them to find work, and their family connections are often lost, making it difficult for them to find a "place to belong." Such difficulties cause elderly criminals to become homeless, and the impoverishment they experience in their homelessness may lead them to commit crimes. In other words, although it is possible to erase one's criminal record and live a life of homelessness, those lives would be in extreme poverty with an environment that makes it easy to reoffend. Therefore, social welfare support should be implemented in advance of their release from correctional institutions.

In that sense, social welfare support is provided to address the difficulties of these elderly criminals living in the community. However, while a life in the community should be impossible for them, they often end up living in prison. Therefore, the two systems must work together to address differences in the systems' respective views of support that create new challenges, such as how to coordinate and reconcile the two systems' views of support. From a judicial point of view, characterizing elderly criminals as vulnerable individuals to be protected would pose a certain uneasiness, whereas from the social welfare viewpoint, legalizing social services would raise concerns. However, by identifying these differences in the two systems, it is possible to provide collaborative support.

At the same time as enhancing institutional support, we need to carefully observe how society accepts elderly criminals and homeless people. Social reform from a macro perspective, such as creating a society in which criminal offenders are less likely to recidivate, is also necessary (Suzuki, 2015; Sugiyama, 2015). There are also other vital issues, including whether the local community in which they intend to start over in their ordinary lives is a proper place that would prevent them from recidivism and provide them with informal support, as well as issues regarding which stage support and monitoring by experts should be loosened and how to acquire informal and peer support for the parties involved.

The post-modernity in which we live encompasses a society that produces exclusion and harsh punishment rather than inclusion for criminals (Wacquant, 1999/2008; Young, 1999/2007). Thus, it is necessary to examine the extent to which such tolerance is feasible in post-modernity, where punishment is becoming increasingly severe. In today's increasingly fragmented society, inclusion for those who are socially excluded must be considered a social issue.

This research was supported by a grant-in-aid for scientific research (C) "Precipitation process of social exclusion status in Japanese society" (Project No. 26380702, Principal Investigator: Watanabe Kaoru) from 2014 to 2019, as well as by the Toyo University Inoue Enryo Memorial Research Grant in 2021.

Notes

1 Okuda defined a homeless person (rough street sleeper) as a person without home (a loner or a social connection-deprived person) or a person without house (a street sleeper or a person without a residence). Okuda suggested the "systemization of social bonds" as a measure to supplement the lack of social connections (Okuda, 2010: 35–36). Accordingly, the challenge for a society with weak family connections is how to realize the bond capable of providing "sustainable accompanied support."

2 The social welfare corporation, Kawasaki Seifu Fukushikai, has kindly permitted us to use the facility user ledger for our study. We would like to express our sincere gratitude for their cooperation.

References

Abe, A. (2007) 'Gendai Nihon No Shakaitekihaijo no Genzai [Current Situations of Social Exclusion in Contemporary Japan]'. In Fukuhara, H. (eds.) *Shakaitekihaijo/Housetsu to Shakaiseisaku* [*Social Policies on Social Exclusion/Inclusion*], Horitsu Bunka Sha Co., Ltd.

Akiyama, M. (2012a) 'Koureihanzaisha no Seikatsusaiken no Torikumi [Efforts Toward Livelihood Rehabilitation of Elderly Criminals]', *Crime and Delinquency*, 173, pp. 113–125.

Akiyama, M. (2012b) 'Jiritsushienhomu ni okeru Shien no Jissen [Practical Support at Halfway House]', *Homuresu to Shakai* [*Homeless People and Society*], 6, pp. 38–45.

Aoki, H. (2000) *Gendai Nihon no Toshikasou* [*Lower-class Society in Cities of Contemporary Japan*], Akashi Shoten Co., Ltd.

Furukawa, T. (2015) 'Koureihanzaisha no Shalaifukki Shien no Torikumi no Genjou to Kadai: Kyousei to Hogo no Renkei wo Chushin ni [Current Situation and Issues in Efforts of Rehabilitation Support for Elderly Offenders: Focusing on Coordination of Correction and Protection]', *Crime and Delinquency*, 180, pp. 55–69.

Furukawa, T. (2016) 'Koureishahanzai ni kansuru Kenkyu Doukou [Current Situations of Elderly Crime Research]', *Japanese Journal of Sociological Criminology*, 41, pp. 98–104.

Giddens, A. (1992) *The Transformation of Intimacy: Sexuality, Love and Eroticism in Modern Societies*, Matsuo, K. and Matsukawa, A. trans. (1995), Stanford University Press; Jiritsushobo Ltd.

Hamai, K. (2011) *Jisshouteki Keijiseisakuron: Shin ni Yukouna Hanzaitaisaku he* [*Empirical Theory of Criminal Policy: Toward Genuinely Effective Remedy for Crime*], Iwanami Shoten Publishers.

Hosoi, Y. (2012) 'Koureihanzaisha no Gaiyou to Kadai [Overview and Issues of Elderly Criminals]', *Crime and Delinquency*, 173, pp. 6–36.

Ishida, M. (2011) *Koritsu no Shakaigaku: Muen Shakai no Shohousen* [*Sociology of Isolation: A Guide for a Life in Society of Indifference*], Keiso Shobo Publishing.

Ishida, M. (2018) *Koritsu Fuan Shalai: Tsunagari no Kakusa, Shounin no Tsuikyu, Bocchi no Kyoufu* [*Society in Fear of Isolation: Disparity in Connection, Pursue of Approval, and Fear of Isolation*], Keiso Shobo Publishing.

Iwata, M. (2008) *Shakaitekihaijo: Sanka no Ketsujo/Futashika na Kizoku* [*Social Exclusion: Lack of Participation and Unstable Connection*], Yuhikaku Publishing Co., Ltd.

Kinoshita, D. (2018) 'Shihou to Fukushi no Renkei niyoru Shihou no Fukushika no Riskufakuta to sono Eikyou ni kansuru Kentou [Discussion of Risk Factors and Impacts of Welfare Practice in Justice System by Coordination of Justice and Welfare Systems]', A Society for Prison Reform eds. (Doi, M., Masaki, Y., Mizuto, M., and Morihisa, C. (eds.) *"Shihou to Fukushi no Renkei" no Tenkai to Kadai* [*Development and Challenges in "Coordination of Justice and Welfare Systems*], Gendaijinbun-sha Co., Ltd., pp. 115–135.

Maruyama, S. (2018) *Hinkonmondai No Shin Chihei: <Moyai> No Soudan Katsudou No Kiseki* [*A New Horizon of Poverty Issues: Tracks of Counseling Activities at <Moyai>*], Junposha Co., Ltd.

Mashiko, C., Miyazawa, S., Tachioka, M., and Mizuuchi, T. (2012) 'Keijishisetsu Shusshosha no Chiikishakai Teichakushien: Atarashii Seifuthinetto no Kenshou/Daiichidan [Support for Settlement in Local Communities for People Released from Correctional Facilities: First Inspection of a New Safety Net]', *Homuresu to Shakai* [*Homeless People and Society*], 6, pp. 7–19.

Ministry of Justice. (2008) 'Part 7 The Circumstances and Attributes of Elderly Offenders and Their Treatment', *White paper on crime 2008*, pp. 27–45.

Nihei, N. (2011) 'Nihongata Seikatsuhosho Sisutemu no Saihen to Minshuto Seisaku no Ichi: Futatsu no "Kojinka" no Hazama de (Sinpojiumu Houkoku Seiken Koutai de Kazoku wa Kawaruka) [Reformation of Japanese Style Social Security System and Position of Policies of Democratic Party of Japan: Between Two "Individualizations" (Symposium Report: Will Family Change from Change of Government?)]', *Annals of Family Studies*, 36, pp. 61–75.

Okuda, T. (2010) 'Poverty of Social Bond and Crime: Considering Crime and Rehabilitation of Offenders Through Practice in Supporting Homeless People', *Japanese Journal of Sociological Criminology*, 35, pp. 21–37.

Oota, T. (2008) 'Koureihanzaisha no Jittai to Taisaku: Shogu to Yobou no Kanten kara [Situations and Measures for Crime by the Elderly: From Treatment and Prevention Perspectives]', *Jurist No. 1359*, pp. 116–127.

Oota, T. (2009) 'Koureihanzaisha no Jittai to Taisaku [Situations and Measures for Crime by the Elderly]', *Security Service Review*, 11, pp. 126–161.

Research and Training Institute of the Ministry of Justice. (2007) *Research Department Report 37 Koureihanzaisha no Jittai to Ishiki ni kansuru Kenkyu: Koureijukeisha oyobi Koureihogokansatsutaishousha no Bunseki* [*Research on Situations and Awareness of Elderly Offenders: Analysis on Elderly Prisoners and Probationers/Parplees*], Research and Training Institute of the Ministry of Justice.

Sugiyama, H. (2015) 'Keimusho Shusshosha tou no Shuuroushien ni tuite: Kyouryoku Koyounushi no motodeno Shuurou no Kakudai ni mukete [Employment Support for Released Inmates: Toward Employment Expansion in Collaboration with Supporting Corporations]', *Crime and Delinquency*, 180, pp. 89–107.

Suzuki, T. (2015) 'Saiba Hanzai no Genjo to Taisaku [Current Situation and Countermeasures of Cyber Crimes]', *Dai 8 Kai Konpyuta Hanzai ni Kansuru Shirahama Sinpojiumu Houkoku* [*The 8th Shirahama Cyber Crime Symposium Report*], https://www.jstage.jst.go.jp/article/shirahama/8/0/8_0_26/_pdf/-char/ja

Tachi, Y. (2009) 'Koireisha no Hanzai wa Naze Zouka shitanoka? [Why Have Crimes by the Elderly Increased?]', *Tsumi to Batsu* [*Crime and Punishment*] *46-2*, Nihon Keijiseisaku Kenkyukai, pp. 45–60.

Wacquant, L. (1999) *Les Prisons de la Misère, Édition Raisons d'agir* [*The Prisons of Misery, Reasons to Act Edition*], Mori, C., and Kikuchi, K. trans. (2008), Shin-Yo-Sha Publishing Ltd.

Watanabe, K. (2010) *Jiritsu no Jubaku: Homuresu Shien no Shakaigaku* [*Curse of Self-reliance: Sociology of Support for the Homeless*], SHINSENSHA Co., Ltd.

Young, J. (1999) *The Exclusive Society: Social Exclusion, Crime and Difference in Late Modernity*, Aoki, H., Itoh, T., Kishi, M., and Murasawa, M. trans. (2007), RAKUHOKU-Publications.

Section II

Characteristics of Elderly Criminals Based on Surveys on Elderly Inmates in Japan (Survey Conducted in 2012, 2016, and 2017)

7 Survey of Elderly Inmates

Outline and Results of Research on Elderly Male and Female Prisoners (2012 Survey, 2016 Survey, and 2017 Survey)

Bunri Tatsuno

Kokushikan University, Japan

7.1 Summary of the elderly inmate surveys (2012 survey, 2016 survey, and 2017 survey)

The crime situation in Japan since the beginning of the 1990s has been characterized by a decrease in juvenile delinquency and an increase in cases committed by the elderly. Regarding the number of arrests by age group for criminal offenses, the number of those aged 65 and above has remained high, whereas other groups have shown downward trends since 2017. The occupancy rate of the elderly in the total number of arrests has been rising almost consistently (by 22.8% in 2020). The occupancy rate of elderly recidivists among apprehended criminals has also been increasing, by as high as 53.8% for those aged 65 to 69 and 50.7% for those aged 70 and above (both 2017 values).

This increase in crimes committed by the elderly and the increase in recidivist rates have had an impact on the situation of prison inmates.

Figure 7.1 shows chronological changes in the yearly total of inmates in penal institutions in Japan and the percentage of the elderly among them. The total number of inmates has been decreasing since 2007, whereas the number of elderly inmates has been increasing, nearly up to 13%. This trend is more pronounced in female inmates, whose occupation rate has reached nearly 20% of the total inmate population (Figure 7.2).

One of the characteristics of elderly inmates is the high percentage of those who have been in prison more than once. The percentage of those who have served more than once among elderly male inmates remains high, around 70% (less than 60% for non-elderly inmates). For women, the percentage of both elderly and non-elderly inmates remains around 50%. The frequency of multiple admissions means that the offenders are repeat offenders, indicating that they have problems with their living conditions after release. What do elderly inmates think about while in prison, and how do they envision their lives after release? Are they not disillusioned or depressed by the fact that they have been in prison multiple times? Are they worried that things will not go well after their release? If so, it is necessary to develop measures to make their life after

DOI: 10.4324/9781032669519-10

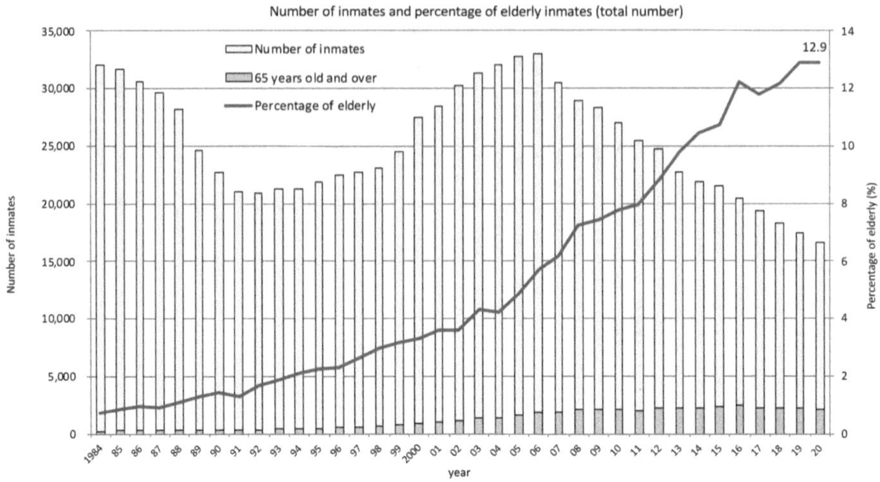

Figure 7.1 Number of inmates and percentage of elderly inmates (total number).
Source: White Paper on Crime 2021.

release as secure as possible and to help them have a better outlook for the future while they are in prison.

Therefore, in this study group, we conducted a multi-questionnaire survey over several years to understand the actual conditions of elderly inmates, find out the background behind their repeated imprisonment, and clarify what kind of awareness and anxiety the inmates have during their stay in prison.[1] A summary of the survey is below.

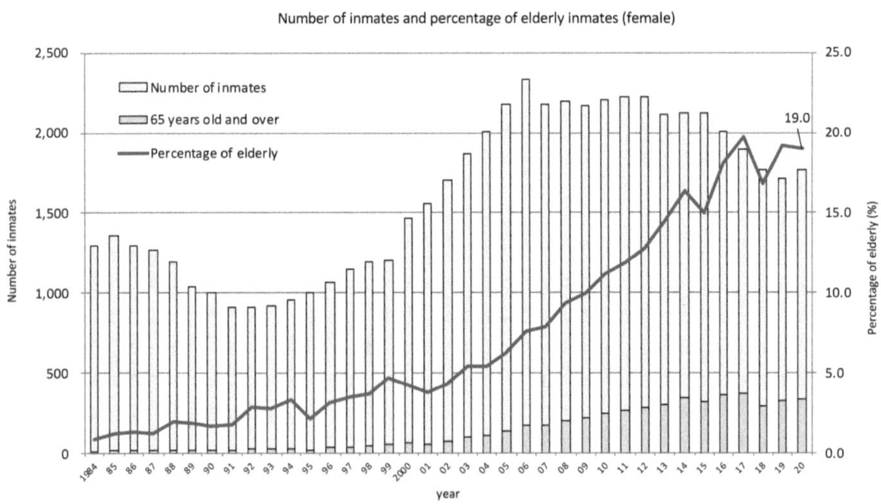

Figure 7.2 Number of inmates and percentage of elderly inmates (female).
Source: White Paper on Crime 2021.

The main items of the survey instrument are as follows.

Attribution items (including criminal history), living situation before entering prison, psychological and medical symptoms during adolescence, social and nonsocial experiences before the age of 30 years, self-image at the time of the offense, feelings of insecurity, circumstances leading to the offense, ability to care for a life partner/supporter at the time of the offense, impact of the offense on self and surroundings, prospects for life after release, and attitudes toward prison.

The survey included as many open-ended questions as possible to gain a broad understanding of the actual situation of older prisoners. The survey was designed and administered in such a way that the subjects were asked to reflect on their own life history, focusing primarily on their relationships with their families, perceptions of their lives, and mental health concerns, and to answer these questions as specifically as possible in their own words.

The summary of the Questionnaire Survey of Correctional Institution Inmates is below (Table 7.1).

1. Collaborating institutions: Correctional Bureau of the Ministry of Justice, Toyo University, and Kokushikan University
2. Survey target setting: The target institutions and sample size were selected according to the number of elderly inmates. For the first survey, male and female inmates aged 65 years and over were targeted, and for the second and third surveys, female inmates aged 40 years and over were targeted.
3. Method of conducting the survey:

   a. A sample number of questionnaires and collection envelopes (sealable type) were sent to the person in charge of the target prisons.
   b. The survey forms and collection envelopes were distributed to inmates of the specified sex and age.
   c. Prisoners filled out the survey form by themselves during their free time.
   d. Whether or not they cooperated with the survey, the forms were placed in the collection envelopes and handed to the person in charge, who only checked the envelope for foreign objects before sealing it.
   e. The collected envelopes were packed up and returned to either Toyo University or Kokushikan University.
   f. Data were compiled, tabulated, and analyzed by the study group.

7.2 Results of and discussion concerning the 2016 survey

7.2.1 Survey outline and method (2016 survey)

7.2.1.1 Survey outline

This survey was designed to ask participants to respond to specific items concerning their own life histories while reflecting on their relationships primarily with family members, their awareness of life-related matters, their psychological insecurities, and confronting their past as much as possible. It was conducted

Table 7.1 Questionnaire survey of correctional facility inmates

	2012 Survey	*2016 Survey*	*2017 Survey*
Survey period	December 2012–March 2014	August 2016	November–December, 2017
Number of facilities surveyed	56	8	2
Number of samples	Men and women over 65 years 700 samples	Women over 40 years 542 samples	Women over 40 years 550 samples
Number of valid responses	Total 635 Male 495 Women 87 Unknown 53	Female 438	Female 377
Valid response rate	90.7%	80.8%	68.5%
Survey Target Facilities	Sapporo, Sapporo Prison Branch, Obihiro, Abashiri, Tsukigata, Aomori, Miyagi, Akita, Yamagata, Fukushima, Fukushima Prison Branch, Mito, Tochigi, Kurobane, Kitsuregawa Rehabilitation Center, Maebashi, Chiba, Ichihara, Fuchu, Yokohama, Niigata, Kofu, Nagano, Shizuoka, Toyama, Kanazawa, Fukui, Gifu, Kasamatsu, Nagoya, Mie, Shiga, Kyoto, Osaka, Kobe, Kakogawa, Harima Rehabilitation Center, Wakayama, Tottori, Matsue, Shimane Asahi Rehabilitation Center, Hiroshima, Yamaguchi, Iwakuni, Tokushima, Takamatsu, Matsuyama, Kochi, Fukuoka, Fumoto, Sasebo, Nagasaki, Kumamoto, Oita, Miyazaki, Kagoshima, Okinawa (When the facility name is XX Prison, "prison" is abbreviated.)	Sapporo Prison Branch, Fukushima Prison Branch, Kasamatsu Prison, Wakayama Prison, Kakogawa Prison, Iwakuni Prison, Saijo Prison Branch, Fumoto Prison	Tochigi Prison, Mine Rehabilitation Center

The results of the 2016 and 2017 surveys are discussed below. The results of the 2012 survey will be presented in Chapter 8.

Note:

Each of the surveys was funded by the following MEXT "KAKENHI" grants.

Survey 2012

Principal investigator: Yoko Hosoi, sub-investigators: Bunri Tatsuno, Takashi Furukawa, et al., Research term: 2011–2013, Research category: Fundamental research (C), Research field: Coexistence and exclusion

2016 and 2017 Surveys

Principal investigator: Yoko Hosoi, Research assistant: Bunri Tatsuno, Research organization: 2014–2019, Research Category: Fundamental Research (A), Research Field: Neo-Gerontology to elucidate the world in which these participants live and identify triggers for criminality to paint a precise picture of elderly female inmates broadly.

The survey form comprised questions whose contents included the following: items on attributes (including criminal history), living conditions before imprisonment, psychological and medical symptoms during puberty, social and non-social experiences up to 30 years of age, self-conception corresponding to the time of the most recent commission of a crime, sense of insecurity and developments leading to crime, ability of life partners and supporters to provide care at the time of the commission of a crime, impact that the commission of a crime had on the participant and those associated with the participant, life after release from prison, awareness of and thoughts about life after release from prison, and awareness and thoughts about prison.

7.2.1.2 Survey protocols

This survey was administered to female inmates aged 40 years and above, housed in one of eight nationwide penal institutions (institutions primarily housing female inmates)[2], who entered prison between January and June 2016. Institution workers distributed the survey form to respondents, each of whom then completed this form, enclosed it in an envelope, and returned it to an institution worker. Completed forms were then collected and sent back in a batch. The survey was conducted with the consent of respondents on an anonymous basis between August 1 and 31, 2016. The number of valid response forms received was 438, and the valid response rate was 80.8%.

*7.2.2 **Survey results (2016 survey)***

7.2.2.1 Basic attributes of respondents (Table 7.2)

Several characteristic points were observed in the 12 attributes applied to the 438 respondents in this survey, divided into the elderly (aged 65 years and above) and non-elderly groups (aged 40–64 years). The proportion of the elderly and non-elderly groups was 21.9% and 71.5%, respectively, showing a result more or less in line with that of all inmates across the country. Since the purpose of this survey was to obtain a precise picture of elderly people, results of non-elderly people were used for comparative purposes. In terms of types of offense committed, "theft" accounted for 77.1% of the elderly group, while illicit drugs and theft accounted for 47.6% and 43.8%, respectively, in the non-elderly group. Regarding the distribution of the number of times each respondent had been imprisoned, a substantial number of respondents in the non-elderly group indicated either the first time or two to four times, whereas many in the elderly group indicated five times or more. The average number of years before re-offence was 5.25 for the elderly group, which was approximately two years longer than the non-elderly group (3.23 years). No difference was observed in the types of crime committed.

Table 7.2 Attributes of respondents

			Age bracket		*Type of crime in question (*)*	
			Elderly group	*Non-elderly group*	*Theft*	*Illicit drugs*
			65 years or older	*40–64 years*	*40 years or older*	
1	Breakdown of respondents in terms of age (sample size: n = 438)	n: actual number of persons	96	313	216	157
		Percent of sample size (%)	21.9	71.5	49.3	35.8
2	Current age	(N)	96	313	211	156
		average age	71.6 years	49.0 years	58.8 years	47.0 years
3	Type of crime in question	Theft	77.1	43.8		8.3
		Illicit drugs	5.2	47.6	6.3	
4	Current sentence	(N)	84	313	198	153
		average	1.94 years	2.19 years	1.83 years	2.37 years
5	Age at the time this crime was committed	(N)	94	310	208	157
		average age	70.2 years	48.1 years	58.0 years	46.1 years
6	Number of years between the previous release of the respondent from prison and the commission of this crime	(N)	25	157	88	96
		average	5.25 years	3.23 years	3.50 years	3.37 years
7	Number of times the respondent has been imprisoned	First time	27.1	31.9	31.5	22.9
		2–4 times	27.1	39.9	33.3	49.0
		5 or more times	10.4	9.3	10.2	12.7
8	Educational background	Dropped out of or graduated from primary school	2.1	1.0	1.8	1.3
		Dropped out of or graduated from junior high school	45.8	34.5	35.2	45.2

(*Continued*)

Table 7.2 (Continued)

			Age bracket		*Type of crime in question (*)*	
			Elderly group	*Non-elderly group*	*Theft*	*Illicit drugs*
			65 years or older	*40–64 years*	*40 years or older*	
		Dropped out of high school	9.4	21.1	12.0	28.0
		Graduated from high school	35.4	31.0	38.0	18.5
		At least enrolled in junior college or university	5.2	10.5	10.2	7.0
9	Did the respondent have a husband or partner at the time of the commission of this crime		37.5	62.6	48.6	69.4
10	Whether or not the respondent had been living with someone else at the time of the commission of this crime	Yes	60.4	71.9	68.1	70.1
		No	33.3	24.6	27.3	26.1
11	Relationship with person with which the respondent had been living	(N)	58	225	147	110
		Husband or partner	56.9	62.2	55.1	63.6
		Child	58.6	47.1	55.8	43.6
12	Current state of health	Healthy	19.8	36.4	27.8	36.9
		I'm not particularly healthy but neither am I sick	43.8	31.3	35.6	31.2
		Prone to illness or having difficulties dealing with illness	29.1	27.2	31.1	28.6

(*Continued*)

Table 7.2 (Continued)

			Age bracket		*Type of crime in question (*)*	
			Elderly group	*Non-elderly group*	*Theft*	*Illicit drugs*
			65 years or older	*40–64 years*	*40 years or older*	
		Often receive assistance or nursing care	–	0.3	–	–

Notes:

1. Where no population parameter (n) is indicated, the sample size is as follows: elderly group (n = 96), non-elderly group (n = 313), theft (n = 216), and illicit drugs (n = 157).
2. Percentage distributions are not indicated for respondents not belonging to the above age brackets or for non-respondents to any given question.

Breakdown table goes right below.

* Breakdown of types of crime in question (multiple responses) (%).

	Theft	*Illicit drugs*	*Fraud*	*Relating to automobile operations*	*Murder*	*Physical assault and causing injury*	*Robbery*	*Other*	*Unknown*
Sample size (n = 438)	49.3	35.8	6.3	4.1	1.6	1.4	0.7	3.4	7.1

Regarding educational background, 45.8% of respondents in the elderly group indicated that they had graduated from junior high school, followed by 35.4% who had graduated or dropped out from high school, respectively. In contrast, similarly-sized segments of the non-elderly group indicated that 34.5% of them had graduated or dropped out of junior high school, and 31.0% had graduated from high school, respectively. One thing to note is that the number of high school drop-outs was higher in the non-elderly group than in the elderly group. The option to drop out of high school possibly was not as familiar to those who currently belong to the elderly group. In addition, the percentage of high school dropouts among respondents from the non-elderly group convicted of illicit drug-related offenses was notably high at 28.2%. As for whether or not respondents were living with someone else at the time of the offense in question, "living with someone else" accounted for a more significant percentage of respondents in the elderly group, most of whom also indicated that they were living with a child. In looking at the current state of health, the number of those who responded "healthy" was relatively low in the elderly group. However, in combination with "I am not particularly healthy, but neither am I sick," it accounted for 64% of responses, revealing that many respondents were not experiencing health-related problems in their daily lives.

7.2.2.2 *Living conditions and awareness of the participants*

Focusing on the living expenses of the inmates, most of the elderly group relied on "pension" (62.5%) before imprisonment, followed by "savings" (20.8%), "welfare" (19.8%), "income from work" (18.8%), and "income from husband/partner" (18.8%). In contrast, 57.5% of the non-elderly group cited "income from work," followed by "welfare" at 37.1%. Among the non-elderly group, 51.4% of the respondents were unemployed because they were receiving public assistance. In addition, 34.6% of them said they were unable to work because of illness.

Among those who were not working at the time of the crime, which consisted of 19.0% (one in five) of all the participants, they said they were "having extreme financial difficulties."

With regard to their plans to cover living expenses after release from prison, those in the elderly group who replied "pension" and "savings account" exhibited an increase at 67.7% and 31.3%, whereas those who replied "work income" and "husband/partner's income" showed a decrease at 10.4% and 16.7%, respectively. In contrast, the non-elderly group saw a significant decrease in "work income" (36.4%) and increases in "husband/partner's income" (30.7%) and "welfare" (43.1%).

7.2.2.3 *"Concerns about life" and "Important things to me"*

83.3% of the elderly group and 88.2% of the non-elderly group responded that they were "troubled" at the time they committed this crime. Said troubles referred to "own health" at 42.5% and "recidivism" at 41.3% for the elderly group, followed by "family relations" at 27.5%, "family health" at 25.0%, and "daily living expenses" at 20.0%. In the non-elderly group, 44.9% selected "own health," followed by 43.8% for "family relations" and 38.0% for "daily living expenses".

The top concern for both groups after release from prison was "own health" (67.7% for the elderly group and 51.4% for the non-elderly group). At the same time, "family health" and "relationship with family" were higher among the non-elderly group at 47.3% and 46.6%, respectively. The concern regarding "daily living expenses" at 34.2% was nearly twice as high in the elderly group as the non-elderly group. Approximately half of the non-elderly group were unemployed and receiving public assistance. The elderly group, in contrast, receives a fixed amount of "pension" regularly; thus, although they are struggling to make ends meet, they are less worried about financial issues than the non-elderly group.

7.2.2.4 *"Mental state in periods of adolescence and young adulthood" and "Experiences of social and Non-social behaviors"*

It was noted in the 2013 White Paper on Crime (Ministry of Justice, 2013) that many female inmates had experiences of being abused in the past, trauma from sexual abuse, and problems of eating disorders. In this survey, respondents were asked whether they had experienced “psychological and medical symptoms” and “non-social behavior” in their teens, 20s, and 30s. Overall, the non-elderly group shows a higher number of experiences. The reason may be related to the fact that the non-elderly group is more likely to have experienced illegal drug use as a type of crime. Table 7.3 shows the experience of the non-elderly group in terms of “theft” and “drugs.” Almost

Table 7.3 Conduct and medical conditions experienced into one's thirties (theft and illicit drug-related offenses committed by members of the non-elderly group)

		Non-elderly theft group (n = 137)	*Non-elderly illicit drug group (n = 149)*
1	Nail-biting or skin-peeling	27.0 %	35.6 %
2	Atopic dermatitis	12.8	13.1
3	extreme shyness	23.2	26.6
4	OCD	10.9	10.7
5	Chronic pain	8.8	4.0
6	Anger attacks	15.3	20.5
7	Menstruation cramps, irregular menstruation, or PMS	43.5	51.7
8	Excessive anxiety or hyperventilation	20.4	26.8
9	Eating disorder (binge eating)	18.2	18.8
10	Eating disorder (anorexia)	14.6	14.8
11	Domestic violence or verbal abuse (perpetrator)	15.3	22.1
12	Domestic violence or verbal abuse (victim)	21.9	35.6
13	Bullying (perpetrator or victim)	19.7	26.2
14	Laziness	22.6	31.5
15	Running away from home	33.6	63.5
16	Misconduct	31.4	63.1
17	Shoplifting	47.0	46.9
18	Non-shoplifting form of theft	21.9	30.2
19	Smoking (heavy)	47.4	71.8
20	Compulsive shopping	31.4	38.3
21	Sexual relations with unspecified members of the opposite sex	21.9	37.6
22	Sex addiction	5.8	11.4
23	Alcoholism or illicit drug addiction	25.5	61.1
24	Addiction to pachinko, mahjong, horse-racing, or other forms of gambling	19.0	40.0
25	Addiction to gaming	12.4	24.2
26	Provision of sex trade-related services	9.5	21.5
27	Compensated dating (received compensation)	10.7	18.8
28	Compensated dating (provided compensation)	2.2	3.4

all of the experiences are high in the "drug" category. In other words, the "drug" group experienced various psychological symptoms and problematic behaviors during their upbringing. This is a phenomenon that transcends age groups.

7.2.2.5 *Social networks and isolation*

Being "lonely" is often mentioned concerning elderly criminals. In this survey, the participants were asked who were the "people who were expected to provide support" and "people who actually provided support," and the choice of "family members including husbands/partners" was the most dominant reply in both the elderly and non-elderly groups, while the choices of "friends" and "professionals" were minimal. In other words, when they have no one in the broad sense of "family member," they have very few people to turn to for advice, and they do not expect to receive support from anyone else. As a whole, they do not expect much consultation or help when they are in trouble, and in fact, they do not receive any. This seems to be indicative of "social isolation."

7.2.2.6 *Profile of elderly first-time inmates*

Out of the 438 respondents in this survey, 26 were imprisoned for the first time after they became elderly (65 years and above). We sought to paint a profile of these respondents by attempting to ascertain the circumstances that led them to become imprisoned in the latter half of their lives and figure out what sorts of lives they had led up to that point in time. Those with a criminal past consisted of 16 respondents, among whom the earliest age at which a crime was committed was 27 years. The remaining ten respondents led lives utterly free of the taint of a criminal background; 11 respondents were in their sixties, 14 in their seventies, and one in their eighties. One respondent was convicted of homicide, while the remaining 25 respondents had engaged in theft.

Let us examine what points were most commonly indicated primarily in responses to free-answer questions. (1) Concerning living conditions, most respondents indicated that they received pension payments. In addition, respondents indicated that they made use of savings, assistance from family members and relatives, and the income earned by husbands and partners. While nine respondents indicated that they received welfare, only two lived on welfare payments alone. However, all but a single respondent noted that life was hard. Causes of theft (shoplifting) commonly indicated consisted of "I wanted goods," "I could not restrain myself," and "I did it for my family." Others included "I was upset at the time because of a quarrel with my family" and "I shoplifted to speak to a police officer about and escape from my husband's violence." (2) When asked how they were taking their current situation in prison, some respondents described the difficulties they experienced in their lives in prison: "My first time in a group life was more horrible and harsher than I had imagined," "I was surprised to see so many young inmates," and "It was difficult to be ordered or admonished by prison guards who were young enough to be my daughter or grandchild." At the same time, respondents regretted causing grief to their own families (children and grandchildren). However, very few respondents cared much about themselves in one way or another. (3) Another free-answer question presented was a question tasking them to identify their most trying experiences in life to date. Many respondents indicated domestic violence by husbands and family-related difficulties (such as an illness, debt, problems with members of the opposite sex, and nursing care), whereas no respondent indicated their own crime or imprisonment as their most trying experience in life. In contrast, when they were asked about their happy experiences, many respondents indicated marriage and childbirth. (4) Regarding a question concerning their life after release from penal institutions, except for one respondent who indicated that she wanted to live a quiet life apart from family members after being released from prison, a typical response was: "I want to live and help each other with my child who would be my guarantor (if I can be forgiven)," followed by replies indicating an intent to reside in a halfway house or public welfare facility.

7.2.3 Comparison with elderly male inmates – Comparison with the 2012 survey

The results of this survey were compared with those of the "2012 survey" by combining items and subjects common to the two surveys. The following are the two items that showed differences between elderly female and male inmates.

i For female inmates, the majority of the crimes were theft (76.0%) for the elderly, while for male inmates, in addition to theft (32.9%), assault/injury (16.8%) and drugs (15.0%) were the main types of crime (results for females are from the combined 2016 and 2012 surveys, and for males are from the 2012 survey).
ii Living expenses prior to release differed significantly between men and women, with 39.4% of men reporting "income from work," 27.7% "pension," and 27.3% "welfare," whereas 57.4% of women reported "pension," 24.1% "income from work," 19.7% "savings account," and 17.5% "welfare," in that order.

An even more significant difference was the plan to cover living expenses after release from prison. While men cited "work income" at 30.5% in addition to "welfare" at 42.6% and "pension" at 36.0%, women overwhelmingly cited "pension" at 61.8%. Another 26.3% expect "savings," 22.4% expect "welfare," and 14.7% expect "income from work," which is less than half of the male respondents.

When asked about their "hopes for life after release from prison," the most prominent responses were "I want to live a life centered on work" for men and "I want to live with my family" for women.

7.2.4 Conclusion of this section

Points clarified through the results of the 2016 survey are outlined below.

i Respondents in the elderly group (female inmates aged 65 years and above) exhibited a lower level of criminality than the non-elderly group (female inmates between the ages of 40 and 64 years), as demonstrated by the fact that their dominant crime was mostly a minor offence such as theft. This was also demonstrated by the fact that many respondents, in identifying what troubled them at the time they committed the crime in question, indicated that they feared and were concerned about the possibility that they might re-offend. These respondents' thoughts about their crimes (and the possibility of re-offending) to this extent on their own can be seen as evidence that they reflected considerably on what they did while in prison even though they could not stop themselves from re-offending in the end. In contrast, respondents from the non-elderly group were more concerned about the relationship with family and daily living costs to a greater extent than the possibility of re-offence. While this may be indicative of just how difficult their situation was, it could nevertheless suggest that they were not particularly inclined to control themselves concerning crimes.

ii Respondents in the elderly group indicated that the things that mattered most to them were: "I must suffer for the crime I committed," "I must hide I was in prison," and "I should make amends to the victim." Respondents from the non-elderly group indicated that they valued "having hopes for the future" and "becoming independent or engaging in a job." The former sought to distance themselves from their crimes and live quiet lives in peace, whereas the latter regarded the link between themselves and their crimes as an opportunity to step up in their lives. It is evident that they possessed levels of desire and enthusiasm concerning living for the future. For this reason alone, it is possible to suppress recidivism and promote a desire for greater independence on the part of respondents by improving their living conditions (in terms of family relationships and life-related issues), providing them with support for securing a job, and reinforcing their connection with society. To help respondents maintain their motivation, the understanding and support of those surrounding them are vital.

iii Inmates tied to theft differ from those tied to illicit drugs across age groups. Respondents tied to illicit drugs exhibited high proportions for almost all attribute-related items, including educational background (high school dropouts), unemployment (welfare, no financial difficulties), dwelling type (rented housing, rented apartment), marital status and family (divorce, cohabitation, abortion, recipient of domestic violence, extramarital affair), and psychological symptoms and behaviors experienced in their thirties. Even for misconduct behaviors in adolescence, differences between the responses of inmates tied to theft and those tied to illicit drugs were evident. With the same being applicable to the elderly group and the non-elderly group, the problems of illicit drugs can be seen in these observations.

iv As can also be seen in the 2012 survey, comparisons between male and female elderly inmates reveal that female respondents thought the relationship with their family was most important in terms of what concerns or difficulties they had at the time they committed their crime, whereas male respondents indicated that things that most concerned them were problems at work. A similar trend can be seen for post-release concerns. This trend is even more pronounced when we see the gap between male and female respondents concerning living costs. Many female respondents indicate, both before and after imprisonment, that they expect to cover living costs with pension payments, savings, and welfare, whereas male respondents indicated welfare and pension payments, followed by employment income. Male individuals seek to maintain connection to society through work, even when they reach old age (at the age of 65 years). Female individuals, in contrast, seek to lead a life based on a family foundation.

7.3 Results of and discussion concerning the 2017 survey

7.3.1 Survey outline and method (2017 survey)

7.3.1.1 Survey outline

Based on the results obtained in the past two surveys, a questionnaire incorporating more free-answer questions targeting female inmates was used in the third survey conducted between November and December 2017. It was administered at two female penal institutions (Tochigi Prison and Mine Rehabilitation Program Center) subjecting female inmates (excluding those who the facilities believed could not complete the survey without difficulties based on the nature of their treatment or sentence) aged 40 years and above (as of the time of the questionnaire form distribution).

7.3.1.2 Survey protocol

With the cooperation of the Ministry of Justice's Correction Bureau, this survey was administered to female inmates aged 40 years and above, housed in two penal institutions between November and December 2017. Institution workers distributed the survey form to respondents, each of whom then completed this form, enclosed it in an envelope, and returned it to an institution worker. Completed forms were then collected and sent back in a batch.

The survey was conducted with the consent of respondents on an anonymous basis. The number of valid response forms received was 377.

7.3.2 *Survey results (2017 survey)*

7.3.2.1 *Basic attributes of respondents (Table 7.4)*

In dividing the 377 respondents in this survey by age group, the proportions of elderly (aged 65 years and above) and non-elderly groups (40-64 years of age) were 19.4% and 67.1%, respectively, of all respondents. In this survey, differences between facilities mirrored differences between age groups due to

Table 7.4 Attributes of respondents

			Age bracket		*Type of crime in question (*)*	
			Elderly group	*Non-elderly group*	*Theft*	*Illicit drugs*
			65 years or older	*40–64 years*	*40 years or older*	
1	Breakdown of respondents in terms of age (sample size: n = 438)	n: actual number of persons	73	253	123	94
		Percent of sample size (%)	19.4	67.1	32.6	24.9
2	Current age	(N)	73	253	74	94
		average age	73.5 years	49.5 years	60.5 years	47.6 years
3	Type of crime in question	Theft	64.4	26.5		4.3
		Illicit drugs	2.7	36.4	3.3	
4	Current sentence	(N)	55	208	95	86
		average	3.50 years	3.07 years	1.95 years	2.17 years
5	Age at the time this crime was committed	(N)	68	250	115	93
		average age	67.3 years	45.9 years	57.8 years	45.5 years
6	Number of years between the previous release of the respondent from prison and the commission of this crime	(N)	12	57	29	30
		average	2.42 years	3.30 years	19.31 years	4.40 years

(*Continued*)

Table 7.4 (Continued)

			Age bracket		*Type of crime in question (*)*	
			Elderly group	*Non-elderly group*	*Theft*	*Illicit drugs*
			65 years or older	*40–64 years*	*40 years or older*	
7	Number of times the respondent has been imprisoned	First time	45.2	70.4	50.4	57.4
		2-4 times	20.5	20.6	23.6	29.8
		5 or more times	9.6	5.1	5.7	12.8
8	Educational background	Dropped out of or graduated from primary school	2.8	0.8	0.8	1.1
		Dropped out of or graduated from junior high school	28.8	22.6	25.2	34.1
		Dropped out of high school	12.3	17.8	16.3	25.5
		Graduated from high school	23.3	29.6	30.1	17.0
		Dropped out of graduated from junior college or dropped out of university	19.2	23.0	18.7	20.2
		At least graduated from university	5.5	5.5	4.1	2.1
9	Did the respondent have a husband or partner at the time of the commission of this crime		35.6	62.8	41.5	62.8
10	Whether or not the respondent had been living with someone else at the time of the commission of this crime	Yes	50.7	80.6	64.2	75.5
		No	34.2	15.8	28.5	19.1

(*Continued*)

Table 7.4 (Continued)

			Age bracket		*Type of crime in question (*)*	
			Elderly group	*Non-elderly group*	*Theft*	*Illicit drugs*
			65 years or older	*40–64 years*	*40 years or older*	
11	Relationship with person with which the respondent had been living	(N)	37	204	79	71
		Husband or partner	70.3	59.8	58.2	54.9
		Child	37.8	58.3	48.1	56.3
12	Current state of health	Healthy	30.1	49.8	35.0	44.7
		I'm not particularly healthy but neither am I sick	32.9	24.5	31.7	26.6
		Prone to illness	9.6	9.1	10.6	9.6
		Having difficulties dealing with illness	16.4	12.3	14.6	16.0
		Often receive assistance or nursing care	2.7	0.8	0.8	1.1

Notes:

1. Where no population parameter (n) is indicated, the sample size is as follows: elderly group (n = 73), non-elderly group (n = 253), theft (n = 123), and illicit drugs (n = 94).

2. Percentage distributions are not indicated for respondents not belonging to the above age brackets or for non-respondents to any given question.

* Breakdown of types of crime in question (multiple responses) (%)

	Theft	*Illicit drugs*	*Fraud*	*Murder*	*Robbery*	*Physical assault and causing injury*	*Relating to automobile operations*	*Other*	*Unknown*
Sample size (n = 377)	32.6	24.9	11.7	8.8	4.2	1.6	1.1	8.8	15.9

restrictions on the ages of inmates placed by the facilities at which this survey was administered. In terms of offence types of all respondents, theft, illicit drugs, and others accounted for 32.6%, 24.9%, and 43.5%, respectively (it should be noted, however, that the four respondents who answered both "theft" and "illicit drugs" were double counted). In terms of the distribution of the number of times each respondent had been imprisoned, the percentages for once only, two or more times, and unknown times were 59.4%, 24.4%, and 16.2%, respectively.

In terms of educational background, junior high school graduates and high school graduates in the elderly group accounted for 31.6% and 35.6%, respectively. In contrast, junior high school graduates and high school graduates in the non-elderly group accounted for 23.4% and 47.4%, respectively, indicating a higher percentage at the upper educational background. However, respondents who graduated from university accounted for 5.5% in both groups. In comparing offence types between thefts and illicit drugs, the percentage of junior high school graduates was notably high at 34.8% among those corresponding to illicit drugs in the non-elderly group.

As for whether a respondent was living with someone else at the time of the crime in question, a high percentage of respondents in the non-elderly group, equal to 80.6%, answered affirmative. Regarding their health conditions at the time of the survey, the percentage of those who answered "healthy" was relatively low in the elderly group. However, in combination with "I am not particularly healthy, but neither am I sick," it accounted for 63.0% of responses, revealing that many respondents were not experiencing health-related problems in their daily lives.

7.3.2.2 Living conditions of the participants and living expenses after release

Regarding the living conditions of respondents before imprisonment, nearly half of them (50.9%) answered that they were "not having trouble"[3] to the question "whether or not it was difficult to make ends meet to pay the electricity and other bills," and the percentage of those who answered that they were "having trouble"[4] was also high at 35.0%.

When separated by age group and crime, 52.1% of those in the non-elderly group had committed "theft" stated that their living conditions were challenging. Conversely, although 18.2% of those who had committed "theft" in the elderly group stated that their living conditions were challenging, the majority of them (75.0%) said they were not, making it difficult to determine whether difficulties in their everyday life were the cause of the theft.

Regarding the financial source to cover living expenses at the time of the crime, many in the elderly group cited "pension" (49.3%), while many in the non-elderly group cited "income from work" (50.6%). Incidentally, many of those in the elderly group who had committed "theft" depended on "pensions" (56.8%) and "husband/partner's income" (27.3%) to cover their living expenses. Those in the non-elderly group who were tied to "illicit drugs" were more likely than those in the other groups to depend on "welfare" (46.7%) for their living expenses.

Regarding their plans to cover living expenses after release from prison, most of those in the elderly group chose "pension" (58.9%), "savings account" (38.4%), and "welfare" (23.3%). In contrast, many of those in the non-elderly group chose "income from work" (72.7%). The percentage was exceptionally high (75.0%) among those tied to "illicit drugs" in the non-elderly group, with many of them relying on work after their release from prison.

7.3.2.3 "Concerns about life" and "Things that are important to me"

A relatively high proportion at 78% (74.0% of the elderly group and 82.6% of the non-elderly group) of respondents answered that they were "troubled or worried" at the time of the crime. The most common concern was "own health" (44.4%) in the elderly group, whereas "family relations" (43.5%) and "daily living expenses" (38.8%) were relatively common in the non-elderly group.

Likewise, the most common concern after release from prison was "own health" for both the elderly and non-elderly groups (67.1% of the elderly group and 69.2% of the non-elderly group). Approximately the same proportion of the non-elderly group selected "daily living expenses" (64.4%) and "work problems" (62.8%). Other than these, the items that were answered by more than 30% in the non-elderly group included "relationships with children" at 44.3%, "relationships with neighbors and workplace" at 42.7%, "relationships with friends" at 35.1%, "loneliness" at 33.2%, "relationship with parents" at 32.0%, "debt payment" at 29.6%, "lack of a trusted advisor" at 29.3%, and many others. In contrast, the only item to which more than 30% of the elderly group responded was "relationship with children" at 31.5%. In the elderly group, 67.1% of their worries and concerns were related to "own health."

With respect to type of offense, approximately 70% of both "theft" and "illicit drugs" groups cited "own health," whereas more than half of the "illicit drugs" group also cited "daily living expenses" at 62.8%, "work problems" at 58.5%, and "relationship with children" at 51.1% as their concerns.

7.3.2.4 Psychological state during puberty and adolescence and experience engaging in social and non-social conduct (Table 7.5)

In examining past experiences, responses mostly consisted of smoking, shoplifting, and compulsive shopping. Respondents whose offenses corresponded to illicit drugs also exhibited high values for other experiences, with a majority indicating the following: running away from home (63.8%), depression (53.2%), domestic violence or verbal abuse (53.2%), sex with unspecified members of the opposite sex (53.2%), and addiction to pachinko, mahjong, horse-racing, or other forms of gambling (50.0%). Incidentally, 89.4% of respondents tied to "illicit drugs" indicated "smoking" experience and 77.4% of them indicated that they experienced it in their teens. Other experiences

Table 7.5 Experiences to Date

		Age bracket		*Type of crime in question*	
		Elderly group	*Non-elderly group*	*Theft*	*Illicit drugs*
		65 years or older	*40–64 years*	*40 years or older*	
	(N)	*73*	*253*	*123*	*94*
1	Smoking (120 cigarettes per day or more)	13.7 %	67.6 %	38.2 %	89.4 %
2	Shoplifting	39.7	59.3	69.9	64.9
3	Compulsive shopping	21.9	51.4	38.2	60.6
4	Depression	20.5	44.3	33.3	53.2
5	Domestic violence or verbal abuse as victim	24.7	44.7	32.5	53.2
6	Being bullied	12.3	44.7	39.0	41.5
7	Running away from home	13.7	47.0	27.6	63.8
8	Alcohol or illicit drug addiction	11.0	42.7	9.8	89.4
9	Misconduct	6.8	42.7	18.7	67.0
10	Sexual relations with unspecified members of the opposite sex	8.2	39.9	23.6	53.2
11	Self-harm or suicidal behavior	11.0	34.8	22.8	46.8
12	Laziness	6.8	37.2	19.5	46.8
13	Addiction to pachinko, mahjong, horse-racing, or other forms of gambling	16.4	33.6	20.3	50.0
14	Non-shoplifting form of theft	16.4	26.1	30.1	29.8
15	Binge eating	2.7	26.1	16.3	30.9
16	Domestic violence or verbal abuse against family	6.8	22.5	13.0	34.0
17	Mania	6.8	19.8	13	23.4
18	Being harassed	5.5	18.6	11.4	25.5
19	Addiction to gaming	5.4	19.0	8.9	33.0
20	Sex addiction	1.4	19.0	5.7	29.8
21	Stress disorder brought about by PTSD	2.7	15.0	9.8	20.2

Note: In order from most highly indicated to least highly indicated.

with high values aside from smoking among inmates tied to "illicit drugs" included being bullied (87.2%), running away from home (86.7%), and shoplifting (85.2%). It can be said that members of the illicit drugs group had experienced various psychological symptoms, experiences as victims, and experiences in terms of problematic behavior while growing up.

7.3.2.5 Life after release from prison, social network, and isolation

Regarding how they would like to live after their release from prison, the most common responses were "avoid committing crimes again" (74.0% of the elderly group and 79.4% of the non-elderly group) and "avoid causing trouble to others" (67.1% of the elderly group and 77.1% of the non-elderly group). The non-elderly group provided responses such as "live with family" (62.1%) and "focus on work" (60.9%), whereas more than half of the elderly respondents selected no other two options.

Among the 208 respondents (55.2% of the total) who answered, "live with my family" regarding how they would like to live after their release from prison, 65.4% cited "own health," 51.5% "work problems," 51.4% "daily living expenses," and 42.3% "relationships with neighbors and workplace," as their "concerns and worries" after release.

In contrast, of the 76 respondents (20.2% of the total) who answered that they would like to live alone after their release from prison, 72.3% of them (68.5% of the total) cited "own health," and "daily living expenses," 50.0% cited "work problems," 48.7% cited "relationship with children," 44.8% "not having a trusted advisor," and 43.4% "loneliness," as concerns in their post-release lifestyle. Those who will live alone after release from prison are more concerned about living expenses and health than about being lonely.

7.3.2.6 Self-efficacy

Let us examine the measurement results of self-efficacy from the standpoint of preventing recidivism. Self-efficacy consists of experiences of past successes and failures. It is said to affect expectations that one can adaptively deal with a new situation that has not been previously experienced. In other words, it is a measure of the extent to which one perceives being capable of adapting to life after prison.

The measurement results of overall self-efficacy among female inmates[5] are explained here. In comparing these results with values obtained after surveying members of the general public, we see that there is no significant difference in terms of average values. The distribution of values is also more or less the same between these two groups. There are not, in fact, many people who feel pessimistic about life after prison. Many believe that they are capable of adapting successfully to life after prison. Thus, there is no difference between the results obtained through a survey administered to these inmates and the results obtained through a survey administered to members of the general public.[6] In addition, no significant difference can be seen in average values corresponding to female inmates between the elderly group and the non-elderly group. While one might typically believe that becoming imprisoned causes self-efficacy to decline and inmates to feel pessimistic about their ability to cope with situations, the results of a survey administered to female inmates suggest that levels of self-efficacy do not differ between inmates and members of the general public and that inmates who are optimistic about their coping ability are as common as members of the general public who feel likewise.

This survey (614 respondents): average 69.00, standard deviation 12.80, minimum value 31, maximum value 111, skewness -.001, kurtosis .388
Women (861 respondents): average 75.31, standard deviation 13.42, minimum value 27, maximum value 113, skewness .093, kurtosis .361

7.3.3 Conclusion of this section

Points clarified through the results of the 2017 survey are outlined below.

i As also clarified in the 2016 survey, inmate groups tied to theft and illicit drugs in a way that goes beyond age groups differ from one another. In particular, respondents tied to illicit drugs indicated, to a significant extent, high values in most items regarding psychological symptoms and behavior that they may have experienced in the past. The illicit drugs group indicated that they had experienced various psychological symptoms, had experiences as victims, as well as experiences of problematic behaviors when growing up, exhibiting their evident problems. However, these experiences can be perceived more as underlying factors behind convictions for illicit drugs than as consequences of illicit drug use.

ii Regarding concerns and anxieties relating to post-release life harbored by inmates, differences can be seen between the non-elderly (female inmates aged between 40 and 64 years) and the elderly groups (female inmates aged 65 years and above). While "own health" was indicated to a significant extent by respondents in both groups, many in the non-elderly group indicated concerns regarding living costs, work, and their relationship with their children and others in their lives, whereas few of those in the elderly group indicated such responses. It can be surmised that ties to others grow fewer with age. Thus, there remains uncertainty in terms of adequate accommodation of supports for the prevention of recidivism and the assistance for independent living in situations requiring connection with others.

iii Concerning self-efficacy, no differences between the results obtained in this survey and those obtained in a survey administered to members of the general public could be discerned. Thus, it is not the case that imprisonment causes a majority of inmates to engage in self-denial or lose self-confidence. It is, therefore, possible to believe that individuals are capable of living effectively after they are released from prison. There is, however, the possibility to make inmates to face past failures in a negative light in such a way that they would have difficulties in motivating themselves to improve. For example, let us look at the example of illicit drug use.

The inmates tied to illicit drugs need to understand the problems associated with how they lived to date and ascertain specific ways to abstain from illicit drug use. However, since such inmates will typically be confident that they can manage to live with no real difficulties after being released from prison, they might not have a sufficient level of determination to change themselves.

7.4 Summary of the "Survey of elderly inmates"

The Study Group has conducted a series of questionnaire surveys on elderly inmates over several years since 2012 to understand their conditions. The primary surveys can be classified by year of implementation: the 2012 survey, the 2016 survey, and the 2017 survey.

The 2012 survey was administered to elderly inmates (male and female) aged 65 years and above in 56 penal institutions nationwide and received 635 valid responses. In this survey, a comparison was made between men and women, and the results showed that women showed a stronger sense of penitence about life after release than men, such as "not to re-offend" and "not to cause trouble to others," and that they expressed their hopes for their lives, such as "to live with my family" and "to live a joyful life." The results showed that the female penitents' desire to live with their family and to live a joyful life were stronger.

The 2016 survey was conducted among female inmates aged 40 and above in eight penal institutions housing female criminals nationwide and received 438 valid responses. In this survey, the results were compared between the elderly group (aged 65 or older) and the non-elderly group (aged 40–64). It was found that the non-elderly group was more likely to be "unemployed" and "receiving welfare benefits," while the elderly group was less anxious after release from prison than the non-elderly group because they receive a certain amount of "pension" money. In addition, a comparison of "hopes for life after release" with male prisoners in the 2012 survey showed that while men "want to live a life centered on work," more women "want to live with their families."

Based on the previous survey results, the 2017 survey was conducted at two women's correctional institutes using a questionnaire with more free-answer questions, and 377 valid responses were received from female inmates aged 40 and above. In this survey, questions were asked about inmates' self-efficacy from the perspective of recidivism prevention. In general, it is believed that prisoners' sense of self-efficacy declines, and they tend to view their ability to cope with things negatively. However, the results of this survey showed no difference in self-efficacy from that of the general population, and those who viewed their ability to cope with things positively did not differ significantly from the general population.

Through the above multiple surveys, we clarified the actual conditions and attitudes of the female inmates, especially concerning their lives before and after their release from prison, through comparisons between male and female inmates and between elderly and non-elderly groups. The survey results indicate that female inmates have a strong sense of looking back on what they have done and taking a positive view toward the future, as well as a strong sense of seeking connections with others. For such awareness to continue after their release from prison, the understanding and support of the people around them are vital. In this sense, providing public and non-public assistance targeting people around these inmates should be vital to help them support these inmates to rehabilitate.

Notes

1 Acknowledgments: We would like to thank the Department of Corrections of the Ministry of Justice for their generous cooperation in this survey.
2 The eight institutions targeted for this survey consisted of the following: Sapporo Prison – Sapporo Prison Branch, Fukushima Prison – Fukushima Prison Branch, Kasamatsu Prison, Wakayama Prison, Kakogawa Prison, Iwakuni Prison, Matsuyama Prison – Saijo Prison Branch, and Fumoto Prison Branch.
3 total of "not at all" and "not very much"
4 total of "somewhat so" and "very much so"
5 This question was common to the 2016 and 2017 surveys; responses were aggregated and non-responses were excluded, such that results for 614 respondents were used.
6 An Investigation to Measure Characteristic Self-Efficacy (Kenichi Narita, Yoshiko Shimonaka, and Katsuji Nakazato; Research on Pedagogical Psychology 43(3)) is based on results obtained for 1,524 respondents between the ages of 13 and 92 years residing in the Tokyo Metropolitan area.

Reference

Ministry of Justice. (2013). 2013 White Paper on Crime, p. 180.

8 Typology of Elderly Male & Female Prisoners on Their Awareness

From Results of 2012 Survey and Free-Answer Survey

Yoko Hosoi

Toyo University, Japan

This chapter summarizes the results of two surveys conducted in 2012. The overview and results of each survey are described in the relevant sections: 1) the four types of elderly convicts – "the 2012 survey," and 2) the previous term of elderly convicts (over 40 years old).

8.1 Four types of elderly convicts – "the 2012 survey"

8.1.1 General characteristics of the survey results

Overall, the following nine characteristics were identified. (1) Aside from health issues, "daily living expenses" was the most common concern for the male convicts, and "family relations" was the most common concern for the female ones. (2) Regarding living expenses after release from prison, "public assistance" was the most common concern for the males, while "pension" was the most common one for the females. (3) Aside from health issues, the most essential object after release from prison was "family" for the females, and "job" and "ability to make a living" for the males. (4) Regarding prison, both men and women wanted to be "released from prison as soon as possible." (5) And for the reason as to why, both the male and female convicts answered that they "detach from prison," while the female followed with "I have a family waiting for me." (6) The most common answer for females is "children" as a guarantor, followed by "none" for male and "offenders rehabilitation organization." (7) "Theft" was the crime for which the majority of both male and female convicts were sentenced to prison. Two out of three of the female respondents were convicted of "theft." (8) Regarding the cause of the crime, the male answered that they "wanted money," while females answered that they "wanted items," (9) Regarding past crimes, the female convicts overwhelmingly reported "theft," while the males reported "theft" followed by "fraud," "injury," and "drugs."

DOI: 10.432/9781032669519-11

8.1.2 Categorization of elderly convicts

In order to understand the characteristics of elderly inmates, this chapter categorized the male and female inmates according to their responses to the "Self-perception" item in the 2012 survey. The survey covered 635 men and women over 65 years of age.

The categorization procedure was as follows.

1 Principal component analysis was conducted using the subject's individual "self-perception" (23 items that they think apply to them) responses as variables, and the scores of the top two principal component axis variables with the strongest explanatory power for individual similarity were organized to obtain their trends.
2 The scores of the principal component loadings, which indicate the distance relationship between individuals on the first and second axes calculated by principal component analysis, were used as variables, and a cluster analysis was conducted to create four typologies for each subject.
3 The created typologies of individuals were incorporated and cross-tabulated with other survey items, and based on the results, the characteristics of each typology were analyzed and given a typology name (typology names are based on the analysis of crosstabulation results with other survey items by cluster typology).

Based on the results of the survey, Japanese elderly convicts were classified into four types: "stable," "self-reliant," "dependent on others," and "insecure." Multiple statistical methods were performed on the data obtained from the convicts (635 respondents), focusing on the results of Question 19 on "Self-perception"; two axes were extracted - the strength of "Relationships" and "trust in people and society." The results of the cluster analysis showed four groups: Group 1 ("Stable" 15%), Group 2 ("Independence-oriented" 30%), Group 3 ("Dependent on others" 21%), and Group 4 ("Unstable" 31%). Briefly describing the characteristics of each group, the first group is relatively stable in terms of spouse, family, work, economy, and housing and resembles the general elderly population. The second group is similar to the first group; however, their economic, familial, and housing conditions are not as good as those in the first group. The third group consists mainly of female convicts. Many of them lived with their families before they entered the prison and sought "dependence on others" even after their release. Compared to the other groups, the fourth group has the most unstable living conditions. They have been receiving social welfare assistance, such as public assistance, and will receive public support after release, including support centers for settlement in local communities (Table 8.1).

8.1.3 Four types (groups) and their sense of life

Convicts in the first group, i.e., "stable" type, answered with the option "having family support" when asked "what is important for me in the future"

Table 8.1 Four types of elderly convicts

	Total		*Group 1: Stable*			*Group 2: Self-reliant*			*Group 3: Dependent on others*			*Group 4: Unstable*		
	Actual number	*(%)*	*Actual number*	*(%)*	*χ2*	*Actual number*	*(%)*	*χ2*	*Actual number*	*(%)*	*χ2*	*Actual number*	*(%)*	*χ2*
Composition of categories	635	100.0	93	14.6		193	30.4		133	20.9		198	31.2	
Overall	635	100.0	93	100.0		193	100.0		133	100.0		198	100.0	
F1Gender														
Male	485	78.0	79	84.9		159	82.4		95	71.4	F	156	78.8	
Female	87	13.7	12	12.9		25	13.0		27	20.3	B	23	11.6	
Unknown	53	8.3	2	2.2	G	9	4.7	F	11	8.3		19	9.6	
Question 1: Employment status at the time of crime														
Employed	235	37.0	58	62.4	A	77	39.9		52	39.1		42	21.2	H
Unemployed	310	48.8	19	20.4	H	93	48.2		58	43.6		134	67.7	A
Question 1 SQ2 Reason for unemployment														
*All who answered "Unemployed"	310	100.0	19	100.0		93	100.0		58	100.0		134	100.0	
Unable to work due to illness	87	28.1	4	21.1		23	24.7		23	39.7	C	36	26.9	
Looked for a job but could not find one	138	44.5	6	31.3		52	55.9	B	14	24.1	H	64	47.8	
Didn't feel like working	38	12.3	1	5.3		8	8.6		5	8.6		22	16.4	
Not in need of money	42	13.5	7	36.8	B	9	9.7		13	22.4	B	12	9.0	
Unknown	18	5.8	1	5.3		6	6.5		4	6.9		7	5.2	

(*Continued*)

Table 8.1 (Continued)

		Total		Group 1: Stable			Group 2: Self-reliant			Group 3: Dependent on others			Group 4: Unstable		
		Actual number	(%)	Actual number	(%)	χ2	Actual number	(%)	χ2	Actual number	(%)	χ2	Actual number	(%)	χ2
Question 2: Type of residence at the time of crime															
	Owned home	162	25.5	52	55.9	A	33	17.1		33	24.8		39	19.7	F
	Owned condominium	19	3.0	2	2.2		4	2.1	H	6	4.5		7	3.5	
	Rented condominium	90	14.2	10	10.8		39	20.2		24	18.0		17	8.6	G
	Apartment	136	21.4	5	5.4	H	45	23.3	B	31	23.3		52	26.3	C
	Rented house	64	10.1	12	12.9		14	7.3		16	12.0		19	9.6	
	Friend's or acquaintance's house	34	5.4	2	2.3		16	8.3		7	5.3		7	3.5	
	Rehabilitation facility	12	1.9	1	1.1		3	1.6	C	4	3.0		4	2.0	
	Homeless	34	5.4	1	1.1	F	7	3.6		2	1.5	G	23	11.6	A
	Other	68	10.7	7	7.5		27	14.0		8	6.0	F	25	12.6	
	Unknown	16	2.5	1	1.1		5	2.6		2	1.5		5	2.5	
Question 3: Living, marital, income and healthy status															
Living status	Living alone	333	52.4	22	23.7	H	118	61.1		53	39.8	H	134	67.7	A
	Have a spouse	189	29.8	55	59.1	A	41	21.2		56	45.1	A	32	16.2	H
	Had income	416	65.5	84	90.3	A	13	67.9		96	72.2		98	49.5	H
	Healthy	220	34.6	48	51.6	A	65	34.2		51	38.3		50	25.3	H
Question 7: Did you have any financial difficulties before imprisonment?															
	Financial difficulties	92	14.5	36	38.7	A	15	7.8		23	17.3		16	8.1	G
	Not at all	133	20.9	30	32.3	A	44	22.8	H	29	21.8		27	13.6	G
	Not much	243	38.3	18	19.4	H	85	44.0		58	43.6		77	38.9	
	Sometimes	157	24.7	9	9.7	H	48	24.9	C	21	15.8	G	74	37.4	A
	Always	10	1.6	0	—		1	0.5		2	1.2		4	2.0	

(Continued)

Table 8.1 (Continued)

		Total		*Group 1: Stable*			*Group 2: Self-reliant*			*Group 3: Dependent on others*			*Group 4: Unstable*		
		Actual number	*(%)*	*Actual number*	*(%)*	*χ2*	*Actual number*	*(%)*	*χ2*	*Actual number*	*(%)*	*χ2*	*Actual number*	*(%)*	*χ2*
Question 9: How did you make a living before imprisonment?															
Living expenses	From work	233	36.7	65	69.9	A	74	38.3		50	37.6		41	20.7	H
	Pension	196	30.9	49	52.7	A	52	26.9		43	32.3		50	25.3	F
	Personal savings	51	8.0	10	10.8		16	8.3		15	11.3		9	4.5	F
	Personal property	16	2.5	6	6.5	B	3	1.6		3	2.3		3	1.5	
	Debt	27	4.3	1	1.1		13	6.7		2	1.5		11	5.6	
	Support from family and relatives	48	7.6	9	9.7		13	6.7	C	9	6.8		14	7.1	
	Received public assistance	160	25.2	4	4.3	H	49	25.4		36	27.1		67	33.8	A
	Other	68	10.7	3	3.2	G	28	14.5		14	10.5		21	10.6	
	Unknown	20	3.1	0	–		2	1.0	C	3	2.3		10	5.1	
Question 11: How would you like to live after release from prison?															
Desired life after release from prison.	I want to live a work-oriented life.	174	27.4	41	44.1	A	56	29.0		41	30.8		33	16.7	H
	I want to live without concern or stress.	198	31.2	41	44.1	A	65	33.7		36	27.1		53	26.8	
	I want to live a life that makes the most of my hobbies.	133	20.9	36	38.7	A	42	21.8		25	18.8		29	14.6	G
	I don't want to bother anyone anymore.	406	63.9	64	68.8		139	70.5		89	66.9		111	56.1	G
	I want to live with my family.	142	22.4	46	49.5	A	31	16.1	C	46	34.6		19	9.6	H

(*Continued*)

Table 8.1 (Continued)

	Total		*Group 1: Stable*			*Group 2: Self-reliant*			*Group 3: Dependent on others*			*Group 4: Unstable*		
	Actual number	*(%)*	*Actual number*	*(%)*	$\chi 2$	*Actual number*	*(%)*	$\chi 2$	*Actual number*	*(%)*	$\chi 2$	*Actual number*	*(%)*	$\chi 2$
I want to avoid committing crimes again.	424	66.8	63	67.7		141	73.1	G	80	60.2		130	65.7	
I want to live in a nursing home.	40	6.3	2	2.2	F	11	5.7	C	9	6.8		16	8.1	
I want to live a cheerful life.	264	41.6	56	60.2	A	88	15.6		59	44.4		55	27.8	H
I want to live without anyone to tell me what to do.	66	10.4	16	17.2	B	19	9.8		10	7.5		20	10.1	
I want to respect moral obligation and humane feelings.	86	13.5	26	28.0	A	26	13.5		17	12.8		15	7.6	G
Unknown	4	0.6	0	—		0	—		0	—		0	—	

$\chi 2$-test Plus A-1% B-5% C-10% D-20%
Minus H-1% G-5% F-10% E-21%

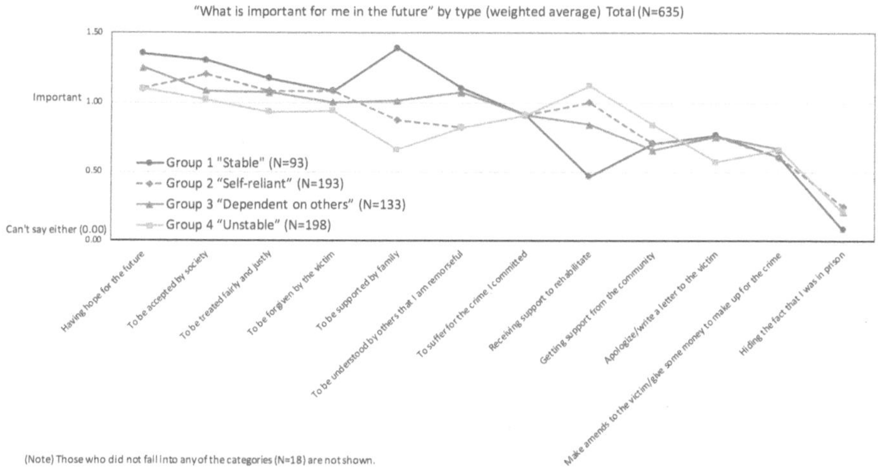

Figure 8.1 "Important objects in the future" (by type).

(Question 20), whereas those in the fourth group, i.e., "unstable" type, listed "receiving public assistance" as the priority (Figure 8.1).

8.1.4 Characteristics of female elderly convicts

Based on the survey results obtained from 87 female convicts, the following characteristics can be attributed to elderly female convicts: (1) 40% were high school graduates; (2) 40% were currently married; (3) over 80% were "healthy" or "not so healthy but not seriously ill"; (4) 35% were working (full- or part-time) before entering the prison; (5) 44% were not working before entering the prison, and the reasons were "could not find work" and "did not have money problems"; (6) 90% of the respondents have been married; (7) 52% of the respondents (comprising twice the male convicts) answered "pension" as the cost of living before entering prison; (8) "Relationship with family" was the most common problem before entering prison; (9) "I was the one who was depended on" and "the one who was trusted" before prison term; (10) more than half of the respondents answered "pensions" and "savings" as their life expense after release from prison; (11) "Not to re-offend," "Not to cause trouble for others," and "Want to live with family" were the most frequent responses for their life after release from prison; (12) the most critical concern after their release from prison was "family relations"; and (13) the most essential factor they would pay attention to after their release from prison is "health," followed by "family."

The results show that the elderly female convicts prioritized "family" and cannot be considered without "family (Figure 8.2)." Therefore, how they can organize and repair their relationships with their families seems to be the most crucial factor.

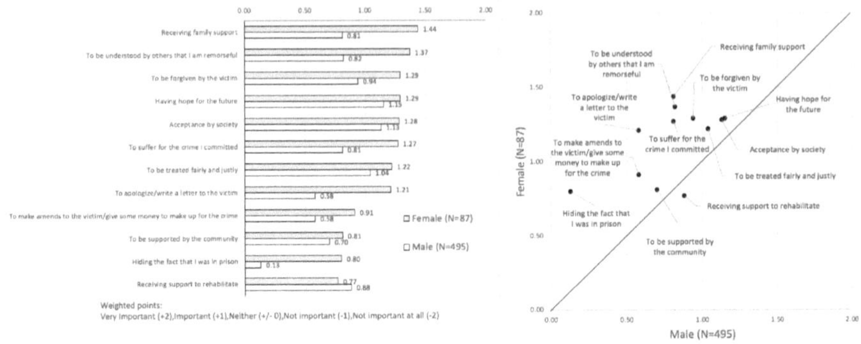

Figure 8.2 "Important objects in the future" (Question 20) by gender.

Finally, a comparison of "what is important to me in the future" (Question 20) between males and females revealed the following points. While males placed more importance on "work" and "life skills," females selected "family" and "socializing," indicating that, in general, they consider human relationships to be important.

8.2 Through a "free-answer survey" of previous term's elderly convicts (40 years and older)

8.2.1 Characteristics of the subjects' persons and the survey method

1 105 male convicts (over 40 years old) were asked to speak freely in response to a questionnaire to look at the life history of elderly convicts from a different angle. The form was enclosed in a letter through a specific not-for-profit organization (NPO) and returned to us.
2 The survey items were their experiences of crime and delinquency (from their teenage years to the present) and their family relationships during that time. Attention was paid to the objective circumstances, perceptions, and evaluations. We took them chronologically, followed their life histories, and patterned them (Figure 8.3). We ascertained "crime-promoting factors" from them while looking at "crime-deterrent factors" (things that keep them away from committing crimes).
3 For the 105 male convicts, we constructed several patterns of their life histories, looking at the factors that promote and discourage crime: 64 (61.0%) were in their 40s, 26 (24.8%) in their 50s, 12 (11.4%) in their 60s, and 3 (2.9%) in their 70s or older.
4 Life history of convicts in the previous term and four patterns (precipitating and preventing events) (Figure 8.5)

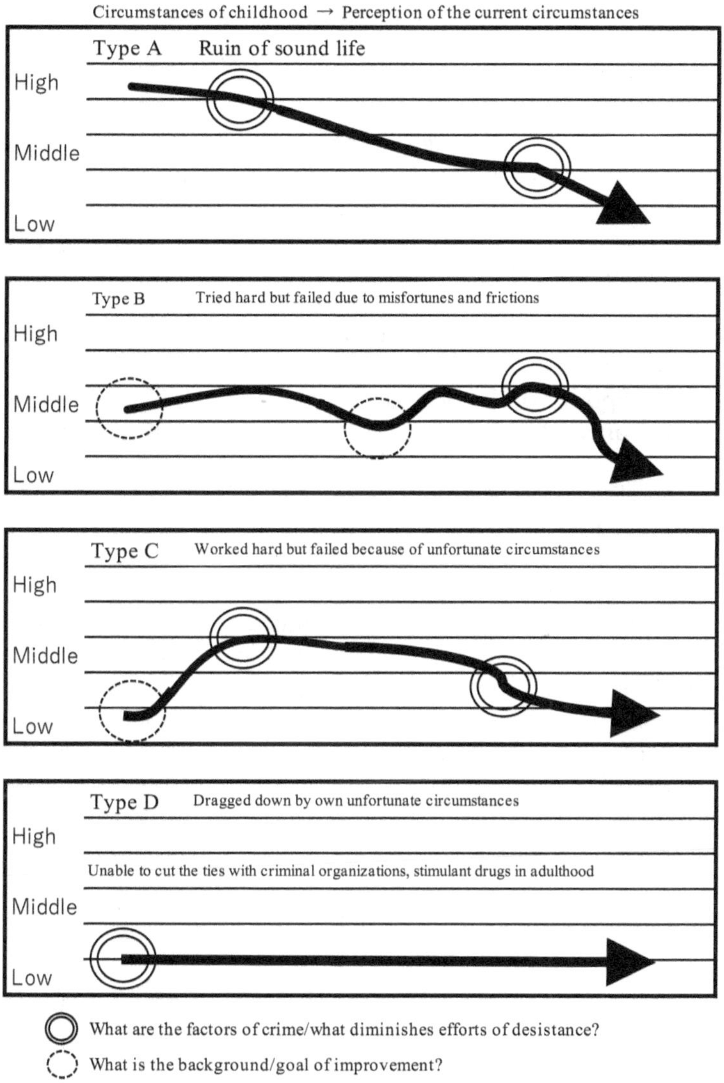

Figure 8.3 Life history and four patterns of the early-stage elderly.

8.3 Discussion

1 In this section, based on the results of the "Questionnaire Survey," a principal component analysis and a cluster analysis of the elderly inmates were conducted. As a result, two axes were found and four groups were extracted: "stable type," "independent type." "dependent type," and "unstable type" groups.

Comparing the "what is important" to the "stable" and "unstable" types, the "stable" type emphasizes "family support," while the "unstable" type emphasizes "receiving assistance for self-support," indicating that the "unstable" type expects public assistance. The "unstable" type received public assistance before serving their prison sentences, and they consider it important to receive assistance from society after their release from prison.

2 This study focused on "Questionnaire Survey" and "Interview Survey" for understanding elderly prisoners, and the "Open-ended Questionnaire Survey" was conducted with prisoners between 40 and 65 years old. In this survey, we asked them to reflect on their life in prison. Then, by arranging the crimes and delinquencies in chronological order and finding routes close to and relatively far from crime and delinquency, we read what was in the free descriptions of the prisoners and established "life history types" of Japanese prisoners (Figure 8.4). Then, while setting up each type, we identified the factors (social, economic, and psychological) that led them to crime and delinquency and the factors (social, economic, and psychological) that prevented them from committing crimes or acts of delinquency, even temporarily.

The results showed that one in five prisoners in their 60s had relatively affluent childhoods with no major problems with parents, siblings, or relatives, but did not have much mental satisfaction. In their 30s and 40s, while living in poor conditions, "the void in their hearts widened." Then, the group became decreasingly energetic, took the first step toward becoming criminals, and finally became prisoners. However, prisoners of another group who had been in low-income family environments during childhood and felt alienated from their parents did not receive their love until their 20s. As a result, many of them became yakuza. These groups "in between" have had a different start in life, experiencing its ups and downs but gradually becoming frustrated and imprisoned.

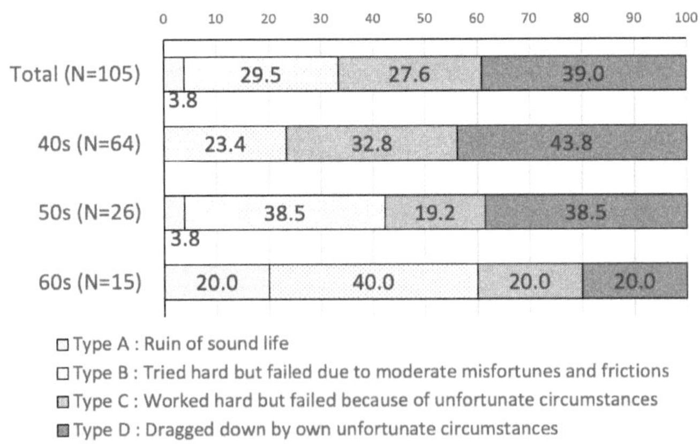

Figure 8.4 Changes in their life history by pattern.

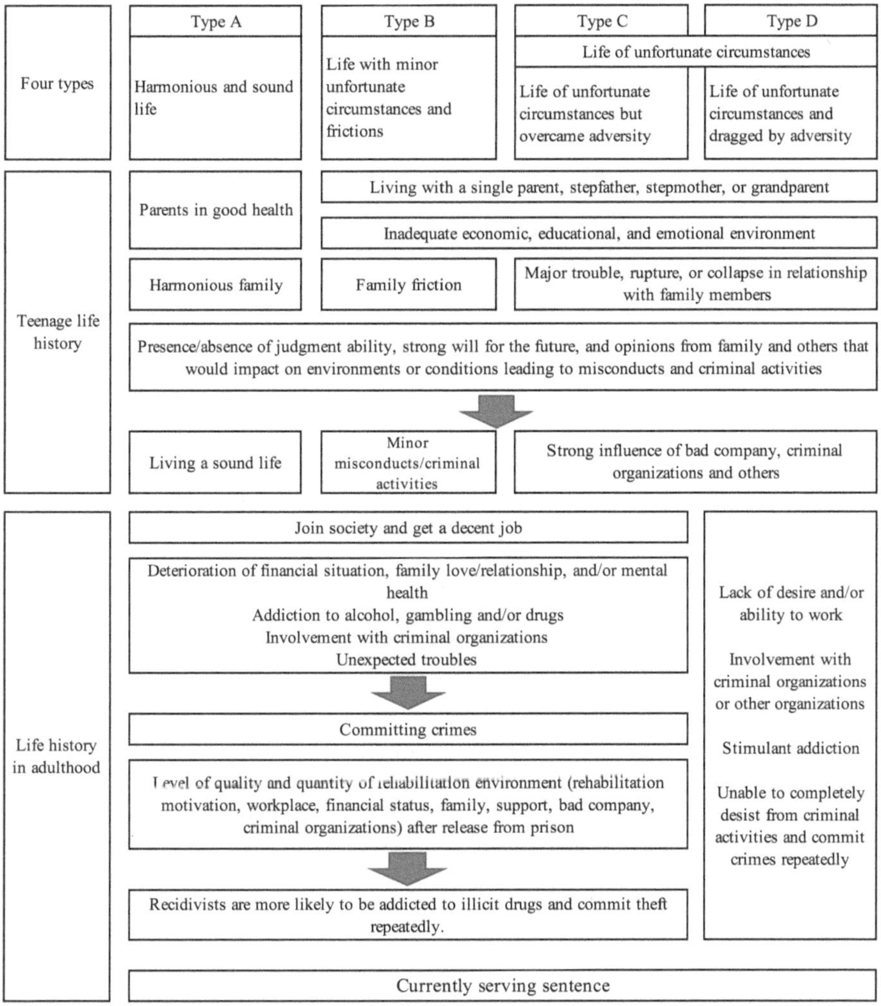

Figure 8.5 Relationship between crime promotion and prevention in the life history by typology.

The factors that lead to crime and delinquency in each type and the factors that impede the flow toward crime are intricately intertwined and often unrefusable or unacceptable despite the prisoners' efforts. However, by observing their life histories chronologically, we will examine whether some "event" or "encounter with others" did not impede the flow to crime, and what were the circumstances and conflicts that kept those who were able to encounter such events and opportunities yet keep away from crime. The idea was reinforced that those who were compelled to continue to commit crimes at an older age should stop as soon as possible.

3 Elderly female convicts in Japan, compared to their male counterparts, answered most of the items in the "Important Objects in the Future" question as important, including "suffering for the crimes I committed." This indicates that women are willing to face up to the crimes they have committed. Among the items, "receiving family support," "To be understood by others that I am remorseful," and "To be forgiven by the victim" are also considered to be important.

However, a recent trend has been noted of an increase in recidivism among elderly female offenders. The survey shows that elderly female offenders are willing to confront their crimes, but if it does not contribute to preventing recidivism, further investigation should be necessary to clarify what is behind this trend of increase in recidivism.

4 These are the realities (life careers and attitudes toward life) of elderly prisoners in Japan as revealed by the two surveys. Finally, as indicated at the beginning of this section, we will mention what has slightly reduced the number of criminal cases and the arrest rate over the past few years.

The first factor is the notice issued by the Ministry of Health, Labor and Welfare in 2011. Prisoners are now able to apply for public assistance in their place of residence and are guaranteed a livelihood immediately after release from prison.

The second is the existence of regional community support centers[1], which were institutionalized in 2009 and finally established nationwide in 2011.

The third is the enhancement of facilities for housing inmates after their release from prison. In addition to conventional rehabilitation facilities, there are also independence preparation homes[2]. Private facilities include "NPO Motherhouse," a self-help organization, and "Maaru" (formerly NPO Kubari no Kai), an entity and support group that cooperated with this study. It remains to be seen how useful these facilities will be in preventing recidivism among elderly prisoners.

Notes

1 Information about support centers for settlement in local communities is as follows: On April 01, 2011, the Ministry of Health, Labour and Welfare revised the notification (Public Notice No.246 of the head of the Social Bureau of the Ministry of Health and Welfare as of April 01, 1963), which determined local governments providing public assistance for those released from prison as "location of prison," for the first time in 50 years and switched to a policy of placing responsibility on local governments to which those released from prison apply for public assistance, which helped provide seamless welfare services for those released from prison with difficulty in independence because they are handicapped or elderly.

2 Self-reliance assistance homes have made use of open beds at facilities managed by NPO or other organizations for urgently securing accommodations and supporting independence since 2011. Self-reliance assistance homes are registered in a probation office, which entrusts employers with accommodations, provision of meals, everyday lifestyle guidance, and other services as needed. The number of registered employers as of March 31, 2014, was 289 (increased by 53 (22.5%) over last year), and the actual number of persons entrusted in 2013 was 1,278 (2014 White Paper on Crime).

9 The Needs of Restorative Justice for Senior Criminal Women in Japan

Kaoru Umezaki

Saitama Prefectural University, Japan

In Japan, the number of criminals aged 65 years and above has steadily increased. This chapter discusses the status of senior criminal women in Japan in relation to the need for restorative justice practices. To this end, a series of surveys was conducted on elderly criminal women in 2016 and 2017, and the data were analyzed accordingly. As shown in Table 9.1, those who had been convicted for the first time at the age of 65 years and above were extracted from the analysis data, total number for which was 53. According to the analysis results, shoplifting was the dominant crime among them, which indicated that all those aged 75 and above were shoplifting offenders. Their academic backgrounds ranged widely, some of whom had even finished four years of university education. Nearly half a century ago, most Japanese women had to quit their education much earlier than what is expected of them today. This is because, if they wanted to get married, higher education could interfere with their engagement. Thus, their academic backgrounds in the analysis results do not represent their age.

Regarding their financial situation, the mode of total and discretionary income was 100,000 JPY and 20,000 JPY, respectively, and food costs could probably be included in the latter. Therefore, it is estimated that women aged 75 years and above cannot afford to buy anything much more than the bare minimum of groceries, such as snacks and beverages. In fact, many of the items most shoplifted by elderly criminal women were rice crackers, candy, cosmetics, and other petty commodities, indicating that their main reason for stealing was to save money; however, their true motivations seemed be poverty, combined with complex reasons, such as isolation and cognitive impairment.

If these women have cognitive impairments, they need appropriate medical care, not imprisonment; they should be transferred from the penal institution to a nursing home or comprehensive support center. If they are in financial distress, they need financial support, which would require them to apply for assistance from public institutions, where they could receive various types of social support.

Regardless of their age at the time of first incarceration, the following were the most common responses, in order of most frequent, regarding what these women thought was most important about the future after release from penal institutions: "support from family," "having hope for the future," "writing a

DOI: 10.4324/9781032669519-12

Table 9.1 Crime, education history, and financial situation of participants

Crimes	Shoplifting, theft	Fraud	Burglary	Murder (DV)	Assisted suicide	Other	Unknown	Total (%)
	41 (77.4)	1 (1.9)	1 (1.9)	3 (5.7)	1 (1.9)	2 (3.8)	4 (7.5)	53 (100.0)
Education history	Compulsory education	Dropout from high school	High school graduate	Junior college, professional dropout	Junior college graduates	University graduates	Unknown	Total (%)
	23 (43.4)	4 (7.5)	16 (30.2)	2 (3.8)	7 (13.2)	1 (1.9)	0 (0.0)	53 (100.0)
Financial situation	Income (average)	Income (median)	Income (mode)	Income over 75years (mode)	Discretionary income (average)	Discretionary income (median)	Discretionary income (mode)	Discretionary income over 75years (mode)
	¥211,064	¥120,000	¥100,000	¥30,000	¥127,514	¥30,000	¥20,000	¥20,000
Reasons for unemployed	Illness	Housework	Not hired	No intention	Welfare recipients	Other	Unknown	Total (%)
	4 (7.5)	3 (5.7)	4 (7.5)	5 (9.4)	9 (17.0)	13 (24.5)	20 (37.7)	53 (100.0)

letter to apologize to the victim," "having people around you who understand your remorse," "changing yourself," "rehabilitation assistance," "suffering yourself," "hiding the fact that you were sentenced," and "acquire regular jobs to live independently." Therefore, we found that many of these women sought support from their families rather than living independently with social support.

9.1 Severe punishment, medicalization, or restorative justice?

Restorative justice, also known as victim-offender mediation, is an excellent way to protect and restore the victim's rights. However, for elderly women criminals in Japan, it requires complex and sensitive considerations in its application.

In the European Union, the Victims of Crime Directive (Directive 2012/29/EU), establishing minimum standards on the rights, support, and protection of victims of crime was adopted on October 25, 2012 (Suemichi, 2014). This directive established minimum standards on the rights, support, and protection of victims' rights, especially those of children and older adults. It also encouraged cooperation between Members States.

Japan's elderly female criminals are perpetrators. However, they are also victims of Japanese society in the sense that they have been forced into such a situation.

Looking at the social problem of elder abuse in Japan, perpetrators are overwhelmingly the sons of their victims. This social problem is symbolized by the so-called "8050 problem," in which the son of HIKIKOMORI, in his 50s, withdraws into his home for a long time, supported by his parents who are in their 80s. It has been a while since the necessity of early detection and intervention in domestic elder abuse was voiced among relevant public service organizations. However, most interventions have been practiced in the form of continuous watchful waiting until the elderly person's life is in danger, resulting in separation and protection. Even in the early detection cases, few of them are confirmed as abuse incidents, and most are judged as watch-over cases or subjected to the adult guardianship system. Parents, in the absence of public financial support available for their children, sometimes prefer to offer their pension to the child to protect them. The victims of abuse are overwhelmingly mothers.

It is important to examine how the poverty of today's elderly women, who once lived during Japan's period of rapid economic growth, has arisen. In Japan, many women are granted property in their husbands' names, even though these are jointly owned. Property built with the husband during the period of high economic growth, even property in his name, can be used by the wife without major problems when he is alive.

However, the property in the husband's name belongs to him. Though it might seem that the property is jointly held by both the husband and wife, the property is his. The wife has no right to decide how much she can inherit after his death. Moreover, pension is a system of payments to individuals, so the husband's portion is withheld after his death; however, basic living expenses, such as housing, utilities, communication, water, and sewer bills, which were shared when the husband was alive, will not be cut in half upon his death. It is easy to understand that this portion will weigh heavily on the wife's living expenses after his death. Nevertheless, who could anticipate today's Japanese society? The benefit amount of the Old-Age Basic Pension under the Japanese National Pension System is below the minimum standard under the Public Assistance Law "to maintain the minimum standards of wholesome and cultured living" guaranteed in the Constitution of Japan.

The imprisonment of elderly Japanese women is a social problem, and we should reconsider appropriate measures to help them recover from their repeated offenses in which they can be both perpetrators and victims. Prison sentences harm the elderly women's relationship with their families and isolate them socially. If their repeated shoplifting can be diagnosed as kleptomania, then prison sentences that isolate them from society would serve nothing but worsen the addiction; it would never suppress their urge of stealing (Matsumoto, 2018). Should we continue with the severe punishment of imprisonment? If their repeated offenses are due to their cognitive decline, isn't it possible that what we should provide them with is appropriate medical care, not the punishment? Restorative justice, not the harsh punishment by imprisonment, should be the answer in such cases of elderly women's repeated shoplifting that has historically complexed backgrounds, in which the difference between perpetrators and victims is somewhat vague (Umezaki, 2019). If we can introduce restorative justice, we can consider suitable social treatment for the elderly in our society. Punishment alone cannot create a safe and happy future.

Concerning shoplifting, which is a prevalent offense among elderly female prisoners, could restorative justice be introduced as social treatment in the early stages before they are sentenced? The approach should heal the victimized and the wounded exhausted by life's hardships and provide them with necessary welfare support measures. Thereafter, they could face themselves as perpetrators and work with the community to find ways to redeem themselves. At this point, it should be distinguished from medicalization by focusing on kleptomania's symptoms.

Restorative justice in the community, as is being attempted in Finland and other countries, will restore relationships with the family and community and create a place in the community. Japanese women need to be independent; the treatment provided through restorative justice may serve elderly women in becoming self-reliant and not relying on families alone.

References

Matsumoto, T. (2018) *Yakubutsu Izonshou* [*Drug Addiction*], Chikumashobo Ltd.

Suemichi, Y. (2014) 'Victimology in the World (20)Protection of the Rights of Victims of Crime in EU: Summary of the Directive 2012/29/EU of European Parliament and of the Council Establishing Minimum Standards on the Rights, Support and Protection of Victims of Crime', *Japanese Journal of Victimology*, 24, pp. 45–60.

Umezaki, K., (2019), *Shufukuteki Taiwa Talikng Circle Practice Manual* [*Restorative Dialogue Taking Circles Practice Guide Japanese version*], Harushobo Co., Ltd.

10 Social Position and "Self Perception" of Elder Female Inmates

Yoko Hosoi

Toyo University, Japan

Bunri Tatsuno

Kokushikan University, Japan

10.1 Awareness of the problem

Who are the women who are repeat offenders? This chapter uses the findings of sociological stratification studies to understand elderly female offenders who repeatedly commit crimes. In analyzing the Sui class structure of today's Japanese society, Hashimoto focused on the fifth class, the "underclass," in addition to the previous four classes.

The term "underclass," according to Hashimoto, has been used in class and poverty studies for quite some time, especially in the United States, to refer to the poor who make up the lowest strata of urban society. However, its usage has differed from period to period and from theorist to theorist, and its common denominator is that of people who are placed in a state of persistent and inescapable poverty. In particular, Dahrendorf, R. referred to the "underclass" as those who are deprived or restricted in their citizenship rights due to the decline of the welfare state (Hashimoto, 2018a: Chapter 2). Therefore, using this concept of "underclass," we will attempt to infer the relationship with the main topic of this chapter, "middle-aged and elderly female offenders," based on data on the attributes, attitudes, life experiences, and self-perceptions of "underclass" women in Japan.

As a second step, we will clarify the characteristics of female criminals through a comparison with "general women" over 40 years old, from results of a survey conducted by online questionnaire in 2009. We will examine what differences exist between offenders and non-criminals, or whether there are not so significant differences.

10.2 Women of the "underclass," a new class in Japanese society, as seen in the SSM survey of sociology

According to Hashimoto, Japanese society today, especially in the past 30 years, has seen the disparity (between the poor and rich, between winners and losers, etc.) widen year by year, and the structure of the society has

DOI: 10.4324/9781032669519-13

undergone changes. In particular, a large disparity has been formed among the "employed," who make up the majority of society's members. The structure of Japanese society has a high-currency elite at the top who work for large corporations, but at the bottom are many low-wage, unstable "non-regular workers," and their numbers continue to increase, which has become a major source of social unrest (Hashimoto, 2018b).

Hashimoto called the rest of these non-regular workers—excluding part-time housewives who work as household helpers, part-time executives and managers, and qualified and skilled professionals— the "underclass" to describe the class structure in Japan today, and focused on a new class (the "underclass" follows the existing "capitalist class," "new middle class," "formal working class," and "old middle class").

Those belonging to the "underclass" account for about 15% of the working population, both male and female, and are expanding rapidly. The poverty rate, especially among women, has reached almost 50%. The majority of jobs are manual, sales, and service occupations. Among women, about a quarter are clerical, sales, service, and manual workers. Family formation is difficult, with 66.4% of men never married and a majority of women never married, but an additional 43.9% have experienced separation and bereavement. This contributes to poverty. Only 18.6% of the whole population are satisfied with their lives.

10.3 Female prisoners and the underclass

In order to consider the relationship between underclass women and female prisoners in Japan, we tentatively defined the underclass as "those who have no husband or partner and who work as fixed-term contract workers, dispatched workers, or part-time workers." The following is a list of those prisoners who were selected.

The following information on the 34 prisoners was examined: type of crime, previous experiences, financial situation, financial resources for living expenses, psychological concerns and worries, educational background, and self-perception.

The age structure of the underclass was dominated by those in their 50s (32%), followed by those in their 40s (26%), accounting for approximately 60% of the total. The non-underclass, conversely, has the largest percentage of those in their 40s at 36%, followed by those in their 50s at 22%. The underclass is more likely than the non-underclass to be single, at 29.4%.

In terms of the composition of cohabitants, the underclass has no "husband/partner," but 85% of the cohabitants have children, which is a significant factor. Depending on the age of their children, they are likely to face many challenges such as educational expenses, pocket money, and family relationships during difficult times.

In terms of type of job experienced so far, the underclass is less likely to have long-term employment, such as in the service industry, and a greater variety of occupations. This also creates a cycle of inability to acquire specialized knowledge and skills, making it difficult for them to become professionally independent.

In terms of the crime, the underclass is characterized by the fact that "theft" accounts for half of the total (50%), 90% of which is "shoplifting," followed by "drugs" at 29%. Other, violent crimes are less common. The non-underclass has a smaller percentage of "theft" (30%) and "drugs" (25%), with fraud and violent crimes being relatively more common. It should be noted that "shoplifting" is a major issue in today's society and one that is related to the issues of the underclass.

Regarding the question "Was it difficult to make payments for electricity, gas, water, etc.?", relatively few (29%) respondents in the underclass thought so, suggesting that they may have been suffering financially.

Regarding mental anxiety and worries, many inmates generally felt anxious and worried. Almost 97% of the underclass felt anxiety or distress in almost all shells, and 77% of the underclass "felt very much," much higher than the 61% of the non-underclass.

Regarding financial resources for living expenses, the underclass seems to consider "income from work" as the primary source of financial resources for living expenses (71%), both at the time of admission and after release from prison. This is followed by "savings (27%)," "family support (21%)," and requests for "public assistance (24%)."

With regard to self-perception (the way of living and thinking that they believe applies to them), the underclass is characterized by a much higher number of respondents who were "willing to work" than the non-underclass.

When education is examined in terms of cumulative composition (%) from higher education, the underclass has only 3% of those with a college degree or higher, but about half of those who dropped out or graduated from junior college or vocational school (47%), about twice as many as the non-underclass (25%).

This is the most difficult condition in an educated society, and one that makes it difficult to attain a senior position in a large company. On the other hand, it shows the reality that these women are valued by society as important workers with a certain level of education as non-regular workers.

10.4 "Female prisoners" and "general female workers"

10.4.1 Sample composition

Next, in order to examine the characteristics of female prisoners, we will compare female prisoners and women in general. The participants were 737 female inmates, 568 of whom were "40-65 years old" and 169 of whom were "65 years old and above;" and 389 females from the web survey, 202 of whom were "40 years old and above" and 187 of whom were "65 years old and above."

10.4.2 Comparison of the two groups (in terms of employment, cohabitants, and education)

With regard to employment status, more than half of both female inmates and general females were "not working," including housewives. Many female inmates were working as "dispatched or part-time workers," while many general females were working as "fixed-term contract workers." Among general females aged 65 and over, "full-time housewife" accounted for 63%, a particularly high percentage.

The reasons for not working differ significantly between female inmates and general females. Female prisoners are more likely to rely on "social security" such as "welfare" and "pension" included in the "other" category. "Welfare" is the most common reason given by about half of female inmates under age 65, and 23% of those over age 65. Among females in general, "welfare" is rarely cited.

The percentage of female inmates who live with a roommate is more than 80% for general females, but about 10 percentage points less for female inmates. By age group, the proportion of female inmates under 65 years old is about 10% higher than that of those 65 years old or older, both for female inmates and general females. Almost all general females live with their husbands/partners, but the difference between the female inmates and the general females is large, at around 60% for both "under 65" and "65 or older.

The composition of educational background is the item with the largest difference between "female inmates" and "general females". However, general females are the subjects of the web-based survey, and their educational background tends to be slightly higher.

Among female inmates, "Junior high school graduation" is the most common. It is especially common among those aged 65 and over. Among general females, almost all shells are "high school graduates" or above.

Among female inmates "under 40-64 years old," "high school or dropout graduation" accounts for half of the total. Among those "65 years old or older," 40% each of "junior high school graduation or lower" and "high school dropout/graduation," together accounting for 80% of the total.

Among women in the "40 to 65" age group, approximately 40% of the general female population has graduated from college or university, and 30% have dropped out of or graduated from junior college or vocational school, bringing the total to 70% of the highly educated group. In the "65+" age group, 50% of the respondents are "high school dropouts/graduates" (Figure 10.1).

Finally, we compare female inmates and the general female population in terms of self-perception. For self-perception, female inmates were asked to select "what was true for me at the time of the offense" for the question choices, while the general female population was asked to select "what was true for me at the time of my survey responses" (MA).

1 Comparison between female inmates "over 40" and general females (Figure 10.1)

Compared to the general population, prisoners are more "trusting" but "less likely to rely on others." They are more active than the general

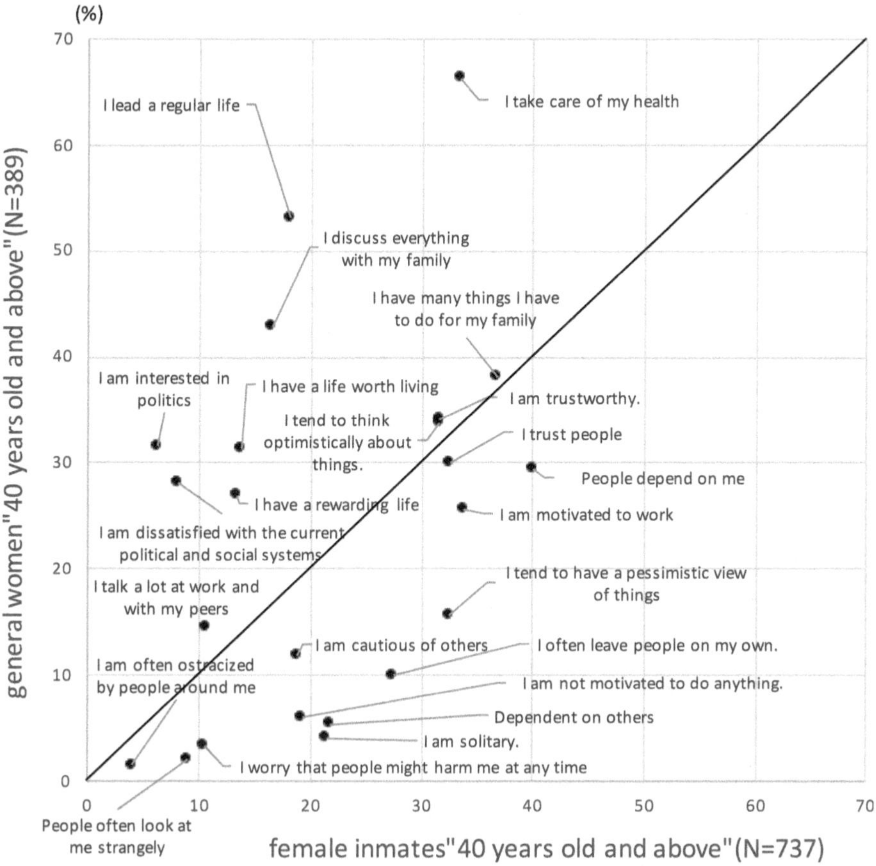

Figure 10.1 Comparison between female inmates "over 40" and general females.

population, with a strong "work ethic" and a "regular lifestyle," and it can be said that this gives rise to a variety of desires and ways of thinking. Both groups have a strong desire to live, but the general population has a stronger relationship with their families.

2 Comparison between female inmates aged between 40 and 65 and general females (Figure 10.2)

Female inmates listed many more items than the general female population. This may be due to the fact that they have more opportunities to think about themselves and have a higher level of interest.

Female inmates were more likely to say that people depend on them, that they often do things for their families, that they trust people, that they are motivated to work, and that they are optimistic, indicating that they are more confident about their relationships and work, etc. On the other hand, they were equally likely to say that they are pessimistic. These items are much higher than in the general female population.

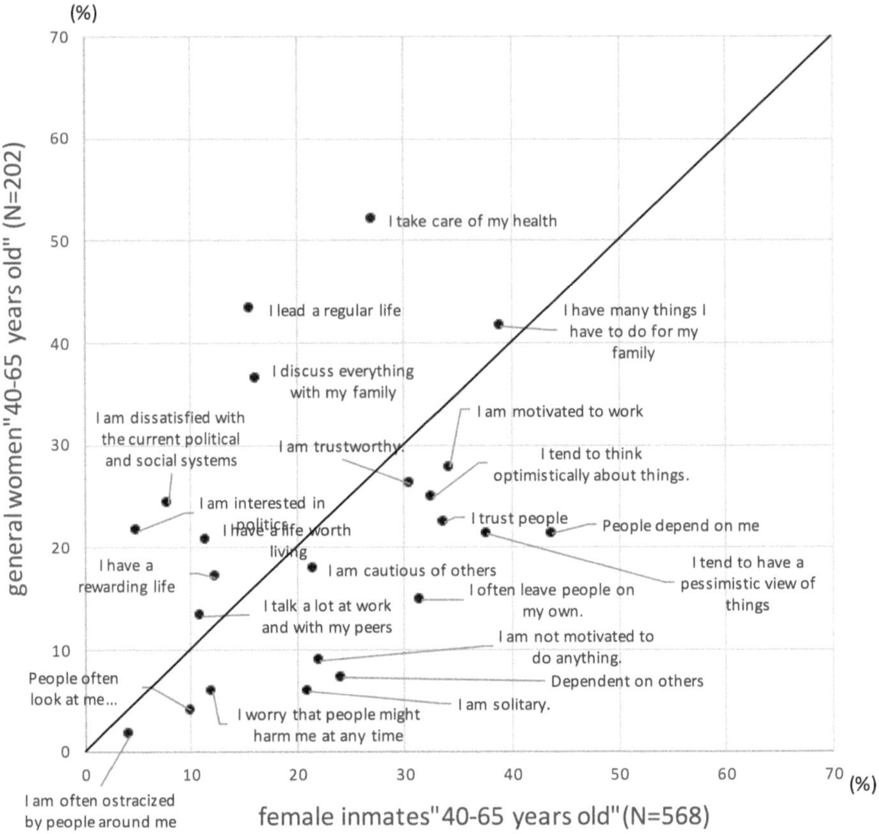

Figure 10.2 Comparison between female inmates aged between 40 and 65 and general females.

Among the general female population, "Pay attention to my health," "lead a regular life," "often do things for my family," and "discuss everything with my family" were frequently cited, far exceeding those of the inmates, suggesting that they have a strong relationship with their families. In addition, "dissatisfied with politics," "a purpose in life," "life with a sense of purpose," "interested in politics," and other positive aspects of life and awareness were also seen, although in smaller numbers.

3 Comparison between female inmates aged 65 and older and general females (Figure 10.3)

Contrary to the "40–65" age group, female inmates in the 65+ age group are below general females in all major categories. Female inmates are more likely to "pay attention to own health" (57%), followed by "motivated to work," "trustworthy," "dependable," "have a lot to do for my family," and "optimistic" in the following 40% range. Women in general are particularly interested in "taking care of my health" (81%) and "living a regular life" (64%).

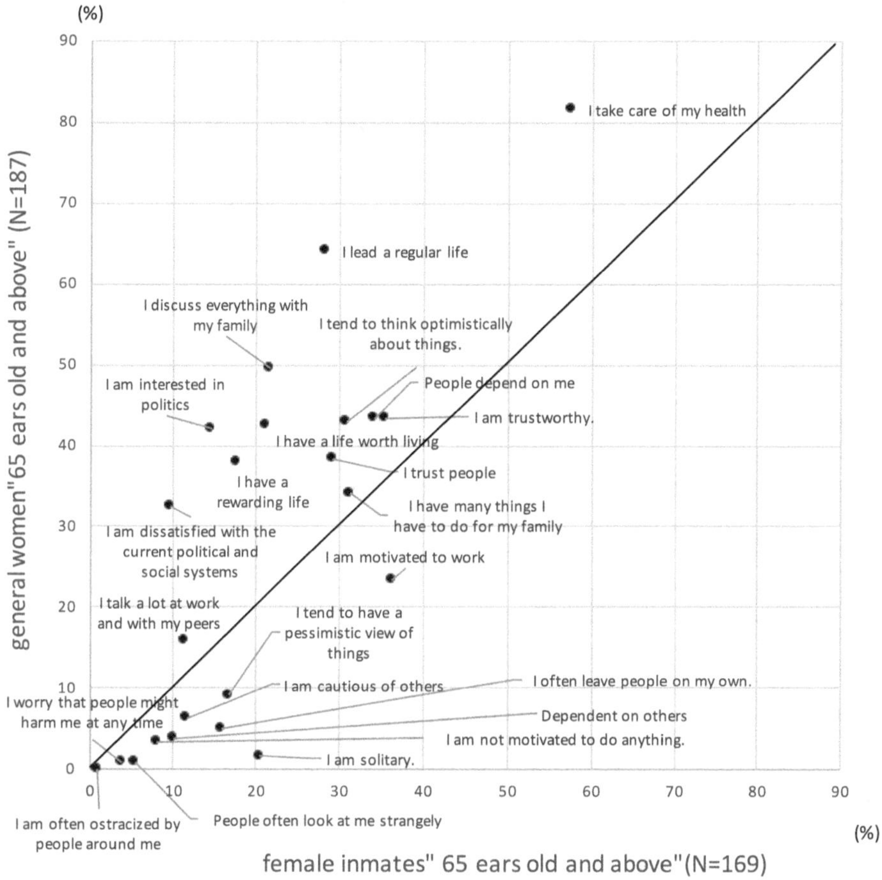

Figure 10.3 Comparison between female inmates aged 65 and older and general females.

This is followed by more positive life and awareness items such as "discuss everything with my family," "have a life worth living," and "am interested in politics."

10.4.3 Comparison between the two groups (problems and anxieties)

The female inmates' opinions were related to the time of the crime, while the general females' opinions were related to what was troubling or worrisome at the time of their responses. Note that the items asked in this question differ between the female inmate survey and the web-based general population survey, so it is difficult to make a strict comparison between female inmates and general females, but the figures for female inmates are also included in the numerical table (Table 10.1).

Table 10.1 Troubles/Anxiousness

	Female inmates[a]			*General women*[b]		
	Total	*40–65 years old*	*65 years old and above*	*Total*	*40–65 years old*	*65 years old and above*
Total(N)	737	568	169	389	202	187
Yes	84.2	85.7	79.3	72.0	79.2	64.2
No	10.4	8.5	16.6	28.0	20.8	35.8
N.A.	5.4	5.8	4.1	–	–	–

[a] Did you have anything you felt bad or worried about when you committed the crime?
[b] Did you have anything you felt bad or worried about now?

The proportion of female inmates and general females who have problems or concerns is almost 70% to 80%, but the proportion of female inmates is about 10 percentage points higher than that of general females in each age group, and the proportion of "40 to 65 years old" is higher than that of "65 years old or older" (Tables 10.1 and 10.2).

The most common problems and concerns of the general female population are "my health," "retirement planning," and "family health," at 70% of the total. The "40 to 65" age group also cited "planning for retirement," "own health," and "family health" as concerns, as well as "current assets" and "future income prospects" as economic concerns, with the "40 to 65" age group feeling particularly anxious about "planning for retirement." In addition, respondents aged 65 and older were more concerned about disasters and accidents than those aged 40 to 65.

10.5 Conclusions

In this chapter, we looked at the characteristics of older female inmates by taking three groups of women (underclass women, female inmates, and women in general) and comparing them to each other. The following are the conclusions obtained.

1 For women, the turning point in whether or not to flow into the underclass is the "separation and bereavement" from their husbands/partners that they experience in their late 20s and early 30s. They become single mothers, and the "non-regular employment" they engage in to make ends meet often intensifies their subsequent difficulties in life. Many prisoners also have higher rates of "separation and bereavement" and "single motherhood" than women in general. In the course of their lives after release, unstable jobs, joblessness, and paths to poverty are common to underclass women.
2 In the "self-perception" by female inmates, more than 90% of them give "marriage" and "childbirth" for "the 'happiest' thing in my life." This is

Table 10.2 Description of the trouble/anxiety

	Female inmates			*General women*		
	Total	*40–65 years old*	*65 years old and above*	*Total*	*40–65 years old*	*65 years old and above*
Total(N)	*621*	*487*	*134*	*280*	*160*	*120*
1. My health				72.9	68.8	78.3
2. Planning for Old Age				62.5	76.9	43.3
3. Family member's health				55.0	55.6	54.2
4. Current income and assets				36.4	47.5	21.7
5. Prospects for future income and assets				33.9	43.8	20.8
6. Disasters and accidents				22.1	20.6	24.2
7. In the family's life (employment, marriage, etc.)				20.7	25.6	14.2
8. Family and kinship relationships				15.0	19.4	9.2
9. Neighborhood and community relations				7.1	7.5	6.7
10. In my life (employment, marriage, etc.)				5.7	9.4	0.8
11. Crime damage				5.4	6.3	4.2
12. Work and personal relationships at the place of employment				4.6	8.1	0.0
13. Problem on a business or family business				1.4	2.5	0.0
14. Successor to a business or family business				0.4	0.0	0.8
15. Crimes committed				0.4	0.6	0.0
16. Others				2.9	1.9	4.2
17. D.K.				0.7	1.3	0.0
1. My health	41.2	40.7	13.3			
2. Relationship with a family member	39.8	43.5	26.1			
3. Daily living expense	34.5	38.4	20.1			
4. No reliable person to consult	26.9	29.6	17.2			
5. Family member's health	26.6	27.7	22.4			
6. Recommitment of shoplifting and theft	24.6	21.1	37.3			
7. My character	23.5	26.5	12.7			
8. Loneliness	22.7	25.7	11.9			

(Continued)

Table 10.2 (Continued)

	Female inmates			*General women*		
	Total	*40–65 years old*	*65 years old and above*	*Total*	*40–65 years old*	*65 years old and above*
Total(N)	*621*	*487*	*134*	*280*	*160*	*120*
9. Dependence on drug	21.6	26.9	2.2			
10. Debt repayment	21.3	23.8	11.9			
11. Husband's or partner's character and behavior	21.3	24.2	10.4			
12. Problem on business	20.8	24.2	8.2			
13. Relationship with a relative	18.7	20.3	12.7			
14. Tendency to shop	16.9	19.3	8.2			
15. Relationship with a friend	15.3	17.7	6.7			
16. Losing my vigor	13.4	12.9	14.0			
17. Heterosexual relationship	11.4	14.2	1.5			
18. Relationship with a neighbor and workplace	11.3	12.1	8.2			
19. Child's character and behavior	11.0	12.1	6.7			
20. No reliable person to consult	8.7	9.4	6.0			
21. Dependence on alcohol	6.9	8.2	2.2			
22. No tomb	4.6	4.5	4.3			
23. Others	7.3	7.7	7.6			
24. Nothing special	0.3	0.3	0.2			
25. NA	0.6	0.3	-			

the same for both underclass women and women in general. The problem is what comes after. For women in general, "family relationships" and "family problems," including children, follow them throughout their lives. For women in prison, their children's "disabilities, delinquent behavior, and failed lifestyles" weigh heavily on them. On the other hand, for underclass women, their children's "economic deprivation (non-regular work, unemployment, etc.)" and "unmarried/mentally dependent" affect their lives. At the same time, general women are not so much concerned or motivated about society and life, but their relationship with their families is less subject to their worries and anxieties.

3 Among women, those who are between 40 and 65 years old (middle-aged women) and those older (65 years old and over), it can be pointed out that the issue of women's own economic independence (work and

family finances) has a significant impact on their lives, especially among the former group. Both inmate women and underclass women appear to be struggling with "work," which forms the basis of their lives. Behind this, we can see that the unstable and low-paid employment of "non-regular employment" and "part-time work" constantly creates mental anguish. This is a common problem for men. In comparison, elderly women, both inmates and underclass, basically have pensions, and the shortfall is covered by "non-regular employment" and "part-time work," and they do not suffer as much from mental anxieties. However, behind the "shoplifting" that is often seen among the elderly inmates, it can be seen that they are suffering from another kind of psychological anguish due to the lack of support for their families living with them and the "savings" that ordinary women have.

4 The majority of the elderly underclass women are receiving pensions, but at the same time they are working informal jobs. Moreover, half of them are satisfied with their jobs. This is because they are happy with the contribution they make to the livelihood of their children and grandchildren who live with them. Older prisoners are also forced to engage in "part-time work" while receiving pensions, partly because of a lack of savings, but above all because of financial support for their own families.

5 Among female prisoners, a comparison of 34 women from the underclass of prisoners (no husband/partner, part-time employment, part-time work) and 335 other non-underclass women showed that the underclass women "had the desire to work," "had more to do for their families," and "had more to do for their own health." They were more likely than non-underclass women to say that they were paying attention, suggesting that they were working hard at their jobs in a positive manner, for their families, and for their own health. It can also be seen that they spend less time with those around them and can be isolated. Among the female inmates, the underclass women take on more responsibility for themselves, work hard, and show a particularly strong indication of an active lifestyle.

References

Hashimoto, K. (2018a) *Andaakurasu Aratana Kasoukaikyu no Shutsugen* [*Underclass: The Emergence of a New Lower Class*], Chikumashobo Ltd., 2018.

Hashimoto, K. (2018b) *Shin Nihon no Kaikyu-shakai* [*New Japanese Class Society*], Kodansha Ltd.

Shirahase, S. (2005) *Joshi Koureishakai no Mienai Kakusa: Gender, Sedai, Kakusa no Yukue* [*Invisible Disparities in the Aging Society of Women: Direction of Issues regarding Gender, Generations, and Disparities*], Tokyo, University of Tokyo Press.

Section III

Trends and Issues in Elderly Crime from Around the World

11 Trends in Crimes Committed by the Elderly and Laws Regarding "Sexual Crimes" in New Zealand

Masaharu Senzu

Tokiwa University, Japan

11.1 Introduction

This chapter outlines the current circumstances of elderly prisoners and relevant laws regarding sexual crimes in New Zealand.

The most dominant crime among elderly convicts in Japan is offenses against property, as discussed later in this chapter. Although sexual crimes are not very prevalent in Japan, they are widespread in New Zealand. In addition, the ethnicity of elderly convicts of sexual crimes consists mainly of Pakeha New Zealanders, whose ancestors came from Europe. This differs from the finding that most inmates in New Zealand's penal institutions are Maoris, the country's indigenous people.

In light of these points, the present chapter first outlines the current situations of elderly convicts, followed by the discussions regarding relevant laws and relief measures for the victims under 16 of sexual crimes in New Zealand.

This chapter will provide valuable information to characterize elderly convicts and legislate relevant laws against sexual crimes in New Zealand.

11.2 The current situation of elderly convicts in New Zealand

First, I examine the current circumstances of elderly convicts in New Zealand according to the "Annual Sentenced Prisoner Population for the latest Fiscal Years" (http://nzdotstat.stats.govt.nz/wbos/Index.aspx?DataSetCode=TABLECODE7322&_ga=2.74750034.1132967788.1519736266-306366456.1490536581) (Accessed: April 13, 2020) in "Stats NZ" (https://www.stats.govt.nz/) (Accessed April 13, 2020)[1].

Table 11.1 shows the number of elderly convicts (unless otherwise noted, "elderly convicts" mean inmates aged 60 years and above, and the same applies hereafter) for the past ten years in New Zealand according to the crime(s) they committed. The first point to be mentioned as the characteristics of elderly convicts in New Zealand should be the number of prisoners convicted of sexual assault and related offenses. For the past ten years, the number of particular offenses has consistently ranked at the top in each fiscal year (FY)[2]. In the case of FY 2018 (from 2018 to 2019 in the calendar year), 51 out of

DOI: 10.4324/9781032669519-15

Table 11.1 Annual sentenced elderly prisoner population for the latest fiscal years

Year	*2009/10*	*2010/11*	*2011/12*	*2012/13*	*2013/14*	*2014/15*	*2015/16*	*2016/17*	*2017/18*	*2018/19*
Total offences	*105*	*126*	*141*	*165*	*135*	*144*	*168*	*144*	*174*	*147*
Homicide and related offences	3	3	3	3	0	3	6	0	3	3
Acts intended to cause injury	0	9	6	9	6	6	9	12	9	9
Sexual assault and related offences	45	39	57	66	57	66	72	36	60	51
Dangerous or negligent acts endangering persons	9	0	..	3	0	..	0	6	0	..
Abduction, harassment, and other related offences against a person	..	3	3	3	6	3	..	6	6	6
Robbery, extortion, and related offences	..	..	..	0	..	..	0	0	..	0
Unlawful entry with intent/burglary, break and enter	3	3	..	3	3	3	6	..	0	6
Theft and related offences	3	9	9	6	6	9	6	3	3	6
Fraud, deception, and related offences	6	12	18	6	9	12	12	9	12	12
Illicit drug offences	3	15	15	12	6	12	9	12	9	6
Prohibited and regulated weapons and explosives offences	..	3	3	3	..	3	3	3	3	0
Property damage and environmental pollution	..	6	6	6	3	3	6	3	6	3
Public order offences	0	6	6	6	3	3	0	3	6	6
Traffic and vehicle regulatory offences	24	15	15	21	18	9	18	21	27	15
Offences against justice procedures, government security and government operations	12	12	12	12	6	18	18	24	24	15
Miscellaneous offences	..	0	0	0	..	0	3	0	..	..
Inadequate data available	..	..	..	..	..	..	..	..	..	..
Unknown	..	..	..	..	..	..	..	..	..	..

Source: Annual Sentenced Prisoner Population for the latest Fiscal Years (http://nzdotstat.stats.govt.nz/wbos/Index.aspx?DataSetCode=TABLECODE7322&_ga=2.74750034.1132967788.1519736266-306366456.1490536581) (Accessed: April 13, 2020)

the 147 elderly convicts were convicted of sexual assault and associated crimes, comprising one-third of the total number.

Table 11.2 shows the number of inmates (out of all) according to the crime(s) they had committed for the past ten years in New Zealand. Among all inmates in the fiscal year 2018, 360 were convicted of sexual assault and related offenses. Compared to Table 11.1, the percentage of elderly convicts imprisoned for the same crime is approximately 14.2%, whereas the number of all prisoners in the fiscal year 2018 was 7,485, of which 147 were elderly inmates, comprising approximately 2.0% of the prison population. The results above indicate that many elderly convicts in the country committed sexual assaults and related offenses.

The above situation in New Zealand is different from the relevant data regarding the crimes of elderly convicts in Japan. According to the "White Paper on Crime 2019," theft comprises the most significant proportion of elderly convicts aged 65 and above by offense, accounting for 56.5% of all crimes[3]. This is followed by 10.4% violations of the Stimulants Control Act and 6.6% violations of the Road Transportation Act[4]. Although the ages of elderly convicts are defined differently in New Zealand and Japan, distinct features are evident in the number of elderly convicts based on committed crime(s).

Moreover, as a feature of ethnicity, elderly convicts who have committed sexual assault and related offenses in New Zealand are mostly Pakeha. A problem often highlighted in New Zealand's penal institutions is that Maori prisoners vastly outnumber Pakeha. According to the "Annual Sentenced Prisoner Population for the latest Fiscal Years," the number of Maori inmates was 4,506 in all prisoners recorded in the fiscal year 2018, which composed more than half of the total convicts.

However, regarding elderly inmates convicted of sexual assault and related offenses, Pakeha prisoners comprised the majority. Evidently, among 51 elderly prisoners convicted of sexual assault and related crimes in the fiscal year 2018, 39 were Pakeha (of which 36 were male), constituting nearly 80%. In this sense, the number of elderly inmates convicted of sexual assaults and related offenses in New Zealand indicates a unique, distinctive feature that differs from those convicted of other offenses.

According to documents independently obtained by the author from the Department of Corrections[5], 291 prisoners aged 65 and above were in the country as of February 12, 2018; among them, 230 were convicted of sexual assault and related offenses. This demonstrates that the number of elderly convicts aggregated according to the same age definition of 65 years and above, as in Japan, exhibits a similarly high percentage, indicating that approximately 79% of them are in prison due to sexual assault and related offenses[6]. Moreover, 188 of the 230 inmates mentioned above were incarcerated for crimes against victims younger than 16 years[7]. Details of the charges and victims' age groups regarding these offenses by elderly convicts aged 65 and above against victims aged less than 16 years are as follows: the most significant number of 51 were male convicts charged with rape against female victims aged less than 12,

Table 11.2 Annual sentenced prisoner population for the latest fiscal years

Year	*2009/10*	*2010/11*	*2011/12*	*2012/13*	*2013/14*	*2014/15*	*2015/16*	*2016/17*	*2017/18*	*2018/19*
Total offences	*8994*	*8730*	*8085*	*8085*	*7389*	*7626*	*8424*	*9195*	*8742*	*7485*
Homicide and related offences	99	96	63	63	84	69	60	66	57	57
Acts intended to cause injury	1623	1569	1575	1590	1371	1476	1656	1743	1758	1566
Sexual assault and related offences	405	393	393	474	447	435	414	411	462	360
Dangerous or negligent acts endangering persons	123	111	81	72	63	69	66	93	93	93
Abduction, harassment, and other related offences against a person	207	207	183	204	183	216	279	291	318	267
Robbery, extortion, and related offences	498	363	330	351	294	300	333	399	390	348
Unlawful entry with intent/burglary, break and enter	1311	1233	1179	1149	1065	1017	1104	1173	978	792
Theft and related offences	675	741	762	750	681	699	795	972	837	735
Fraud, deception, and related offences	339	273	237	246	219	228	312	357	333	291
Illicit drug offences	648	672	573	603	513	564	567	600	579	468
Prohibited and regulated weapons and explosives offences	129	156	138	135	120	156	210	249	273	249
Property damage and environmental pollution	147	141	135	132	144	117	132	129	129	123
Public order offences	102	126	138	123	111	111	117	99	141	114
Traffic and vehicle regulatory offences	1185	1083	879	816	711	681	672	711	669	468
Offences against justice procedures, government security and government operations	1476	1545	1401	1368	1365	1479	1698	1890	1707	1551
Miscellaneous offences	18	30	18	15	15	9	3	12	12	3
Inadequate data available	3	..	..	..	..	0	3	..	0	..
Unknown	..	..	..	..	..	..	..	0	..	..

Source: Annual Sentenced Prisoner Population for the latest Fiscal Years (http://nzdotstat.stats.govt.nz/wbos/Index.aspx?DataSetCode=TABLECODE7322&_ga=2.74750034.1132967788.1519736266-306366456.1490536581) (Accessed: April 13, 2020)

followed by 28 male convicts charged with rape against female victims aged 12 and above and less than 16, 27 charged with unlawful sexual connections against female victims aged less than 12, 19 charged with unlawful sexual connections against female victims aged 12 and above and less than 16, and 18 charged with unlawful sexual connections against male victims aged 12 and above and less than 16[8].

As shown in the data above, the number of sexual assaults and related offenses committed by elderly convicts exhibits an increasing trend, which was more evident in elderly convicts aged 65 and above, as indicated in the data as of February 12, 2018[9].

11.3 Sexual crimes and laws in New Zealand

In this chapter, the types and statutes of limitations for sexual crimes are discussed to examine the situations of sexual crimes and relevant laws in New Zealand.

11.3.1 Provisions of sexual crimes in the crimes act 1961

In New Zealand, sexual crimes are stipulated in Section 127 and later in the Crimes Act 1961. Specific offenses are as follows:

1. Sexual violation – Section 128 B: This means rape[10] and unlawful sexual connections[11] for which the statutory penalty is imprisonment for a term not exceeding 20 years.
2. Attempted sexual violation and assault with intent to commit sexual violation – Section 129: The statutory penalty is imprisonment for a term not exceeding 10 years.
3. Sexual conduct with consent induced by certain threats – Section 129A: Imprisonment for a term not exceeding 14 years in the case of a sexual connection and imprisonment for a term not exceeding 5 years in the case of an indecent act.
4. Incest – Section 130: Imprisonment for a term not exceeding 10 years if the perpetrator is 16 years or older.
5. Sexual conduct with a dependent family member under 18 – Section 131: Imprisonment for a term not exceeding 7 years in the case of a sexual connection and attempted sexual connections and imprisonment for a term not exceeding 3 years for an indecent act.
6. Meeting a young person under 16 years following sexual grooming, etc. – Section 131 B: The statutory penalty is imprisonment for a term not exceeding 7 years.
7. Sexual conduct with a child under 12 – Section 132: Imprisonment for a term not exceeding 14 years in the case of a sexual connection and imprisonment for a term not exceeding 10 years for attempted sexual connections and indecent acts.

8 Sexual conduct with a young person under 16 – Section 134: Imprisonment for a term not exceeding 10 years for a sexual or attempted sexual connection and imprisonment for a term not exceeding 7 years in the case of an indecent act.
9 Indecent assault – Section 135: The statutory penalty is imprisonment for a term not exceeding 7 years.
10 Sexual exploitation of a person with significant impairment – Section 138: Imprisonment for a term not exceeding 10 years for a sexual or attempted sexual connection and imprisonment for a term not exceeding 5 years in the case of an indecent act.
11 Compelling indecent act with an animal – Section 142A: The statutory penalty is imprisonment for a term not exceeding 14 years. For this offense, it does not matter whether penetration is involved or not.
12 Bestiality – Section 143: The statutory penalty is imprisonment for a term not exceeding 7 years. This offense is completed upon penetration.
13 Indecency with an animal – Section 144: The statutory penalty is imprisonment for a term not exceeding 3 years. The provisions listed above do not include sexual offenses committed outside of New Zealand.

In Japan's Penal Code, there is a provision called "Crimes of Obscenity, Forcible Sexual Intercourse, and Bigamy" in Chapter 22. However, offenses deemed sexual crimes for statistical purposes in the "White Paper" only include Indecency through Compulsion and Forcible Sexual Intercourse[12]. Consequently, the range of sexual crimes is more widely stipulated in New Zealand than in Japan.

11.3.2 The period of the statute of limitations for sexual crimes

Section 25 of the Criminal Procedure Act 2011 establishes the statute of the limitation period for sexual crimes and specifies the deadline for filing a charging document.

In New Zealand, all crimes are classified under categories ranging from 1 to 4 (Section 6 of the Criminal Procedure Act 2011). The greater the number, the more serious the crime. For example, a category 4 offense is a severe one that includes murder, manslaughter, or hijacking; these offenses are crimes listed in Schedule 1 of the Criminal Procedure Act 2011. Regarding the above-mentioned sexual crimes, none represent category 4. Category 3 offenses are those that do not fall under category 4 and are punishable by imprisonment for life or 2 or more years; thus, the previously described sexual crimes fall under category 3.

In the Criminal Procedure Act of 2011, a charging document may be filed at any time for a category 4 offense (Section 25 [1] of the Criminal Procedure Act 2011). For category 3 offenses, a charging document must be filed within 5 years after the date of the crime (Section 25 [2] [a] of the Criminal Procedure Act of 2011) if the statutory penalty is imprisonment (not exceeding

3 years). However, if the term of imprisonment is longer than 3 years, a charging document may be filed at any time, just as in a category 4 crime (Section 25 [2] [b] of the Criminal Procedure Act of 2011). That is, for most of the above-mentioned sexual crimes, a charging document may be filed at any time. This means that statute of limitations does not exist for most sexual offenses.

Hence, for most sexual crimes, the legislative policy on setting a period of the statute of limitations has not been in existence since before the Criminal Procedure Act of 2011. The clauses related to the period of the statute of limitations were already stipulated in Section 10 B of the Crimes Act 1961[13], prior to the enactment of the Criminal Procedure Act of 2011. The particular section stipulated that in the case of (1) the statutory penalty is only a fine with the maximum amount not exceeding 2,000 New Zealand dollars, or (2) the statutory penalty is imprisonment not exceeding 3 years and 10 years have already passed since the date of the crime, criminal proceedings could not be commenced to the next step (except for procedures followed by a trial or a hearing) (subsections 1 and 2 of Section 10 B)[14]. That is, if a case did not fall under the above categories (1) and (2), criminal proceedings could advance to the next phase at any time, regardless of the 10-year restriction. Therefore, filing a charging document was possible 10 years after the crime. Accordingly, even before the Criminal Procedure Act 2011, concerning most sexual crimes for which the statutory imprisonment penalty was more significant than 3 years, a statute of limitations period did not exist.

As is well known, in Japan's Code of Criminal Procedure, only a crime for which the death penalty is imposed does not have a statute of limitations; furthermore, it is limited to those involving the victim's death. Regarding other crimes, a statute of limitations is set forth for each offense (Article 250); for example, 7 years for Indecency through Compulsion and 10 years for Forcible Sexual Intercourse are stipulated (excluding those involving the victim's death).

Considering this point, the provision stipulating that a charging document may be filed at any time for most sexual crimes in New Zealand is quite different from the statute of limitations for sexual crimes in Japan.

Unquestionably, there is the principle of the presumption of innocence in New Zealand, as well as in Japan. Section 25 (c) of the New Zealand Bill of Rights Act 1990 states that everyone charged with an offense has "the right to be presumed innocent until proven guilty according to law." This was the basis for the presumption of innocence in New Zealand. Needless to say, the burden of proof is placed on the prosecutor[15], who must prove the defendant guilty beyond reasonable doubt[16]. Thus, even for crimes without a statute of limitations, evidence may be dispersed and guilt cannot be clarified many years after the incident. Simultaneously, it should be noted that cases with sufficient evidence can prevent a situation in which the prosecution of the crime should be disrupted due to the statute of limitations, even many years after the crime[17].

11.4 Recent legislation related to sexual crimes in New Zealand

Lastly, this chapter will outline the Three Strikes Law and the Child Protection (Child Sex Offender Government Agency Registration) Act as recent legislation related to sexual crimes in New Zealand.

11.4.1 Three strikes law

The "Three Strikes law" generally imposes a maximum penalty equivalent to a felony on offenders who repeat serious offenses three times. In New Zealand, along with establishing the Sentencing and Parole Reform Act of 2010, a provision for repeated serious violent offenses was enacted in Section 86A of the Sentencing Act 2002[18].

In Section 86A of the Sentencing Act, 40 crimes prescribed in the Crimes Act of 1961 were deemed serious violent offenses. Among previously mentioned sexual infractions, crimes considered serious and violent are as follows: (1) sexual violation, (2) attempted sexual violation and assault with intent to commit a sexual violation, (3) a sexual connection with consent induced by certain threats, (4) a sexual connection with a dependent family member under 18, (5) an attempted sexual connection with a dependent family member under 18, (6) a sexual connection with a child under 12, (7) an attempted sexual connection with a child under 12, (8) indecent act on a child under 12, (9) a sexual connection with a young person under 16, (10) an attempted sexual connection with a young person under 16, (11) indecent act on a young person under 16, (12) indecent assault, (13) an exploitative sexual connection with a person with significant impairment, (14) an attempted exploitative sexual connection with a person with significant impairment, and (15) a compelling indecent act with an animal. Thus, three-eighths of the crimes set forth in the Sentencing Act as serious violent offenses are of a sexual nature.

A person found guilty of a serious violent offense will receive the first warning from the court as a strike. When receiving the first warning and being found guilty of a serious violent crime for the second time, the person receives a final warning as two strikes from the court. Simultaneously, they have to serve a complete sentence without parole and will not be released before the sentence expires. Furthermore, a person who is guilty of a serious violent crime for the third time (three strikes) will receive the most severe punishment among statutory penalties, without parole. However, if the second or third offense – confirmed as a felony –is murder, the sentence will be life imprisonment, and in principle, parole cannot be granted.

The Three Strikes law in New Zealand is not as harsh as seen in examples in the United States, where third strike convicts are sentenced to life imprisonment for stealing a few pieces of cookies. In addition, the number of third strike offenders was one each in 2016 and 2017, five in 2018, and six in 2019 (among which those marked the third strike by sexual assault and related offenses were one each in 2016, 2018, and 2019, respectively), remaining a small portion, although it recently showed an increasing trend[19]. At the same time, however, the subject crimes of the Three Strikes law in New Zealand are limited to serious offenses, and thus, the sentence's term might already be as long as the first or second strike. Consequently, more time is necessary to determine the extent to which this law affects the capacity of New Zealand's penal institutions. The Three Strikes law's stance of harsh penalties against serious violent crimes, including sexual offenses, is a manifestation of a harsh attitude toward sexual crimes[20].

11.4.2 Legislation for the child sex offender registry

For legislation regarding the child sex offender registry, information on perpetrators of sexual crimes inflicted on victims under 16 is registered and shared by government agencies, such as the police and the Department of Corrections, due to the establishment of the Child Protection (Child Sex Offender Government Agency Registration) Act 2016[21]. Accordingly, this legislation is not meant to release information on sexual perpetrators, as in the case of Megan's Law.

A subject to registration based on the Child Protection (Child Sex Offender Government Agency Registration) Act 2016 is a person aged 18 and above, found guilty of sexual crimes against victims under 16, sentenced to imprisonment or sentenced to a non-custodial sentence, and made subject to a registration order based on the judge's discretion (Section 7 of the Child Protection [Child Sex Offender Government Agency Registration] Act 2016). Qualifying sexual offenses are categorized from Class 1 to 3 (Schedule 2 of the Child Protection [Child Sex Offender Government Agency Registration] Act of 2016). A person found guilty of a crime ranked as a Class 1 offense is registered for 8 years from the day he/she is released from prison or made subject to a registration order by the judge. A person found guilty of a crime ranked as a Class 2 offense is registered for 15 years from the day he/she is released from prison or made subject to a registration order by the judge. A person found guilty of a crime categorized as a Class 3 offense is registered for life (Section 34, Section 35 of the Child Protection [Child Sex Offender Government Agency Registration] Act of 2016).

Meeting a young person under 16 following sexual grooming is classified as a Class 1 offense among the previously mentioned sexual offenses[22]. The infractions categorized as Class 2 offenses are as follows: (1) sexual conduct with consent induced by certain threats, (2) an indecent act with a dependent family member, (3) an indecent act with a child under 12, (4) an indecent act with a young person under 16, (5) indecent assault, and (6) sexual exploitation of a person with significant impairment. The offenses categorized as Class 3 crimes are as follows: (1) sexual violation, (2) attempted sexual violation, (3) assault with intent to commit a sexual violation, (4) a sexual connection with consent induced by a certain threat, (5) incest, (6) a sexual connection with a dependent family member, (7) an attempted sexual connection with a dependent family member, (8) a sexual connection with a child under 12, (9) an attempted sexual connection with a child under 12, (10) a sexual connection with a child under 16, (11) an attempted sexual connection with a young person under 16, (12) exploitative sexual connection with a person with significant impairment, and (13) an attempted exploitative sexual connection with a person with significant impairment. Naturally, offenses from Classes 1 to 3 are conditioned on victims under 16.

Registered perpetrators are obliged to periodically report information regarding their personal circumstances to the New Zealand Police Commissioner until the required reporting period expires (Section 18 of the Child Protection [Child Sex Offender Government Agency Registration] Act of 2016). If they fail to report without justifiable grounds, make false reports, or provide the wrong information, they shall be fined (Section 39, Section 40 of the Child Protection [Child Sex Offender Government Agency Registration] Act of 2016).

Judging from this legislation thus far, measures have been strengthened to prevent young people under 16 from becoming victims of sexual crimes, at least in New Zealand[23].

11.5 Conclusions

I have briefly seen the current situation of elderly prisoners held in penal institutions due to sexual assault and related offenses in New Zealand, and legislation regarding sexual crimes in the country. In New Zealand, (1) many elderly convicts are in prison due to offenses of a sexual nature, and (2) the issue of young persons under 16 being sexually victimized is considered problematic, and preventive measures are being taken. This point is evident by the fact that many victims of elderly convicts are under 16, as illustrated in the previously mentioned documents that the author independently obtained from the Department of Corrections. In this sense, preventing young persons under 16 from being sexually victimized would decrease the number of elderly convicts held in penal institutions due to sexual assault and related offenses.

It was somewhat regretful that sufficient research and consideration could not be conducted because of insufficient time. However, I will continue to monitor trends in elderly convicts in New Zealand.

Notes

1 "Stats NZ" is New Zealand's official data agency, which performs searches of statistics in the country. A statistical report called Statistics New Zealand used to be issued every other year as well as in the form of a database on the website until around 2010; currently, its publication is now integrated into the website database.
2 The fiscal year in New Zealand is from July 1 to June 30 of the following year.
3 Research and Training Institute of the Ministry of Justice, White Paper on Crime 2019. Showa Joho Process, 2019, p. 333.
4 Research and Training Institute of the Ministry of Justice, supra note 3, p. 333.
5 The Department of Corrections in New Zealand is a government agency equivalent to the Correction Bureau and the Rehabilitation Bureau of Japan's Ministry of Justice.

6 Department of Corrections, "Overview of Current Prisoners Aged 65 Years and Over." A paper received from the Department of Corrections in New Zealand on February 28, 2018.
7 *Ibid.*
8 *Ibid.*
9 An e-mail that the author received from New Zealand's Department of Corrections on February 28, 2018, included the following comment regarding such a trend, "The most important factors are an increase number of older offenders being convicted for serious sexual offences, and the fact that a proportion of older sex offenders are judged to present high risks of reoffending, and therefore are detained in prison to serve a large proportion of the imposed sentence." Moreover, according to an e-mail from March 7, 2018, from a staff of Victim Support (commonly called "VS") – an organization that supports victims on a nationwide scale – "in New Zealand, there is a growing willingness for sexual violations to be reported, either current and historic, and under the Crimes Act (1961) for the alleged perpetrators to be brought to account regardless of age or status, based on sound evidence."
10 In the Act, *rape* means a sexual connection occurring by the penetration of person B's genitalia by person A's penis (1) without B's consent to the connection, and (2) without believing on reasonable grounds that person B consents to the connection (Section 128A of the Crimes Act 1961).
11 In the Act, *unlawful sexual connection* means a sexual connection occurring (1) without person B's consent to the connection and (2) without believing on reasonable grounds that person B consents to the connection (Section 128A of the Crimes Act 1961). Additionally, *sexual connection* means (a) connection effected by the introduction into the genitalia or anus of one person, otherwise than for genuine medical purposes, of (i)a part of the body of another person; or (ii)an object held or manipulated by another person; or, (b) connection between the mouth or tongue of one person and a part of another person's genitalia or anus; or, (c) the continuation of connection of a kind described in paragraph (a) or paragraph (b) (Section 2 of the Crimes Act 1961). Therefore, merely saying *sexual connection* includes vaginal intercourse and *unlawful sexual connection* is separated from rape.
12 Research and Training Institute of the Ministry of Justice, the previously cited white paper, p. 234. As is widely known, due to the Penal Code being partially amended in 2017, rape is currently termed *kyosei-seikoto-zai* in Japanese, which was changed from *gokan-zai* (the crime of raping a woman).
13 In general terms, the Criminal Procedure Act 2011 was passed as a different law from most provisions related to criminal proceedings in the Crimes Act 1961.
14 Robertson B., et al., *Adams on Criminal Law 2010 Student Edition*. Wellington: New Zealand, Brookers, 2010, p. 34.
15 Spiller P., *New Zealand Law Dictionary*. Wellington: New Zealand, Lexis Nexis, 2015, pp. 38-39. Moreover, in general, Crown Solicitors and Police Prosecutors are listed as prosecutors in New Zealand. Crown solicitors mean 17 lawyers nationwide designated by the Crown Law Office. One of their duties is to prosecute serious crimes, such as offenses that fall under the previously mentioned category 4 (furthermore, they are called Crown Prosecutors when carrying out their duties). Police prosecutors are assigned to prosecute relatively minor crimes that do not require prosecution by Crown solicitors. In general, the person engaged in duties relating to prosecution among police officers appears in court as a police prosecutor.
16 *Ibid.*, p. 31.
17 An e-mail the author received on February 27, 2018, from Professor John Pratt at Victoria University of Wellington (Wellington is the capital city of New Zealand) stated: "As far as I am aware, there has been no reform that specifically affects the number of elderly prisoners. There have been more prosecutions of the elderly for

historic sex offences, but this is only because more people are now coming forward with complaints about this conduct." However, it is possible to initiate a lawsuit, even for past sexual crimes, if there is no period of the statute of limitations.

18 There is a paper regarding the Three Strikes law in New Zealand, Oleson J. C. (2015) 'Habitual Criminal Legislation in New Zealand: Three Years of Three Strikes', *Australian and New Zealand Journal of Criminology*, 48(2), pp. 277–292.

19 Ministry of Justice, "Three Strikes Offences." (https://justice.govt.nz/justice-sector-policy/research-data/justice-statistics/data-table) (final confirmation date: Apr. 27, 2020).

20 The *New Zealand Herald*, a leading newspaper in New Zealand, initiated a lobby group that claimed "Three Strikes Bill 'Not Tough Enough'" (http://www.nzherald.co.nz/nz/news/article.cfm?c_id=1&objectid=10631205&pnum=0) (final confirmation date: March 18, 2018) In the article, issued on October 10, 2010, before the Sentencing Act of 2002 and the Sentencing and Parole Reform Act 2010 were passed. Moreover, there are people who insist on making the law even stricter.

21 The explanation for the child sex offender registry system, New Zealand Police, "Child Sex Offender (CSO) Register." (http://www.police.govt.nz/about-us/programmes-and-initiatives/child-sex-offender-cso-register) (final confirmation date: Mar. 18, 2018).

22 Targeted crimes are not always considered sexual offenses according to Article 127 of the Crimes Act of 1961 and include infractions related to sex in some form, such as indecent communication with a young person under 16 (Section 124A of the Crimes Act of 1961: ranked under Class 1).

23 According to the Department of Corrections, *Annual Report 2016/2017*. Wellington: New Zealand, 2017, p. 157, the Department of Corrections introduced the system of a senior adviser, who is engaged in improving public understanding of how communities manage prisoners who have sexually offended children, and smooth reintegration of these inmates. This would be one of the measures against sexual crimes in which children are victimized.

12 "No Country for Old Men" The Experiences of Elderly Inmates in New Zealand

John Pratt

Victoria University, New Zealand

Yoko Hosoi

Toyo University, Japan

This chapter[1] is based on discussions with seven elderly ex-prisoners in New Zealand, talking about their experiences. One way to understand these experiences is by making use of and remodeling Gresham Sykes' (1957) concept of the "pains of imprisonment." He characterized these pains as taking the form of "the deprivation of freedom, goods and services, heterosexual relationships, autonomy" and, perhaps most fundamentally, "the deprivation of security" – since this latter posed the most immediate existential threat to everyday existence. The violent background of many inmates meant that the institution which gave so much emphasis to predictability and routine was, ironically, simultaneously highly unpredictable. To protect themselves and to try to alleviate the other pains of imprisonment, inmates were described by Sykes as making alliances with like-minded others, leading to the formation of typologies such as "gorillas and merchants," "escape artists," "real men," and so on.

But in the early 21st century, any such typologies have to include at least two new characters to take account of the changing nature of prison demographics. In the New Zealand prison vernacular, these consist of, first, "old lags": inmates who have served many years in prison and have been able to adjust to the system and develop survival skills. However, as they become old and frail, their status declines, even if they have previously been gang leaders, and, as with any sign of weakness in prison, they then become vulnerable and exploitable. Second, there are the "broken asses": frequently, although not always, these are older prisoners who cannot cope with their sentence. Their advancing age makes them defenseless against attack, and on admission they become immediate and easy targets for predatory prisoners because a large number of them are also sex offenders. For these "broken asses" in particular, prison is indeed "no country for old men" (McCarthy, 2005). They have been propelled into this strange new land but from which they have virtually no possibility of escape nor the ability to leave by their own volition.

It will be argued that the pains of elderly prisoners necessitate both revisions and extensions to Sykes' "pains," both in terms of the prison experience itself

DOI: 10.4324/9781032669519-16

and, thereafter, life beyond prison. The chapter is based on New Zealand data that involved male prison inmates in this age group[2] completing a self-report questionnaire (a 35 per cent response rate), along with in-depth interviews with seven elderly ex-prisoners (the youngest was 70 and the oldest was 87), all of whom had been imprisoned for sexual offences and, while there, most closely corresponded to the "broken ass" typology. It is accompanied by two qualifying comments. First, the ethnicity of those who completed the survey was 68% "New Zealand European," 16% per cent Maori, and 6% "Other": 77% of them were serving prison terms for sex offences. The ethnicity of the interviewees was 100% New Zealand European. These statistics are greatly out of kilter with the mix of the prison population as a whole (50% Maori, 32% European, 11% Pacific Island, and 7% "Other/Unknown." They are rather more in line with the sex offender population within it, though (Department of Corrections, 2016). The chapter thus relates primarily (regarding the survey) and exclusively (regarding the interviews) to the experiences of New Zealand Europeans. It recognizes that the Maori (and Pacific Islander) experiences, given their more supportive whanau (extended family) links, might well be different.

Second, this chapter defines "elderly" (as opposed to merely "ageing") as being 65+ (as other researchers in this field have done, for example Crawley and Sparks, 2005). Choosing this age is administratively convenient: it is the formal age of retirement in many countries and thereby marks an important point of differentiation in the human life course. At the same time, the 65+ age group is the fastest growing cohort in the prisoner population in many modern societies. The selection of the 65+ group thus allows more concentrated light to be shed on the pains of being old in prison, rather than a wider and more general study of ageing within it.

How has this happened? First, it is one of the consequences of longer sentences, especially the growth of life without parole (van Zyl Smit, 2017). Second, it is a consequence of delayed release. Getting out of prison before the formal end of sentence has become much more difficult. Remission for good behavior (typically one third of sentence) has been abolished in some jurisdictions. Over the same period, parole itself has become much more restricted. A risk aversion imperative dominates proceedings, especially as regards those with a background of sex crime. Third, in the UK, New Zealand, and Australia, it has also been brought about by the punishment of historic sex offences sometimes going back to the 1960s. These offences have involved well-known celebrities, churchmen, sports instructors, school teachers, music tutors, etc. and probably most usually, step fathers and other male relatives of the victims. In the New Zealand survey, 47% of the crimes of the respondents had been committed against family members, friends, and/or acquaintances.

12.1 The pains of imprisonment as experienced by elderly inmates

Elderly inmates, the 'broken asses' in particular, experienced four distinct pains of imprisonment recorded in this research. These are the following:

12.1.1 The pains of amplified exposure to violence and threat

In inmate culture, there is a very strong belief that new elderly prisoners are inevitably sex offenders. As one of the interviewees (designated as H1) explained, "it is commonly believed that if you're an older man and you're in prison, there is a 99 per cent chance it's for sex offences" (H1, 71). This then makes them very likely targets for attack, against which they are virtually defenseless, because of their age and lack of prison experience. Outcasts within the prison, they have neither the ability to build up layers of protection through already existing associations with other prisoners, nor the physical ability to conduct and comport themselves to either avoid unwanted attention or to demonstrate confidence in their ability to ward off attackers:

> [mainstream] was a most unpleasant time. There were many instances when I was fearing for my own safety ... there was jostling and verbal intimidation and threats ... one [prisoner] wrote to my wife and threatened her
> (W2, 71).

> there was a bloke beaten up very badly in the games room by some relatives of the girls he had abused ... he was taken away unconscious, he never came back. Never saw him again.
> (H2, 77).

> somebody came up behind me and kicked me to the side of my head. He broke my nose, eye socket, cheekbone and damaged my teeth in the upper jaw. I even damaged my hip as I fell to the ground.
> (A1, 71).

Their predicament and peril brought little sympathy or interest from mainstream prison staff:

> Corrections staff weren't interested in us as individuals ... some of the behavior and verbal abuse we got form them [the officers], it was like they were there to punish us rather than to keep us in custody and ensure our safety
> (W2, 71).

> White Power boys didn't want me there ... they smashed my TV. Prison management just said, "it's your problem that your TV got smashed."
> (H1, 71).

On occasions, it seems that prison staff went out of their way to put them at risk. H2, (77), found that, on reception to his prison, he had been deliberately placed in a non-segregated yard, where he was immediately singled out and threatened. One officer at least, albeit in cryptic fashion which probably further alarmed and confused this inmate, then came up to him and warned him "not to come back on this wing tomorrow or [I] would be beaten up ... they're [other prisoners] already planning it. Go and see the boss or somebody." Thereafter, his transfer to the sex offender prison by bus (from the mid-North Island to the mid-South Island) became a terrifying 24-hour journey. For his own safety - from attack by other prisoners on the bus - he was placed in a cage with another sex offender but in the same compartment as the other transferring prisoners:

> that was a hell of a trip because we were verbally abused all the time [by the other] prisoners being dropped off at prisons along the way … this was because we were sex offenders
>
> (H2, 77).

To add to their insecurity, cuts to prison budgets had led to reductions in prison staff and greatly reduced their visibility around the wings. Desperate for signs of reassurance and protection that the presence of prison officers might otherwise convey, A1, 71, complained that:

> A whole day could come and go and you never see an officer … they've rebuilt parts of the prison and where the officers hang out, you can't see in. There is no door. There's no window
>
> (A1, 71).

However, the slightest hint of any risk, as identified by key performance indicators against which prison staff and the prison itself would be judged (and as opposed to gratuitous insults or threats from other inmates), would set off a security alert:

> a prison officer said, 'what are you going to do when you get out of prison?' 'After this,' I said, 'I may as well be dead'—so I was put on suicide watch
>
> (W5, 87).

This had serious consequences. It meant that he would be kept under 24 hours per day surveillance, held in a cell with padded walls so that he could not injure himself against them, while all other everyday items except for special, "suicide proof" clothing were also removed from the cell.

12.1.2 The pains of chronic health problems

Ageing is accompanied by the onset of all kinds of chronic illnesses. These fundamentally disrupt the ability of individuals to function in everyday life beyond the prison—let alone the prison itself—without assistance. Amongst the interviewees, H2 (77) reported that he had fourteen operations for multiple organic problems, including gallstones, appendix, prostate issues, and tonsillitis. A1 (71) reported that he was in poor health, suffering, in particular from arthritis, diabetes and high blood pressure (on leaving prison he then developed cancer). W1 (76) was suffering from arthritis ("I can't straighten up because of the pain"). W5 (87) said that "I was a bit handicapped [in prison]. I had to have a walking stick because I kept losing my balance." He was also taking medication for constipation, cholesterol, thyroid problems, and high blood pressure. W4 (83) said that "I have a heart problem and I've got what they call Paget's Disease which is an enlarging of the bones … I'm deaf in one ear and I have a hearing aid in the other to try and boost it." It was only W2 (71) who maintained that he was "in average health for this age"—meaning that "I've just been to the doctor this morning to have some of medicines cut back."

Indeed, the health of some of the interviewees deteriorated significantly during the course of their incarceration:

> my legs swelled enormously, and there was no attention paid to that. I had skin cancer here, there and everywhere and nothing ever happened
> (A1, 71).

> in prison, I was given codeine [for my arthritis] … it didn't help because I was getting worse with it … I managed to swindle—to get me an extra blanket … in prison you've got to think how you are going to survive
> (W1, 76).

> prison officers would not give Paracetamol. I started to deteriorate and all I can put it down to was being enclosed in the pens [yards] and on concrete a lot … there were no green areas for us to walk on
> (W4, 83)

There are in fact plenty of green areas at that prison, but these are fenced off from inmates. Security concerns override issues of age, health, and mobility: all inmates have to move along clearly delineated concrete walkways.

But prison health care staff usually deal with the consequences of violence and addiction in the mainstream. They showed little interest in the chronic health problems of the elderly prisoner cohort:

> nurses wouldn't wash any of [the chronically ill] inmates … they were only pill disher-outers really … it was up to look after ourselves.
> (H2, 77).

The prison diet also exacerbated their ailments and chronic decline:

> food is all carbs [carbohydrates] … all bloody spuds and rice and sandwiches … toast in the morning and porridge or something. Then there a couple of sandwiches for lunch … we had 8 to 10, 12 slices of bread each day in our diet
> (H2, 77).

> the food is not nutritious enough … everybody agreed we needed better food. We used to get 11 slices of bread a day … for lunch we would have three sandwiches. One would be sweetcorn, another would be marmite. I forget the other one now
>
> (W5, 87)

> at X prison the meals were shocking: the potatoes were raw, the pumpkins would be raw
>
> (W4, 83)

Furthermore, there were no opportunities for the elderly to maintain or improve their physical fitness, these consisting in the main of gym-based activities for younger inmates. Only one, W2 (71), reported that "I was able to keep physically active. If I had chosen to, I could have done nothing, but I kept fit and well … lots of walking and calisthenics, press ups and those types of things."

While a small group numerically, the elderly, with chronic ailments, use up a vastly disproportionate amount of prison time and resources. But on such occasions, there is no relenting on security precautions, however unnecessary such concerns might appear to be:

> I went to the hospital [outside prison] twice. I had a cataract removed too… I used to look forward to going out on these trips … here I am, though, half crippled with two prison officers with me all the time. One day I had three prison officers with me
>
> (W4, 83)

12.1.3 The pains of being out of place and out of time

The necessary adjustments they had to make to prison life became symptomatic of the heavily brutalized world in which they now found themselves. Norms and expectations exterior to the prison were reversed, overturned, or distorted:

> we only had small yards to wander around and exercise in. Getting supplied with food was really disgusting. They would put your tray outside your door and then someone would come through and your cup of tea would be in a plastic container which they had taken out of the prison urn, which must have had tomato sauce or something and the sauce gets into the plastic … there was only one chair in the cell and one prisoner had to sit on the toilet to eat his meal while the other sat on the chair
>
> (W4, 83).

These "broken asses" were thus out of place in this world that had been constructed on the assumption that all inmates would be mobile and able to move around large, multi-storied buildings that have no lifts, move from wing to wing to work without difficulty, and so on. And it was a world where, when not being directly threatened themselves, the elderly were constantly subjected to displays of highly aggressive masculinity. The bedlam of life on the wings was described as follows:

> a pretty awful experience because the other guys would scream and shout and kick the door and have their radios going all night at full blast
>
> (W5, 87).

But the elderly were also out of time. Because of their age, there was very little work. This had the additional consequence of them not being able to earn any extra money to supplement the prison diet, buy toiletries, put money on their phone cards, and so on, as employed inmates were able to do. A1 (71) thus said that "there was nothing for older people. I was a cleaner in the medical unit for a while." W4 (83) spent his time "cleaning the toilets and the concrete tables in the yard."

There was little else by way of mental stimulation. The educational programmes that were provided were of the most basic kind, suitable only for the barely literate. Elderly prisoners, though, as the survey confirms, tend to have a significantly higher standard of education—38.7% of the New Zealand respondents had completed their secondary school education and another 8% had graduated from university. The interviewees commented, for example, that

> there were no programmes except one that I went on which was not really necessary—a Maths and English course. I did that at [X prison] mainly to get out of the cell ... the woman [that is the teacher] didn't even know how to do fractions
>
> (W4, 83).

It became imperative to get out of mainstream as soon as possible. Some opted to be placed in segregation for their own safety, although they then found that this further restricted their opportunities to do anything at all:

> there was nothing to do but read ... we were often locked in our cells 22 hours per day in segregation
>
> (W3, 70).

> we were locked up an awful lot. We had a meal at 3.30 pm and then we were locked up from 4.30 in the evening until 8.30 the next morning. Then we had breakfast and we were allowed out into the small yard until we had lunch at 11.00 am
>
> (W5, 87).

The latter comment also illustrates the "other-worldliness" of the prison—dinner at 3.30 pm and so on. This unique timetabling suits the shift changeovers of prison officers but has no correspondence with mealtimes beyond the institution, making adjustment to it for first time elderly prisoners particularly difficult.

A much better option than segregation, however, was for them to seek sanctuary in the limited areas within the New Zealand prison system that can provide this: Faith Based Units, the most widespread of these, high dependency units or a small (around 100 beds) sex offenders' prison. In these carefully guarded spaces, despite watching and circling predatory inmates waiting at their boundaries, prison life was transformed into something much more like a care home for the elderly or a hospice since it also housed those who would die in prison. These sites were also staffed by much more sympathetic prison officers and medical staff:

> what was good about it [the high dependency unit] was that they had caregivers looking after us and they had a nurse who was available more or less on tap … the other prisoners were of a similar age to [to me] (W4, 83).

> the hours were better there [the high dependency unit]. We were allowed out of our cells at 6.30 am and then locked up about 8.00 pm which was really good. You could wander around, you could go back to your cell by yourself and have a sleep and you could lock other prisoners out from getting into your room to annoy you … they were single cells with a shower (W4, 83).

> At [the sex offenders' prison], three of us had to be first in the queue for the dining room because we all ate slowly and we were always there. There's things they did like that, and they gave me a job out there in a little garden (H2, 77).

Behavior problems in these settings were likely to be managed by means of medical supervision rather than penal restraints:

> there was one in [the high dependency unit] who was quite bad with dementia. He relies on the girls [nurses] at all times. They take him by the hand and get him organized and tell him it's time to go to bed now and of course, once they get him in there they lock the door on him … He threw a couple of punches at me one day but he was harmless after that … he's been like it for a number of years. He was in there for sex offending (W4, 83).

Furthermore, inmates were now able to help each other rather than having to be constantly on guard against attack, exploitation, or abuse:

> I used to help another old prisoner to shower and that … he used to collapse and he would wet himself and his bed, and for some reason the prison authorities had the idea that he was putting it all on (H2, 77).

> There was one chap in a wheelchair ... I used to down and get him and bring him out for his meals and have a yarn [chat] with him ... but he died on me while we were in there ... we had three that passed away in the period I was up there [three years]. One chap, we didn't have much to do with him. He was a little bit mental, I think.
>
> (W4, 83).

However, these specialized areas of the prison system became not just the most anxiety free part of their sentence but, for many, the most anxiety free part of what remained of their lives.

12.1.4 The pains of release

This was because the pains of imprisonment do not end on release from prison. At the end of their sentence, most had to face up to a new series of concerns related to living alone in a world in which they no longer had any legitimate place. The nature of their offences was likely to have permanently severed existing family relationships:

> Interviewer: "Sounds like relationships with the kids are not so good?"
>
> No, not so good, especially with my daughter and eldest son because the eldest son is the father of my [victim]
>
> (W4, 83).

> One of the conditions of parole is that I'm not allowed to have anything to do with anybody under 16. Well, I've got six grandchildren and 7 great-grandchildren. Four of those are under 16 but I've not seen any of them
>
> (W5, 87).

In practical terms, this meant not mere deprivation of family relationships during their sentence but permanent loss with virtually no possibility, because of their age and circumstances, of rebuilding these on release. W4 (83) who had been married for 58 years, said that the couple had separated after he was sentenced—"the kids got onto her and you know ...". While H1 (71), who had had a wife and six children, was in prison, he was served with a non-molestation order and the bank foreclosed on his house. To receive any housing assistance from the local council on release, he would have to prove he was destitute—but his receipt of a state pension (his only income) precluded this.

While they may thus have regained their sense of physical security on release, their "loss of goods and services, freedom, heterosexual/family relationships, and personal autonomy" did not suddenly materialize for them in the post-prison world:

> it has been a lot harder than I thought. When you're in prison, everything's done for you. Now I'm on my own, and I've got to do my own shopping, cooking and so on, I've found that [since being released], it's much more demanding
>
> (W5, 87).

> it has a bit of a shock when you get out ... the money went straight away. I wasn't sure what was what because of the changes
>
> (W4, 83).

This inmate is referring to the savings he had managed to make while in prison (this would have been very little since standard pay for prisoner labor, if they are working, is only around $20 per week) and a discharge grant of $NZ350, although they cannot claim any social welfare benefits in the first two weeks of release. Yet they had received very little advice about future planning while incarcerated despite—or perhaps because of—the enormity of the challenges they would be facing at the end of their sentence. As W1 (76) put the matter, that "you don't think much about release. All you think of is your own safety while you're there."

For nearly all the New Zealand interviewees (only two of the 10 had resumed living with their spouses/partners), the reality of their lives after release differed greatly from the whimsical expectations of what it would be like for those in the survey population. These aspirations had included "meeting friends" (58.1%), "going shopping" (46.8%), "eating what they wanted" (48.4%), and watching whatever TV programmes they wanted (43.5%). In reality, the most urgent concern on release was finding somewhere to live (they were likely to have lost their homes and much of what savings they might have had as well as family relationships during their sentence). In New Zealand, the provision of material after-care assistance has been contracted out to charities such as the Salvation Army by the Department of Corrections. These charitable organizations, though, offer only short-term accommodation, usually for three months. Furthermore, it is virtually impossible for released prisoners to obtain state housing: much of this has been sold off in recent years and their criminal records anyway preclude them from what little is available. Hence the extreme precariousness of their position on release. W5 (87), released on parole, had been in his hostel for thirteen weeks at the time of interview, which meant that

> I've only got 2 more weeks to go here and after that I've got nowhere to go to yet ... because I've been to prison, people don't want to have anything to do with me.

The best he could hope for was to be returned to prison for breach of parole conditions that being homeless would constitute.

Furthermore, the localities they could move to were restricted because of their offences. W5 (87), planning to live with his sister-in-law when released, found that probation had prevented this "because three or four houses back onto hers and one of them has got children in it."

And even in approved localities, personal autonomy – whom they could see, where they could go etc. – was not suddenly reinvested in them.

> I can't go anywhere near schools. I can't go to a sports venue because there's usually children there, no matter what event it is. I can't go to the swimming pool or anything like that ... theoretically, I can't go anywhere and that's the biggest problem
>
> (W4, 83).

> "I'm not allowed to be in any vicinity where children would be. Obviously, in a church, there are kids there ..." (W3, 70, even though, while in prison, he had been involved in a bible correspondence school).

> I'm not allowed to go near parks, I'm not allowed to go near schools [but] I've never had anything to do with kids in parks, or schools or anything like that
>
> (W5, 87).

While two of the interviewees had been able to return to their spouses and family homes, what kind of life remained for the rest? Some had found solace through religion during the course of their imprisonment and, even though they were prohibited from attending church on release, they continued to participate in local bible study groups. This apart, there was little else left by way of companionship. Their lives had become mere shells, with hopes for a better future all but eliminated. One step from destitution, because of their lack of income, lack of employability, lack of family support, and because of their age and difficulties in finding accommodation, they now found themselves shunned and shut out even by those who themselves had been pushed into the fragile, insecure world that a room in Salvation Army lodging houses offered.

> because of the nature of the conviction [indecent photographs of his stepdaughter], nobody speaks to me. When I'm home at night and I'm alone, I don't have a TV in my room—there's a TV in the lounge but you're surrounded by cigarette smoking, beer drinking, dole-bludging idiots so I don't go in there. So all I can do is sit at my computer, watch you tube videos, something like that, and I just cry. It's terrible
>
> (A1, 71).

12.2 Conclusion

The Society of Captives was written in an era when aggression, threat, provocation, and sometimes lethal violence had become characteristics of prison life, the product of inmate culture in, at least, US maximum security institutions. In the early 21st century, however, elderly prisoners constitute the big growth area in prison populations. Now, the acute dynamics that characterize so much of mainstream prison life—the sudden eruption of violence, security searches, tension between inmates and officers—exist alongside the chronic problems of the elderly: climbing stairs, digesting food, occupying time, their need for access to showers and toilets outside the allotted hours. As their numbers grow, these chronic problems will grow with them, soaking up increasingly disproportionately large parts of prison resources.

This includes the growth of specialist units because the chances of elderly prisoners surviving mainstream prison unscathed are very limited. These units are then attuned to their health, mobility, and other problems, and are where life is lived at a very different pace from the rest of the prison estate. While there may still be violence in these settings, this is more likely to be the product of dementia rather than a prisoner on prisoner vendetta or standover.

What then extends the particular pains of the elderly inmates beyond the prison is the uncertain fate that awaits so many of them on release. In New Zealand, they are likely to spend the remainder of their lives dependent on short-term emergency accommodation as their health continues to deteriorate – usually exacerbated by their time in prison.

Notes

1 This chapter is an abridged version of a chapter with the same title that is published in Crewe, B., Goldsmith, A. and Halsey, M. (eds) (2022), *Power and Pain in the Modern Prison: The Society of Captives Revisited*, Oxford: Oxford University Press.

2 At the time of the survey, there was only one woman in the New Zealand prison system who was aged 65 or over, and she declined to be involved.

References

Crawley, E., and Sparks, R. (2005) 'Hidden Injuries? Researching the Experiences of Older Men in English Prisons', *Howard Journal of Criminal Justice*, 44(4), pp. 345–356.

Department of Corrections (2016) Annual Report to Parliament, Wellington: Government Printer.

McCarthy, C. (2005) *No Country for Old Men*, New York: Anchor Books.

Sykes, G. (1957; 2007) *The Society of Captives: A Study of a Maximum Security Prison*, Princeton, NJ: Princeton University Press.

Van Zyl Smit, D. and Appleton, C. (2016) Life Imprisonment and Human Rights, Oxford: Bloomsbury.

13 The State of Elderly Criminals in Australia

Takashi Furukawa

Otemon Gakuin University, Japan

13.1 Purpose of this chapter

One factor behind the increasing number of elderly criminals is population aging. According to criminal justice statistics, Australia exhibits a similar increasing trend in the number of criminal offenses committed by the elderly as in Japan (Figure 13.1, ABS Website). Simultaneously, the trend should not be understood simply by numbers, because the aging of criminals reflects various other changes in social background aside from population aging. For example, compared to Japan, Australia has better support programs for criminal offenders to reintegrate into society, yet the two countries share the same increasing tendency for elderly criminals. This requires examining other factors, such as the trend in offender rehabilitation. With this in mind, in this chapter, I will provide an overview and consideration of elderly criminals' situation in Australia.

13.2 Aging and social security situation in Australia

13.2.1 Aging population and regional disparities

Here, the population aging process is reviewed according to relevant statistical data from the Australian government. The nation entered an aging society in 1937, when the population aged 65 and above reached 7.04%, which gradually increased and reached 14.18% in 2012 (Figure 13.2, ABS website). The average life expectancy is 80 years and above. Two waves in population policy lie beneath Australia's population aging characteristics. The first wave was gradual population growth after the Australian Federation's establishment in 1901, and the second wave occurred with the acceptance of immigrants after World War II and during the 1980s. Recent population growth has mainly focused on adults, who are considered immigrants. In contrast, the birth rate increase in the youth population remains low compared to the increase in the population aging rate, accelerating the progression of an aging society.

Geographically, there are regional disparities in population sparsity and density over vast land areas. Tasmania and South Australia have the highest

DOI: 10.4324/9781032669519-17

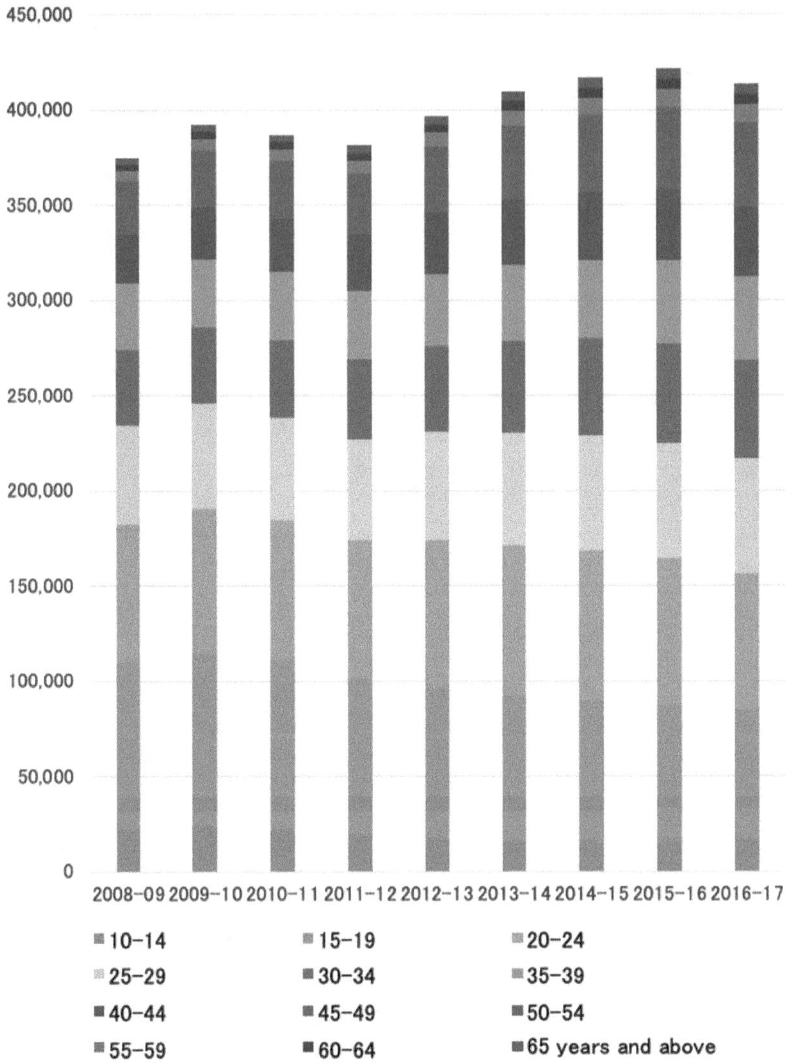

Figure 13.1 Changes in proportions of arrests for criminal offenses by age groups.
Source: ABS Recorded Crimes.

aging populations with low population densities. In contrast, states with metropolitan areas, such as Victoria, exhibit a high rate of population aging and a high population density, indicating a disparity between the metropolitan area and other areas within the state (Table 13.1). In other words, aging in Australia is a combination of aging due to depopulation and aging as an urban problem.

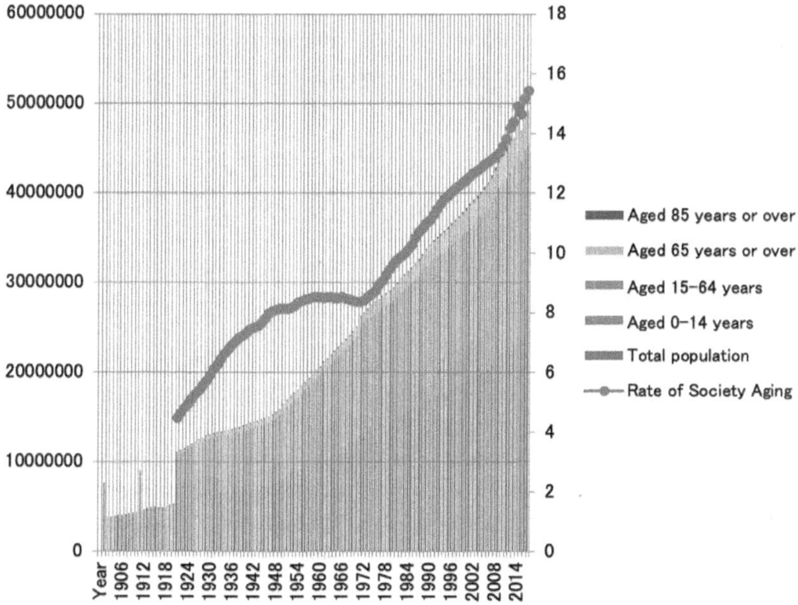

Figure 13.2 Changes in population in three age groups.

Source: ABS Australian Demographic Statistic.

Table 13.1 Aging of the population by state (2017)

	Total	*Aged rate (%)*	*Population density*
New South Wales	7739274	15.73	9.56
Victoria	6179249	15.04	26
Queensland	4848877	14.72	2.62
South Australia	1713054	17.7	1.64
Western Australia	2558951	13.54	0.97
Tasmania	517588	18.73	5.7
Northern Territory	245740	6.87	0.18
Australian Capital Territory	403468	12.19	1711
Other Territories	4608	15.1	67.76

ABS formulated using Australian demographic statistical data (ABS, 2017a).

13.2.2 *Australian social security*

Australia's social security has traditionally operated as a benefit from public financial resources based on income recognition under the remaining influence of the United Kingdom's social security system, the former colonial power. Simultaneously, recent reforms have combined public and private financial resources. The primary management policy is to improve the system's universal social life guarantee and provide consultation support (personal social work) according to individual circumstances, emphasizing respect for individuals. The system is under the jurisdiction of the Department of Human Services (DHS) and provides various services, including care service benefits for physical and mental disabilities, income compensation, pensions, family allowances, and livelihood protection.

Benefits for the elderly include financial assistance for older Australians, which consists of an old-age pension system (Age Pension), a transition service to the old-age pension, a widow's benefit, a pension loan, and a care benefit for the disabled, along with the aid for healthcare expenses and other government and community services (Australian Government Department of Social Services, 2017).

However, these benefit-oriented services have increased expenses, putting pressure on government finances since the 1990s, leading to an economic recession, resulting in stricter system management for income certificates and a shift to the third way (so-called welfare to workfare) of Anthony Giddens. This has led to the introduction of public-private partnerships in the pension system while maintaining the benefits of health care and long-term care services for persons with disabilities. Today, pensions for the elderly are provided for people aged 65 and above in a two-story system consisting of an old-age pension and a retirement pension fund[1].

13.2.3 Pension system and employment policy

The public pension system consists of pensions for persons with disabilities and survivor benefits in addition to pensions for the elderly. The Aged Pension was established in 1908 as the world's first noncontributory (tax-funded) benefit. Today, it operates in combination with other pensions, such as corporate pensions, and the requirements for receiving benefits and asset surveys have become stricter. The benefits are for men aged 65 and above and women aged 63 and above, and beneficiaries receive 25-40% of the average income according to asset survey results. The age at which benefits begin is scheduled to increase to 67 years for both men and women by 2023. If beneficiaries are found to have additional income from employment or asset management according to the asset survey, their benefit amount will be reduced, so that the minimum standard of living of elderly people with low income should be guaranteed.

According to the ABS analysis, 94 million people aged 45 and above had regular jobs in 2016-17, of which 49 million, accounting for 52% of the total, worked for two weeks. Simultaneously, 36 million people retired or left their jobs. Among the elderly, 64% of those aged 65 to 69, and 82% of those aged 70 and above, have left their jobs or retired (ABS, 2017b).

13.2.4 Household composition and residence

Regarding the elderly's living conditions, most men and women owned homes as of 2016. The increase in single-person households is remarkable in the

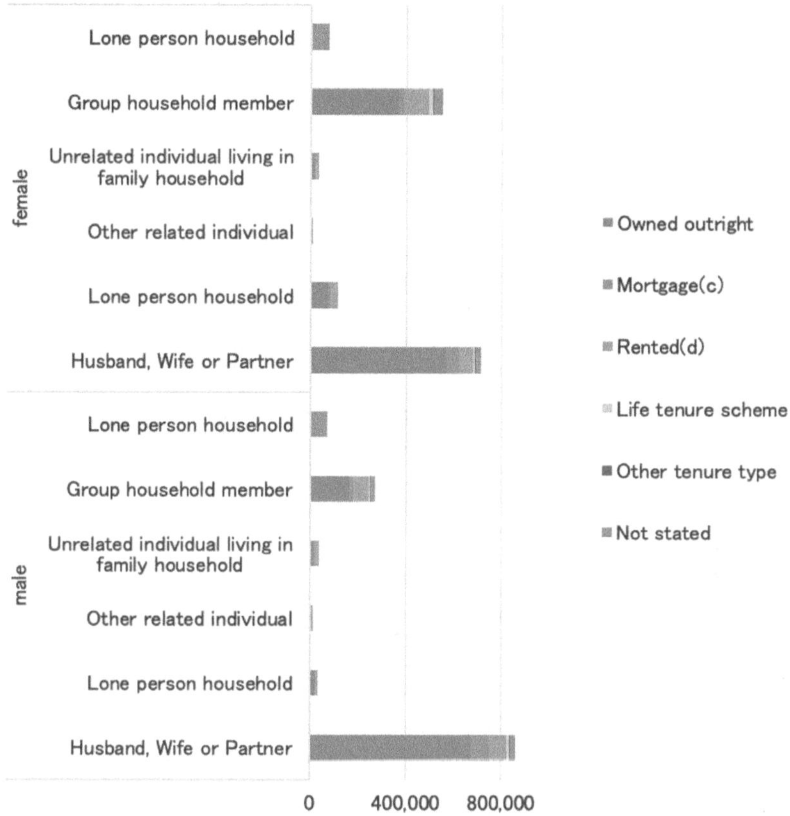

Figure 13.3 Household composition and proportion of elderly people by residence types (2016).

Source: ABS Census of Population and Housing.

household composition of those aged 65 years and above. More than 15% of men and 25% of women for early-stage elderly (65-74 years old), and more than 20% of men and 55% of women for late-stage elderly (75 years and over) live in single-person households (Figure 13.3)[2]. In addition, the federal government provides rent subsidies to low-income earners living in private housing.

Flood (2005) investigated the situation of single-person households and their isolation using the results of a large-scale living statistics survey called the Household, Income, and Labour Dynamics in Australia (HILDA). He found the levels of personal support and the presence/absence of friends would decline for women aged from 35 to 54, but rise again after age 55, and then decline again after age 65. As for men, the levels would be at the lowest during ages 19 to 40, then rise gradually. In other words, social relationships associated with work and care from others are vital for households of singles in their 30s and 40s (Flood, 2005).

In addition, many elderly people in need of long-term care moved into nursing homes up to the 1980s, and community care was being developed to enable elderly people to live at home using medical care services provided by the community-based health care system.

13.3 Situation of elderly criminals

13.3.1 Increase in elderly crimes

Research on elderly crimes in Australia began approximately 20 years ago (ABS, 2005). Here, an overview of elderly crime in Australia is outlined based on data available on the websites of the Australian Institute of Criminology (AIC) and the Australian Bureau of Statistics (ABS). Some corrections were made to the data based on statistical data.

As shown earlier in Figure 13.1, the changes in the number of arrests by police for criminal offenses according to age group exhibit a gradual increase in offenders aged 65 and above. Compared to the rate of change in minor offenders, the rate for elderly offenders shows a striking contrast (Figure 13.4).

Looking at the trends in crime types from the results of 2016 to 2017, sexual assault was the most dominant among offenders aged 65 and above, accounting for 8.29% of all age groups, followed by homicide at 6.62%, other crimes at 3.39%, and possession of illegal firearms at 2.86% (Figure 13.5)[3].

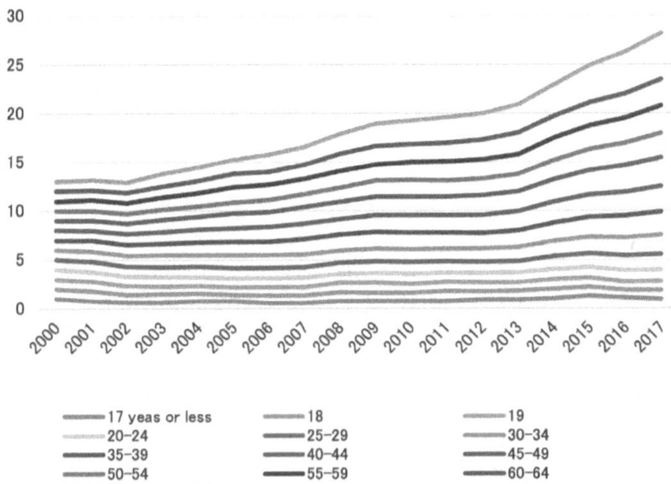

Figure 13.4 Changes in the number of criminal offenders by age groups with the base value of 1 at 2000.

Source: ABS Recorded Crimes

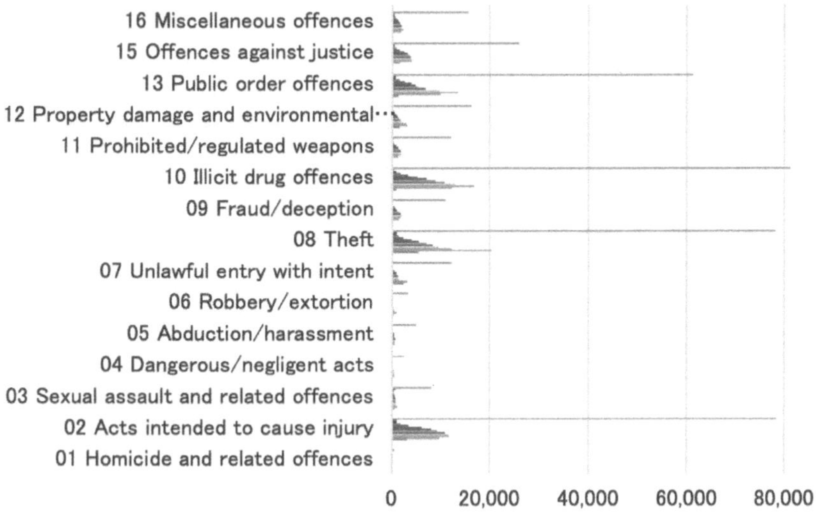

Figure 13.5 Proportions of criminal offenders aged 65 and above by crime types.
Source: ABS Recorded Crimes

13.3.2 Factors behind the increase in elderly crimes

The proportion of elderly inmates in penal institutions in Australia exhibits an increasing trend along with a progressive aging in prison populations (Figure 13.6, Australian Institute of Criminology, 1997–2007; Department of Justice, 2017). Grant (1999) argued the following three factors as causes: aging during imprisonment, aging due to re-offending, and aging due to prolonged sentences. He then investigated the impact of aging inmates on the operation of penal institutions and insisted on the necessity of proper treatment standards and staff training according to the characteristics of elderly inmates (Grant, 1999).

According to an analysis by Baidawi et al., elderly inmates can be divided into the following four types:

- Cases of first offenders being imprisoned for the first time in old age
- Cases of habitual criminals or those who have previously been imprisoned being imprisoned again
- Cases of long-term prisoners who are aging during imprisonment
- Cases of offenders imprisoned for a short period as they grow old

They also identify other distinct groups, including elderly female inmates[4] and indigenous inmates such as Aborigines (Cameron, 2001). They find that the issues of prison administration are, first, health problems; second, mental health and adaptation; and third, treatment cost increases. Regarding other

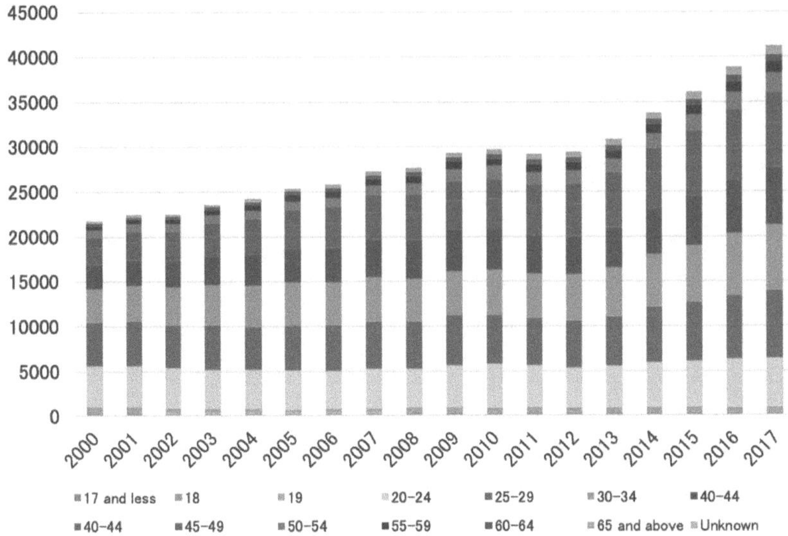

Figure 13.6 Changes in the number of inmates by age group.

Source: ABS Recorded Crimes.

relevant issues in comparison with the research in the UK, they indicate that the fourth issue is the prison environment; the fifth is the sustainability of prison correction; the sixth is the social vulnerability of elderly inmates; the seventh is release and rehabilitation; eighth is the response to particular needs such as nursing and hospice care in prison; and the last is issues of the internal treatment itself, including staff structure, treatment programs, and early release such as parole (Baidawi et al., 2011).

The above suggests not only a direct motive for crime but also a link to elderly criminals' social adaptation. For example, in the housing type shown in Figure 13.3, the more the household compositions are not married couples, the less often the housing types are owned houses, suggesting that households of this type are economically vulnerable to living conditions in complicated social relationships. Furthermore, this may relate to the increase in the number of residents with various cultural backgrounds and the status of social security benefits, but we do not pursue this topic further here.

13.3.3 Relationship with social treatment

Compared with Japan, Australia has a better community correction system for the treatment of criminals. Background factors for the recent emphasis on community corrections include prison overcrowding, criminal convict treatment depending on imprisonment, in-prison treatment inclined toward harsh labor, and financial and spatial limitations regarding criminal treatments.

The system of community corrections with various programs and providers was introduced in response to the situation above as part of the privatization test of the criminal justice system (McCarthy et al., 2000, p. 8).

Social treatment has targeted first-time offenders since the 19th century and has been an essential part of the criminal justice system since a relatively early stage. Paroles and probation in each state would be established through cooperation between the court and police. In Queensland, for example, the Offender Probation Act was enacted in 1886 as part of criminal policy reform, and probation for first-time offenders began. The security situation deteriorated with a rapid increase in the prison population, and there were limitations on what the law enforcement authorities could do; thus, the Parole Act 1937 was enacted.

Later, the need arose to treat sex offenders, leading to the 1945 revision of the Criminal Code that added a probation period for sex offenders, who would be put under probation based on medical and psychological guidance and assessment after release from penal institutes. At first, the probation officer in charge of each case provided guidance. In response to the increase in probation subjects and to enforce the probation system, the Offenders Probation and Parole Act was submitted to the parliament in 1959. From the 1960s to the 1970s, the just deserts model, based on the rehabilitation support of guidance, monitoring, and reward programs, was introduced throughout the federation, and the number of people receiving social guidance increased as a result. In the 1980s, however, the effect of crime prevention measures relying on imprisonment at penal institutions was questioned because of the deterioration of public security despite the budget increase in criminal policy, leading to a trend of enforcing probation programs. In Queensland, social treatment began to change drastically, as exemplified by the enactment of the Social Service Order Program in 1981; the Offenders Probation and Parole Act was revised in 1986, including not allowing fines. Consequently, social treatment, such as social service orders, became a standard treatment for minor offenses. In the 1990s, new technologies such as drug tests and electronic monitoring were adopted, and the content of social treatment increased. In addition, administrative reforms are being promoted amid financial deterioration, and privatization is growing.

The transition described above has been considered a shift in the treatment of criminals who served relatively short detention periods in penal institutions to social treatment, such as probation at a local probation center after release from prison (AIC2008). The author views it differently: first, it provides criminals with much larger opportunities to reintegrate into society and not just a change in criminal punishment; second, it suggests a difference in awareness regarding the supporting staff as well as the organization of social treatment and treatment of criminals based on it; and third, it emphasizes an ideal pattern of community networks. In addition, community care or welfare activities in the local community, such as medical care services, should be the basis for community corrections.

However, the increase in the number of elderly inmates in recent years could be a reflection of changes in the general public's view of crime and politics. It is also possible that community members have become stricter about accepting those with criminal records. For example, the introduction of the Crimes and Other Legislation Amendment (Assault and Intoxication) Act (commonly known as the one punch law) in 2016 in New South Wales could have been influenced by penal populism, as Quiler suggested (Quiler, 2014).

Regarding the social treatment of sex offenders, practical examples of treatment measures targeting elderly criminals, such as community corrections, long-term cognitive-behavioral therapy, and collective treatment attempts in self-help groups, have not yet been identified.

As for the rehabilitation of elderly criminals, their age could be a hindrance to their reintegration into the community, which is probably a cause of the increase in elderly criminals. In addition, a possible correlation between multiple recidivism and excessive reliance on criminals' welfare benefits has been suggested (Giles, 2016; Sherman et al., 2000).

13.4 Conclusion

Studies have suggested the recent increase in criminal offenses by the elderly in Australia is related to changes in social environments, such as increased acceptance of immigrants and social security system reforms. Here, various possible factors for the increase in elderly crimes are discussed, and the author believes that a single factor has not made a decisive contribution to the current situation. Thus, it should be understood as a manifestation of relevant changes in the criminal justice system, as well as changes in the society itself, in which they participate.

Notes

1 The Japanese pension system was established as a social insurance system based on occupation, and the national pension is its primary benefit. However, many people are not eligible to receive this; it is supplemented by the livelihood protection system. In addition, the premiums for public long-term care insurance and medical insurance for people aged 75 years and above are deducted from the pension, resulting in an income decrease in elderly households; some receive nothing. This insufficient social security system is one of the causative factors of the increase in the number of elderly criminals in Japan.
2 Looking at the crime damage situation of the elderly, house invasion and robbery were the most frequent.
3 Most cases involving physical violence from alcohol abuse, which is punishable by law, were committed by young adults. As far as I could tell, there was no connection with criminal cases committed by the elderly. However, in Australia, where the rate of violent and sexual crimes is high, there is intense criticism of violence, especially against that induced by alcohol abuse, and according to Ticehurst, approximately 3% of the population aged 65 and above are alcoholics. Concerns about the situation exist, and some argue that drastic measures are necessary, including medical and judicial interventions (Ticehurst, 1990).
4 As of 2017, 1,017 men and 26 women aged 65 years and above were inmates.

References

Australian Bureau of Statistics (ABS). (2017a) *Census of Population and Housing*. Available at www.abs.gov.au/AUSSTATS/abs@.nsf/DetailsPage/2071.02016?OpenDocument.

ABS. (2017b) *Retirement and Retirement Intentions, Australia, July 2016 to June 2017*. Available at http://www.abs.gov.au/ausstats/abs@.nsf/mf/6238.0.

ABS. (2005) Crime And Safety, Australia. Available at http://www.abs.gov.au.

Australian Government Department of Social Services. (2017) *Review of Australia's Welfare System*. Available at www.dss.gov.au/review-of-australias-welfare-system.

Australian Institute of Criminology (1997–2007), *Crime Facts Info*. Available at www.aic.gov.au.

Baidawi, S., Turner, S., and Trotter, C., et al. (2011) 'Older Prisoners – A Challenge For Australian Corrections', *AIC Trend & Issues In Crime And Criminal Justice No.426* (PDF). https://www.aic.gov.au/publications/tandi/tandi426

Cameron, M. (2001) 'Women Prisoners and Correctional Programs', *Trends and Issues in Crime and Criminal Justice No.194*.

Department of Justice. (2017) Available at www.nt.gov.au/justice/corrservices/community_corrections/index.html.

Flood, M. (2005) Mapping Loneliness in Australia, The Australia Institute, Discussion paper No.76.

Giles, M. (2016) *Study in prison reduces recidivism and welfare dependence: A case study from Western Australia 2005–2010*.

McCarthy, C., Lincoln, R., and Wilson, P. (2000) Privatising Community Corrections: Report for Families, Youth and Community Care, Queensland, Humanities & Social Sciences paper, Centre for Applied Psychology and Criminology, Bond University.

Quiler, J. (2014) 'One-Punch Laws, Mandatory Minimums And 'Alcohol- Fuelled' As An Aggravating Factor: Implications For NSW Criminal Law', *IJCJ & SD*, 3(1), pp. 81–106. Available at www.crimejusticejournal.com.

Sherman, L.W., and Strang, H., et al., (2000) Recidivism Pattern in the Canberra Reintegrative Shaming Experiments (RISE), Centre for Restorative Justice, Research School of Social Sciences, Institute of Advanced Studies, Australian National University. .

Ticehurst, S. (1990) 'Alcohol and the Elderly', *Australian and New Zealand Journal of Psychiatry*, 24(2), pp. 252–260. https://journals.sagepub.com/doi/pdf/10.3109/00048679009077690.

14 Older Prisoners in New South Wales, Australia

Phillip Snoyman

Department of Justice NSW, Australia

Elena Cama, Eileen Baldry, and Carla Treloar

University of New South Wales, Australia

14.1 Background

The number of older prisoners in custodial settings is rising in Australia and elsewhere (e.g., see Beck and Harrison, 2001; LeMesurier et al., 2010; NZDC, 2010; Sabol and West, 2010). The proportion of prisoners in prisons in the state of NSW prisons who are 50 years and older increased 76% between 2000 and 2010 (Stavrou, 2017). The rise may also be attributed to a range of factors, including advances in technology (e.g., DNA matching) enabling police to close historical offences, changes in legislation introducing mandatory sentencing and standard non-parole period, and the increasing number of sex offenders identified in the various Inquiries and Commissions held across Australia over the past decade (Ginnivan et al., 2018).

There is no consensus as to what constitutes an "older prisoner," with age brackets ranging from 45 years and above, to 65 years and above (Baidawi et al., 2011; Turner and Trotter, 2010). The United Nations Handbook on Prisoners with Special Needs (United Nations Office on Drugs and Crime, 2009) notes prisoners' ageing is accelerated due to "chronic health problems, unhealthy lifestyles, alcohol and substance abuse, as well as the stressful effects of imprisonment itself" (p. 123). According to the most recent survey on prisoner health, mental health, tobacco smoking, and alcohol and illicit drug use were health concerns among Australian prisoners (Australian Institute of Health and Welfare, 2019). Almost one-third (29%) of all prisoners, reported having a long-term health condition or disability that limited their participation in daily activities, or education and employment, with a significantly higher rate (42%) of those aged 45 and over reporting disability, three times the rate in the general population (Australian Institute of Health and Welfare, 2019).

Further, the health of Indigenous prisoners remained a significant concern (Australian Institute of Health and Welfare, 2019). The life expectancy for Aboriginal and Torres Strait Islander (Indigenous) people more broadly is estimated at 10.6 years lower than non-indigenous Australians (Australian Institute of Health and Welfare, 2018). Taking this into consideration,

DOI: 10.4324/9781032669519-18

"older prisoners" in Corrective Services NSW are Indigenous people aged over 45 years or Non-Indigenous people aged over 55 years. The differences in definition based on whether the individual is Indigenous or not results in a higher representation of Indigenous prisoners in the older cohort than would otherwise be expected. Although Indigenous people represent around 2% of the general adult population, they are overrepresented in the criminal justice system at 27% of the prisoner population (Australian Institute of Health and Welfare, 2015), but the inclusion of a younger age bracket results in a further overrepresentation of Indigenous people in the older prisoner cohort. While acknowledging this tension, this definition has been adopted to account for the younger life expectancy among Indigenous Australians (Australian Institute of Health and Welfare, 2018). Treating older prisoners as a homogenous group risks neglecting the nuances in individual needs and characteristics (Heckenberg, 2006), and therefore chronological age should not be treated as the sole indicator of these needs and characteristics (Yorston and Taylor, 2006).

14.2 Method

Demographic data were collected from weekly internal Corrective Services NSW (CSNSW) reports compiled by NSW Corrections Research Evaluations and Statistics. The data were collated for one financial year (2017/18) and analyzed using IBM SPSS software (version 19).

Data and analyses from a survey conducted with elderly prisoners in NSW prisons in 2018 are also presented. Surveys were provided to prisoners meeting the definition of older prisoners.

14.3 Results

On a single day in December 2018, there were 12973 sentenced and unsentenced prisoners in NSW. Of these prisoners, 11.85% fit the NSW definition of older prisoners: 29.8% of these were Indigenous and 5.1% were female. There was a reduced number of older females in prison indicating either that females desist from crime earlier than males or possibly reflecting the higher prevalence of older males in prison.

Overall, the average age of older prisoners in the sample was 58.66 years (with a standard deviation [SD] of 8.6), with females being on average 5.1 years younger (53.9 years, SD 6.6) than males (59.0 years SD 8.6). The average age of older Indigenous prisoners was 51.1 years (SD 5.6) and non-Indigenous prisoners was 62.6 (SD 7.1) with 39.2% of older prisoners incarcerated for the first time (Table 14.1).

The average age at which older prisoners entered prison for their current incarceration was 55.3 years (range: 19–87 years).

The oldest male was 90 years old and oldest female in prison was 77 years old. The oldest Indigenous prisoner was 86 years old.

Table 14.1 Percentage of prisoners by age category (most recent incarceration)

Age when currently incarcerated	*Whole Aged cohort*	*Indigenous (45 years and older) 14.3% of all Indigenous prisoners*	*Percentage of prisoners*			
			Indigenous (55 years and older) 2.6% of all Indigenous prisoners	*Non-Indigenous (55 years and older) 9% of all non-Indigenous prisoners*	*Males*	*Females*
45–49 years	10%	21%	6%	5%	10%	11%
50–54 years	28%	66%	10%	10%	28%	44%
55–59 years	51%	87%	36%	33%	50%	67%
60–64 years	76%	97%	82%	64%	74%	89%
65 years plus	88%	99%	94%	81%	87%	97%

Generally older prisoners are incarcerated for longer periods of time, with 12% receiving a sentence of 6-12 months; 10.8% a sentence of 1-2 years; 12.4% a sentence of 2-5 years; and almost 32% sentences greater than 5 years. Over 54% of older non-Indigenous prisoners received a sentence of 5 years or more as have almost 18.6% of older women. Only 8.8% of older prisoners have short sentences of less than 6 months, but 16.3% of older Indigenous prisoners fall into this category, as do 12% of older women.

The top five most serious offences (MSOs), in increasing order, for older prisoners (compared with younger prisoners) are presented in Table 14.2.

In comparison to younger prisoners, older prisoners are 4.4 times more likely to be in prison for "Sexual assault and related offences," and twice as likely to be in for homicide. However, younger people are 1.5 times more likely to be in prison for "Acts intended to cause injury" or "Offences against Justice Procedures, Government Security and Government Operations."

"Illicit drug offences" is the most common reason for older female prisoners (21%) to have been convicted (Figure 14.1). "Acts Intended to cause injury" is the highest MSO for young prisoners, both female (19.7%) and male (25%) and second highest for older female (17.3%) and older male (15.8%) prisoners.

An older offender is twice as likely to be in prison for "Homicide or related offences" for the first time compared with people who have a previous

Table 14.2 Comparison between younger and older offenders' MSO

Most serious offence category	*Younger*	*Older*
Homicide and related offences	4.6%	9.5%
Offences against Justice Procedures, Government Security and Government Operations	16.3%	10.5%
Illicit drug offences	12.5%	13.9%
Acts intended to cause injury	24.5%	15.9%
Sexual assault and related offences	6.9%	30.5%

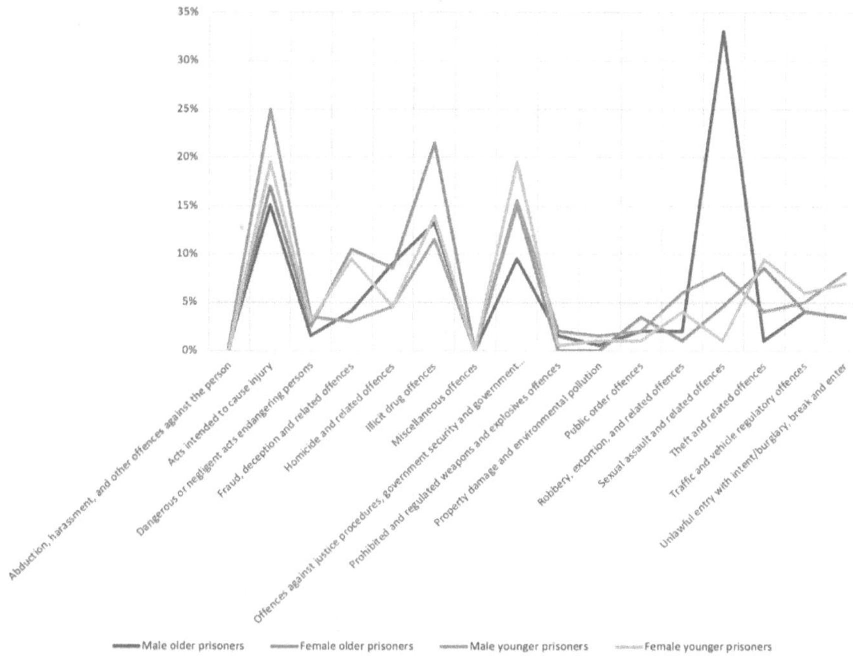

Figure 14.1 Most serious offence category used to describe male and female offence patterns across young and old cohorts.

incarceration (Table 14.3). "Offences against Justice Procedures, Government Security and Government Operations" are eight times less likely to be recorded as an MSO for first time prisoners. First-time older prisoners are almost twice as likely as repeat prisoners to have an MSO of 'Sexual assault and related offences'. These older prisoners may have committed offences decades earlier and are only now being convicted and incarcerated.

The Level of Service Inventory – Revised (LSI-R) is an assessment tool designed to classify a person's risk of general or violent reoffending (not sexual

Table 14.3 MSO for older prisoners first versus repeated time in prison

MSO category	*First time in prison*	*Multiple custodies*
Homicide and related offences	13.4%	6.9%
Offences against Justice Procedures, Government Security and Government Operations	2%	15.9%
Illicit drug offences	15.6%	12.8%
Acts Intended to cause injury	7.7%	21.2%
Sexual assault and related offences	45.6%	20.7%

reoffending) and to identify his or her criminogenic needs (Andrews and Bonta, 1995). Overall, using the LSI-R, 43% of older prisoners have a low risk of reoffending compared to 25% of younger prisoners, and 24% of older prisoners have a high risk of reoffending compared to 37% of younger prisoners. As so many of the older prisoners and fewer young prisoners have committed sex offences, caution should be exercised when using LSI-R scores to predict reoffending for older offenders.

Using the Static-99 Assessment tool for sexual offences, older prisoners are still estimated to have a significantly lower risk of reoffending (28.8% in the medium high to high range compared to 57.9% for younger prisoners).

14.4 Preliminary survey analysis

Preliminary data are presented here from 284 surveys which were completed and returned to the researchers. 91% of the sample identified as male, 2.5% (n=7) identified as female, and 1 identified as transgender. Of those who provided information about their age, (118/284, 42%), the mean age was approximately 65 years for non-Indigenous prisoners and 52 years for Indigenous prisoners. 25% of prisoners identified as Indigenous. 44% had 10 years or less of formal schooling; 7.4% reported highest level of education as completion of secondary school. 24% had a tertiary diploma (trade certificate) while 15% reported undergraduate or postgraduate qualifications. The average age at most recent incarceration was 55 years with a range of 15-85 years. The length of sentence was determined by the longest sentence provided (if there was a minimum and maximum sentence recorded by the participant). The most reported length of sentence was 10 years or more (30%) with a further 19% reporting sentences of more than 5 and less than 10 years. A further 19% did not know their sentence length (for example, the participant was on remand). Fewer participants reported shorter sentences: 11.5% reported sentences of 12 months or less; 4% reported 13-24 month sentences; 7% reported 25-36 month sentences; 4.4% reported 37-48 month sentences; and 5% reported 29-60 month sentences. Two thirds reported living with an illness (64%) and taking prescribed medications (66%). Approximately 6 in 10 prisoners described their current health as either "very good" or "not perfect but not ill often."

14.5 Discussion

Multiple disadvantages experienced by most prisoners prematurely age a person. Factors such as use of alcohol and other substances, lack of stable accommodation, financial hardships, lack of employment opportunities, and other disadvantages associated with poor self-health care all contribute to premature ageing. While this is probably the case, it is important to consider that almost 39%[1] of the non-Indigenous older inmate cohort are in prison for the first time and are unlikely to have experienced disadvantages associated with offending and incarceration. The definition of ageing should uniformly be considered as

65 years except for those prisoners with a prior history of incarceration where both Indigenous and non-Indigenous prisoners are considered older prisoners if 55 years or more. If such a definition was adopted, then 36% of older Indigenous prisoners would be in prison prior to age 55 (like non-Indigenous prisoners), but 82% would be incarcerated by age 60 (28% higher than non-Indigenous prisoners). The implication of this change in definition is that services and programs are more likely to be targeted to a smaller cohort who are more likely to benefit from them.

It may now be useful to discuss the issue of program (treatment) delivery. The most widely published empirical method of considering treatment is that of Risk, Need and Responsivity (RNR). According to the RNR model, the higher the risk of reoffending, the more intense the program and the greater the dosage (number of treatment interventions) required. Treatment should address the factors that drive offending (i.e., criminogenic need) such as criminal history, drug and other substance abuse, antisocial attitudes, and antisocial peers or support systems, to name a few. Finally, the treatment should maximize the inmate's learning style. Looking at the risk for this cohort, the LSI-R indicates that 43% should not get any treatment (aside from those who committed sex offences). Over half of the older sex offender cohort are also low-risk and therefore should not be involved in treatment. There is evidence, though, that this approach to assessing who should attend a program in prison and the very provision of programs in this way are not successful in rehabilitating prisoners. For example, despite the RNR and LSI-R being used for many years now, the recidivism rate across Australia, including in NSW has increased with over 60% of people being reconvicted of an offence within two years of being released from prison (Productivity Commission, 2021). That said, it is likely that a significant proportion of older prisoners will serve their time in prison without receiving a program to address their offending. For this cohort, punishment and deterrence of others are the primary intended outcome of incarceration, although there is no evidence that others or those who are in prison already, are deterred from offending by fear of being caught and going to or going back to prison (Pratt et al., 2008). Their mean age when they reach their earliest possible release date (EPRD) is 68 years with sex offenders being 69.3 years old. They are likely to be released to nursing homes rather than other accommodation in the community. The remaining prisoners assessed as medium to high risk should receive medium or high intensity treatment. Their mean age when they reach their earliest possible release date is 56.5 years with sex offenders being 59.5 years old. Treatment for this cohort is therefore essential as they cannot be released at their EPRD unless they have attended treatment. Some will be considered a risk and will remain in prison well beyond their EPRD and will only be released within a relatively short period of sentence expiry (two years or less) so they can be supervised in the community or when their sentence expires for those for whom it is difficult to find suitable placement.

Data are not available for health-related matters but, as with older people in the community, there are significant health costs attached to this cohort. As many are convicted of sex offences, placement of these prisoners is often in protection areas which tend to be costlier to run. Yet, as they tend to be relatively well behaved in prison, they are not a cohort that receives much attention from prison staff aside from protection areas for about one-quarter of the cohort: bottom bunks for those who are less mobile, access to health facilities and services for those who are not physically well, and access to a range of equipment for those with disabilities. Specific housing is required for those who are frail or dementing, but most older prisoners reside in a range of prisons across the state. Generally, this cohort has diverse needs, and ultimately each prisoner, regardless of age, has his or her case managed as an individual with the goal of safely returning the person to the community.

This chapter has not addressed many of the complex issues for the cohort, including prisoners who transition to the community under supervision; the many services required for reintegration, especially for prisoners convicted of sex offences; and the psychology of ageing in prison. These topics are beyond the scope of this paper but are important factors that need to be considered when addressing the needs of older prisoners.

Note

1 or 48% if both Indigenous or non-Indigenous cohorts are defined as 55 years or older.

References

Andrews, D.A., and Bonta, J.L. (1995) *LSI-R, Level of Service Inventory-Revised User's Manual.* Toronto: Multi-health Systems.

Australian Institute of Health and Welfare [AIHW]. (2015) The Health of Australia's Prisoners 2015. Cat. no. PHE 207. Canberra: AIHW.

Australian Institute of Health and Welfare [AIHW]. (2018) Australia's Health 2018. Australia's Health Series no. 16. AUS 221. Canberra: AIHW.

Australian Institute of Health and Welfare [AIHW]. (2019) The Health of Australia's Prisoners 2018. Cat. no. PHE 246. Canberra: AIHW.

Baidawi, S., Turner, S., and Trotter, C., et al. (2011) *Older Prisoners: A Challenge for Australian Corrections. Trends & Issues in Crime and Criminal Justice No. 426.* Canberra: Australian Institute of Criminology.

Beck, A., and Harrison, M. (2001) *Prisoners in 2000.* Washington DC: Bureau of Justice Statistics. Available at http://bjs.ojp.usdoj.gov/index.cfm?ty=pbdetail&iid=927.

Ginnivan, N., Butler, T.G., and Whitehall, A.N. (2018) 'The Rising Health, Social And Economic Costs Of Australia's Ageing Prisoner Population', *MJA*, 209(10), pp. 422–424.

Heckenberg, D. (2006) *Ageing Prisoners: Significant Cohort or Forgotten Minority?* Master's Thesis. Tasmania: University of Tasmania.

LeMesurier, N., Kingston, P., Heath, L., and Wardle, S. (2010) *A Critical Analysis Of The Mental Health Needs of Older Prisoners: Final Report.* Staffordshire: Staffordshire University.

New Zealand Department of Corrections (NZDC). (2010) *Offender Volumes Report 2009*. Wellington: New Zealand Department of Corrections

Pratt, T., Cullen, F.T., and Blevins, K.R., et al. (2008) *Taking Stock: The Status of Criminological Theory*. New York: Routledge.

Productivity Commission. (2021) *Australia's Prison Dilemma*, Research paper, Canberra.

Sabol, W., and West, H. (2010) *Prisoners in 2009*. Washington DC, Bureau of Justice Statistics. Available at http://bjs.ojp.usdoj.gov/index.cfm?ty=pbdetail&iid=2232.

Stavrou, E. (2017) 'Changing Age Profile of NSW Offenders', *Crime and Justice Statistics*, 123, pp. 1–7.

Turner, S., and Trotter, C. (2010) 'Growing Old in Prison? A Review of National and International Research on Ageing Offenders', *Corrections Research Paper Series No 3*. Melbourne: Department of Justice.

United Nations Office on Drugs and Crime (UNODC). (2009) *Handbook on Prisoners with Special Needs*. UNODC: Vienna. https://www.unodc.org/pdf/criminal_justice/Handbook_on_Prisoners_with_Special_Needs.pdf

Yorston, G.A., and Taylor, P.J. (2006) 'Commentary: Older Offenders—No Place to Go?', *Journal of the American Academy of Psychiatry and Law Online*, 34(3), pp. 333–337.

15 Rehabilitation Services for Elderly Prisoners in Hong Kong

T. Wing Lo

Caritas Institute of Higher Education, Hong Kong

Oliver Chan

University of Birmingham, England

Jeffrey Shing

City University of Hong Kong, Hong Kong

15.1 Introduction

In line with the aging population in Hong Kong, there is a growing number of elderly prisoners aged 65 or above. According to the Correctional Services Department's 2018 annual press conference by the Commissioner, individuals aged 65 or higher sentenced to correctional services institutions in 2017 amounted to 256, a 37% increase compared to 187 in 2005. The daily penal population at correctional facilities in Hong Kong was 8,529 individuals in 2017 (Hong Kong Correctional Services Department, 2018). That means 3% of the total population were elderly prisoners. Based on the newest predictions on the daily average prisoner population, it was estimated that the proportion of prisoners aged 65 or above will increase from 170, which is 2% in 2015, to 410 in 2023, making up 5% of the total prisoner population (Hong Kong Correctional Services Department, 2015). If we re-define old age as 50 years old, the increase is even more alarming. According to a research jointly conducted by Society for Community Organization and City University of Hong Kong in 2015, the number of post-release prisoners aged 50 or higher was increasing, from 1,117 in 2000 (8.68% of total post-release prisoners) to 2,020 in 2013 (21.2%) (Chui et al., 2015).

15.2 The correctional services in Hong Kong

The correctional institutions in Hong Kong are run by the Correctional Services Department, which provide inmates with basic necessities, comprehensive medical, psychological and welfare services, opportunities to engage in useful work, and a decent and healthy living environment. They also provide

DOI: 10.4324/9781032669519-19

education, vocational training, drug addiction treatment, community reintegration programs, and aftercare and support services.

In order to improve the relationship between the prisoners and their family, the correctional institutions organize prisoner-family programs or invite the family members to attend the prisoners' birthday celebration (Lo et al., 2010). However, it is not uncommon for family members to be uncooperative, unsupportive, and refuse to show up, rendering the rehabilitation to be less effective. The correctional institutions also understand the religious and spiritual needs of the prisoners, thus providing a full-time Chaplain to arrange such activities that are supported by volunteers.

The Risks and Needs Assessment and Management Protocol for Offenders was created and implemented to enhance prison management and the quality of rehabilitative programs (Lo, 2017). Since there is a high correlation between crime and unemployment (Britt, 1995; Collins and Weatherburn, 1995; Raphael and Winter-Ebmer, 2001), the correctional institutions provide work programs for drug addicts and prisoners that include a wide variety of industrial activities to help prisoners develop good working habits, discipline, and trade-skills, gain self-confidence, and feel a sense of achievement (Lo, 2008). Approximately 4,452 prisoners were engaged in 130 industrial workshops across 13 trades on a daily basis, while the rest of the prisoners were assigned housekeeping duties like cleaning and kitchen and maintenance work, generating a combined total of HK$460.6 million in products (Hong Kong Correctional Services Department, 2014). However, prisoners of 65 years old and above have lower participation in the vocational training.

The correctional institutions' services continue upon discharge. Inmates of the drug addiction treatment centers will undergo a period of statutory supervision by aftercare officers. The released ex-drug addicts are recalled if they fail to meet the conditions of supervision or relapse to drug taking again because illicit drug use was found to be a risk factor of reoffending (Chan et al., 2016). The Correctional Services Department aims at providing "through-care" for the prisoners (Lo et al., 1997; Kwok, 2007; Lo et al., 2010). Aftercare service starts inside the institutions in order to build a trusting relationship between the officers, prisoners, and the prisoners' families early on because poor interpersonal relationship was identified as a reoffending risk factor among incarcerated male offenders (Chan et al., 2015). Occasionally, some discharged prisoners are placed in hostels run by non-government organizations to assist their adjustment into society after a period of incarceration (Hui and Lo, 2017).

15.3 Tailor-made services for elderly prisoners – The Evergreen Garden

An elderly unit was originally set up in the Ma Hang Prison with special provisions for elderly prisoners, such as the availability of warm showers throughout the year, barrier-free access and ramps, handrails for support, large-print notices, etc. (APCCA, 2014, p. 64). In response to the increase in elderly prisoner population in recent years, especially in accommodating for the various physical, social, and psychological needs of senior prisoners, the Correctional Services Department has promoted an integrated correctional program. They tailored the custodial environment, by adding nurse care and fitness equipment and changing the use of existing facilities into creating "Evergreen Garden" — a tailor-made service for elderly prisoners — housed in the Tai Lam Correctional Institution. In order to provide a suitable supervision and rehabilitation arrangements while using correctional institutions appropriately, the Tai Lam Correctional Institution was renovated in 2015 to cater to the special needs of the elderly prisoners (Hong Kong Correctional Services Department, 2015).

Since the Tai Lam Correctional Institution is a low security prison, it will only imprison lower security grades of C and D types of seniors. Their imprisonment will be less than 3 years, with the average of current imprisoned seniors at approximately 23 months. Seniors with security grades of A and B will continue to stay at Stanley Prison or Lai Chi Kok Reception Center's hospital to serve their sentence. Those correctional institutions can also provide similar care facilities. After the completion of the renovations, the Correctional Services Department transferred prisoners aged 65 or older that fit the security criteria to the Evergreen Garden. This allows the institution to establish a comprehensive rehabilitation scheme with a full package of equipment and program arrangement.

The Hong Kong Correctional Services Department (2015) noted that the newly designed Evergreen Garden was constructed with the needs of senior prisoners in mind, to assist them in building a positive and healthy life through promoting various comprehensive correctional services. The Evergreen Garden is a metaphor for a strong vitality. Cedar and pine are two kinds of evergreen. Their strong and tenacious vitality is what makes them precious, as they remain everlasting. Older prisoners are like seniors, they need to learn how to face the changes to their physical and mental capacities that come with aging. Some of them would feel disappointment and guilt with their crimes, causing psychological and emotional problems. Through the integrated correctional program in Evergreen Garden, the Hong Kong Correctional Services Department (2015) hopes to foster the senior prisoners' vitality, and assist them to develop positive lives.

In terms of rehabilitation, the Hong Kong Correctional Services Department (2015) has collaborated with non-government organizations in creating hobby classes suitable for seniors, including Tai Chi, Chinese calligraphy, and gardening. In addition to the stationary bikes with support handles, there are simple handicraft workshops, senior fitness equipment, and gardening workshops. In order to care for the senior prisoners' mental health, clinical psychologists of the correctional institutions provide psychological counseling and treatment, mental health education, and geriatric mental health care for the seniors (Hong Kong Correctional Services Department, 2015). In terms of vocational training, the correctional institutions have collaborated with the

Employees Retraining Board in creating the Garden Assistant Certification Program (Hong Kong Correctional Services Department, 2015) for those willing to study, allowing senior prisoners to gain gardening skills and knowledge while molding their temperament.

In the physical health aspects, health professionals from the correctional institutions provide body examination regularly for seniors. In particular, in response to the pandemic, the Tai Lam Correctional Institution has strengthened health surveillance. Upon the discovery of a senior prisoner with fever, they will immediately launch the surveillance system and contact the Center for Health Protection when needed. The prisoners can also use the multimedia resource activity room to find information on mental health and health information (Hong Kong Correctional Services Department, 2015).

15.4 Hong Kong elderly prisoners survey

In 2015, City University of Hong Kong conducted research in three correctional institutions where elderly prisoners aged 65 or above were housed. Seventy-six participants were sampled. Of the total, 44.7% each were recruited at Stanley Prison (N = 34 male) and Tai Lam Correctional Institution (N = 34 male), respectively, with the remaining 10.5% recruited at Lo Wu Correctional Institution (N = 8 female).

15.4.1 Socio-demographic characteristics

Out of the 76 participants, 89.5% were male and 10.5% were female (Table 15.1). The education level of this pool of participants was not high, with nearly half of them (48.7%) were either without formal education or primary school dropouts. Slightly more than half of the participants (53.3%) were reported to be married at the time of research. Prior to their current incarceration, living alone (32.9%) in a rented public housing property (46.1%) was not uncommon among these participants. A large majority of them (65.3%) were unemployed prior to current imprisonment, with their common reasons as difficulty in securing a job (22.9%) and their personal health problems (10.4%) (Table 15.1).

15.4.2 Criminal history

Among the participants, most of them were at least 66 years of age (68.9%) when they were incarcerated for the current index offense. The nature of their index offense varied, with most of them being non-sexual in nature (e.g., drug, arson, burglary, blackmail, and tax evasion) and mostly against non-stranger victims (80.9%). A large majority of them (83.6%) committed their offense without any accomplice. Nearly all of the participants (89.3%) were convicted on a non-life imprisonment term. More than two-thirds of the participants (70.8%) were incarcerated for the first time. Indeed, more than half of them (56.2%) only committed their first offense at the age of 65 years or above (Table 15.2).

Table 15.1 Socio-demographics of the participants ($N = 76$)

Variables	*Frequency*	*Percentage of total (100.0%)*
Gender of the participants	($N = 76$)	
Male	68	89.5
Female	8	10.5
Education background	($N = 74$)	
No formal education	9	12.2
Primary school dropout	27	36.5
Primary school completion	8	10.8
Junior secondary school dropout	7	9.5
Junior secondary school completion	9	12.2
Senior secondary school completion	8	10.8
University dropout	1	1.4
Completion of university level or above	5	6.8
Marital Status	($N = 75$)	
Married	40	53.3
Non-married	35	46.7
Living status prior to imprisonment **multiple options permitted*	($N = 76$)	
Living with a partner	35	46.1
Living with children	31	40.8
Living alone	25	32.9
Living with other relatives	3	3.9
Living with at least one parent	2	2.6
Living with others in a halfway house/hostel	1	1.3
Others (e.g., with colleagues, grandchildren)	5	6.6
Living condition prior to imprisonment	($N = 76$)	
Own a private housing unit	14	18.4
Own a government subsidized housing unit	5	6.6
Rented a private/government subsidized unit	9	11.8
Rented a public housing unit	35	46.1
Homeless	1	1.3
Others (e.g., rented room, nursing home)	12	15.8
Employment status prior to imprisonment	($N = 75$)	
Full-time employment	21	28.0
Part-time employment	5	6.7
Unemployed	49	65.3
Reasons for unemployment	($N = 48$)	
Difficulty in securing a job	11	22.9
Personal health issues	5	10.4
Lack of motivation to work	2	4.2
Lack of necessity to work (e.g., own savings)	3	6.3
Others (e.g., old age, past conviction record)	27	56.3

Table 15.2 Criminal history of the participants (n = 76)

Variables	*Frequency*	*Percentage of total (100.0%)*
Age of imprisonment for index offense	(*N* = 74)	
60 years or below	6	8.1
61 to 65 years	17	23.0
66 to 70 years	29	39.3
71 to 75 years	11	14.8
76 years or above	11	14.8
Nature of index offense **multiple options permitted*	(*N* = 72)	
Drug-related	10	13.8
Fraud	5	6.9
Sexual crime/assault/act of violence	5	6.9
Theft	2	2.8
Others (e.g., arson, blackmail, tax evasion)	50	69.4
Offender-victim relationship	(*N* = 68)	
Family member	9	13.2
Friend or acquaintance	2	2.9
Stranger	13	19.1
Other known relationships	44	64.7
Accomplice for index offense	(*N* = 73)	
Yes	12	16.4
No	61	83.6
Imprisonment term	(*N* = 75)	
Life imprisonment	8	10.7
Non-life imprisonment	67	89.3
Number of imprisonments	(*N* = 72)	
One time	51	70.8
2 to 5 times	16	22.2
6 times or above	5	7.0
Age of first offense commission	(*N* = 73)	
18 years or below	2	2.7
19 to 30 years	10	13.7
31 to 40 years	5	6.9
41 to 50 years	4	5.5
51 to 60 years	5	6.9
61 to 64 years	6	8.2
65 years or above	41	56.2

15.4.3 Financial status, health condition, and living arrangement upon release

Financial problems were found not to be a distressing issue to many participants (48.7%) prior to their imprisonment. Most of the participants reported to have received social welfare benefits (47.4%) as their common income source prior to imprisonment, although income generated from their employment was also not unusual (34.2%). However, more participants expected to rely on social welfare benefits (63.2%) as their source of income upon release from prison. In terms of the participants' current health condition, nearly half of them (48.7%) reported that either they are often ill or being diagnosed with a particular disease (Table 15.3).

Table 15.3 Financial status, health condition, and living arrangement upon release (n = 76)

Variables	*Frequency*	*Percentage of total (100.0%)*
Financial problem prior to imprisonment	(*N* = 76)	
Not at all	37	48.7
Not very often	10	13.1
Sometimes	18	23.7
Always	11	14.5
Source of income prior to imprisonment **multiple options permitted*	(*N* = 76)	
Social welfare benefits	36	47.4
No income	32	42.1
Employment	26	34.2
Support from family or relatives	11	14.5
Pension	5	6.6
Savings	3	3.9
Borrowed money	1	1.3
Others	7	9.2
Expected source of income after release **multiple options permitted*	(*N* = 76)	
Social welfare benefits	48	63.2
Support from family or relatives	16	21.1
Employment	8	10.5
Pension	6	7.9
Savings	3	3.9
Interests from assets/property	1	1.3
Others	8	10.5
Current health condition	(*N* = 76)	
In good condition	28	36.8
Not so good, but not often ill	11	14.5
Often ill	6	7.9
Diagnosed with a disease	31	40.8
Personal concern upon release	(*N* = 72)	
Health condition	28	38.9
Employment	4	5.6
Family	24	33.2
Friends	2	2.8
Country	1	1.4
Finance	6	8.3

(*Continued*)

Table 15.3 (Continued)

Variables	*Frequency*	*Percentage of Total (100.0%)*
Place to stay	1	1.4
Self-confidence	2	2.8
Others (e.g., to live a life)	4	5.6
Issues worried about after release **multiple options permitted*	(*N* = 76)	
Health condition	23	30.3
The cost of living	14	18.4
Family relationship	6	7.9
Being alone	5	6.6
Romantic relationship	3	3.9
Employment	2	2.6
Lack of close relationship	2	2.6
Being lazy or idle	2	2.6
Friendship	1	1.3
Financial debt	1	1.3
Lack of motivation to live	1	1.3
Funeral arrangement	1	1.3
Nothing in particular	37	48.7
Expected lifestyle after release **multiple options permitted*	(*N* = 76)	
Live with family	36	47.4
Avoid committing a crime again	31	40.8
Carry out more sport activities	24	31.6
Avoid causing trouble to others	22	28.9
Do as they please	20	26.3
Live a more relaxing life	18	23.7
Involve in a religious activity	17	22.4
Embark on a better moral existence	17	22.4
Work hard	15	19.7
Avoid disappointing those who helped them	15	19.7
Carry out special interest activities	14	18.4
Leave it up to fate	14	18.4
Nothing in particular	10	13.2
Have not thought about it	5	6.6
Live in a home for elderly people	3	3.9
Get married again	1	1.3

To reunite with family (33.2%) and in good health (38.9%) were valued most by many participants upon their release from prison. Indeed, their health condition (30.3%) and the cost of living (18.4%) were commonly considered as issues that they worried about after release from the prison, although a majority of them (48.7%) perceived to have nothing in particular to worry about. Furthermore, nearly half of the individuals expected they would live with their family after release (47.4%) (Table 15.3).

In general, most participants anticipated to live a healthy and crime-free life (e.g., avoid committing a crime again and causing trouble to others and carry out more sport activities; 40.8%, 28.9% and 31.6%, respectively) upon their reintegration into the society later. However, some wanted to go back to do as they please (26.3%). Some participants believed they would focus more on their spirituality by being involved in religious activities or embarking on a better moral existence (17 participants, 22.4%). Some participants preferred to take on a passive role and would do nothing or simply leaving it up to fate (10 and 14, respectively), while others planned to carry out special interest activities (14 participants, 18.4%). Very few individuals had not thought about their lifestyle, might move into a home for elderly, or marry again (5, 3 and 1, respectively) (Table 15.3).

15.5 Conclusion

The findings of our study are drastically different from a previous study conducted by Chiu and associates (2015) because of the use of two different samples. Our study collected samples from existing prisoners still serving their sentences. They came from prisons rather than drug addiction treatment centers. Only 13.5% of the participants committed a drug-related offence. However, Chui's sample was taken from post-release offenders who were mainly drug-addicts and street-sleepers who were served by a non-government organization, the Society for Community Organization. Because of the different backgrounds of the two samples, the results of both studies can complement each other to let readers obtain a clearer picture of the issues faced by elderly prisoners.

Chui's (2015) study found an upward trend in the number of older post-release prisoners aged 50 or above, most of whom were involved in misdemeanors or repeated offense. The study interviewed 50 post-release offenders of this category to understand the causes behind their repeated offense and found that it was due to housing problems. After they were released from prisons, because of the high rental in Hong Kong and infeasibility to live with family, many of them had to camp out in the open or live in bed-space apartments, and easily became addicted to drugs again or returned to the circle of bad friends, resulting in repeated offense. Thus, the research team concluded that drug addiction was the primary cause that prevented them from returning to society. This, combined with the lack of a place to stay and job opportunities, created a vicious cycle leading to repeated offense (Chui et al., 2015).

In our study, several observations can be drawn from the results. First, money was rarely a problem for the majority of the prisoners. Prior to imprisonment, only 14.5% of the participants would always have financial problems, and 23.7% would sometimes have financial problems, despite the fact that near half of the participants had no income or were on welfare benefits. In addition, only about a third of the participants were employed. A majority of the participants expected to be unemployed after their release, as only about 10.5% expected to rely on working as their source of income post-release. Similarly, instead of working, they expected to rely on welfare and/or family to assist them financially. Similarly, that the participants were more likely to choose to engage in "leisure activities" (sports, relaxing life, religious activities) than to work hard also supports this notion. These participants may be planning for their retirement as only a handful of them were worried about employment after their release. All of these responses would explain why older prisoners are less involved in vocational training. This would mean industrial work and vocational training are unnecessary for them, as they are physically incapable and unenthusiastic about working. However, similar to Chui's (2015) study, quite a number of the respondents worried about the high cost of living in Hong Kong.

As with aging, health became a major concern for the elderly prisoners in our study. Though some participants reported to be in good health, nearly half of them were often ill or diagnosed with a disease already. Furthermore, their health condition was consistently the most important concern to them although there was no specific indication as to the type of disease they were diagnosed with. Nonetheless, it is expected that their mental well-being would likely be in good condition as there were few concerns/issues related to companionship (friends, romance or family), finance, or intrinsic motivation to live post-release.

To conclude, the Hong Kong Correctional Services Department has reorganized its rehabilitative services for elderly prisoners by introducing the Evergreen Garden in response to the gradual rise of this population in prisons. Elderly prisoners may benefit from healthy aging workshops. They can have nurses or doctors run health education workshops to raise awareness of diseases or issues that arise with aging. In addition to the hobby classes like Tai Chi, classes on light to medium intensity exercises can improve health and longevity, while also being better than gardening for cultivating good habits since gardening requires a significant amount of space that most households lack. Ideally, having trainers, physiotherapists, or occupational therapists to teach the seniors the proper usage of fitness equipment can prevent injury, or fear from the unknown, and can help them exercise at an appropriate intensity to enhance their physical needs. Correctional institutions should also hire dietitians to provide nutrition classes for these seniors, as healthy eating is a major part of aging and certain diseases. Healthy eating is also a knowledge that can assist them after they leave the institution. For the group of homeless ex-drug addicts who cannot reunite with their family and have to camp on the street, the provision of regular welfare support and counselling services by non-government organizations seem to be the only alternative.

References

APCCA (Asia and Pacific Conference of Correctional Administrators). (2014) *34th APCCA Conference Report*, Victoria, Canada: APCCA. Available at http://www.apcca.org/uploads/APCCA_Report__2014.pdf

Britt, C.L. (1995) 'Reconsidering The Unemployment And Crime Relationship: Variation By Age Group And Historical Period', *Journal of Quantitative Criminology*, 13(4), pp. 405–428.

Chan, O., Lo, T.W., Chui, E., and Zhong, L. (2015) 'Criminal Recidivism of Incarcerated Male Nonviolent Offenders in Hong Kong', *International Journal of Offender Therapy and Comparative Criminology*, 59(2), pp. 121–142.

Chan, O., Lo, T.W., and Zhong, L. (2016) 'Identifying The Self-Anticipated Reoffending Risk Factors of Incarcerated Male Repeat Offenders in Hong Kong', *Prison Journal*, 96(5), pp. 731–751.

Chui, W.H., Fun, Y., and Yap, J. (2015) Resettlement of Elderly Male Ex-Prisoners in Hong Kong: Their Basic Needs and Mental Health. (Report submitted to The Society for Community Organization), Hong Kong: Department of Applied Social Sciences, City University of Hong Kong.

Collins, M.F., and Weatherburn, D. (1995) 'Unemployment And The Dynamics Of Offender Populations', *Journal of Quantitative Criminology*, 11(3), pp. 231–245.

Hong Kong Correctional Services Department (2014) Annual Review 2014. Hong Kong: Correctional Services Department.

Hong Kong Correctional Services Department (2015) *Speech by Commissioner of Correctional Services at Annual Press Conference*. Available at http://www.info.gov.hk/gia/general/201502/16/P201502160301.htm

Hong Kong Correctional Services Department (2018) *Speech by Commissioner of Correctional Services at Annual Press Conference*. Available at https://www.csd.gov.hk/english/news/news_pr/20180227.html

Hui, C., and Lo, T.W. (2017) 'Corrections in Hong Kong'. In Kerley, K.R. (Ed.) *The Encyclopedia of Corrections*, New Jersey: John Wiley & Sons.

Kwok, L.M. (2007) *Services for Rehabilitated Offenders Provided by the Correctional Services Department of Hong Kong SAR*, Hong Kong: Correctional Services Department. (In Chinese)

Lo, T.W. (2008) 'Custodial Sentences And Correctional Services'. In Chui, W.H. and Lo, T.W. (eds.) *Understanding Criminal Justice in Hong Kong*, Devon: Willan, pp. 224–247.

Lo, T.W. (2017) 'Prison and Correctional Services'. In Chui, W.H. and Lo, T.W. (eds.) *Understanding Criminal Justice in Hong Kong*, 2nd Edition, London: Routledge, pp. 311–335.

Lo, T.W., Wong, S.W., and Chan, W.T., et al. (1997) *Research on the Effectiveness of Rehabilitation Programs for Young Offenders: Full Report*, Hong Kong: Government Printer.

Lo, T.W., Wong, S.W., and Chui, W.H., et al. (2010) *Report on Comprehensive Review of the Rehabilitation Centre Program for Correctional Services Department*. Hong Kong: City University of Hong Kong.

Raphael, S., and Winter-Ebmer, R. (2001) 'Identifying The Effect Of Unemployment On Crime', *Journal of Law and Economics*, 44, pp. 259–283.

16 Trends in the Aging Prison Population of England and Wales

Jason Danely

Oxford Brookes University, UK

Natalie Mann

Anglia Ruskin University, UK

Carla Reeves

University of Huddersfield, UK

16.1 Introduction/rationale

This chapter reviews the status of older adult offenders in England and Wales in order to contribute to a comparative perspective on the global phenomenon of aging prison populations and to consider future implications and trends. There are 118 prisons in England and Wales, all overseen by HM Prison and Probation Service (HMPPS), formerly the National Offender Management Service (NOMS). England and Wales currently hold more prisoners than any other Western European country, both in absolute numbers as well as in terms of proportion of the population (Council of Europe 2017)[1]. In October 2021, there were 78,756 prisoners held in England and Wales, or about 167 per 100,000 citizens (Sturge, 2021, 5). Adults over 50 accounted for roughly 17% of the total adult prison population, a 50% increase since 2011 (Sturge, 2021, 12). In recent years, the state of prisons in England and Wales has come under increased scrutiny for overcrowding, poorly maintained structures, violent incidents, and a rapid rise in incidents of self-harm and suicide (HCJC, 2019). The growing numbers of older adults are affected by all of these conditions without adequately resourced special provisions.

This state of mass incarceration in England and Wales did not occur suddenly, but had been gradually taking form since the 18th century. English philosopher Jeremy Bentham's iconic Panopticon design exemplifies this philosophy, and subsequently became a model for prisons around the world (Foucault, [1975] 1995). Over time, prisons produced changes in public attitudes toward crime and punishment that aligned with new understandings of the relationship between citizens and the state (Wacquant, 2009; Fassin, 2017). In the UK and elsewhere, the rise of 'penal populism' (Pratt, 2007) and the quickening pace of the aging society have converged in the

DOI: 10.4324/9781032669519-20

first decades of the 21st century, but still little is understood about the implications of this convergence for offenders, prison staff, and for society at large. Will demographic changes prompt a rethinking of penal policy and procedures? Can cross-national comparisons like those explored in this volume help us to better understand the lives of ex-offenders and the risk of re-offending?

This chapter suggests that as policymakers in England and Wales try to come to grips with their aging prison population, the need for expertise on the lifeworlds of older offenders across the penal and probation system will become increasingly urgent. While serious concerns regarding the treatment of older offenders persist, we also consider possible lessons they might offer as well.

16.2 Background of crimes by older people and incarceration

Over the past two decades, the British prison population has seen a threefold increase in the number of men aged 50 and over being sentenced to a term of imprisonment (Prisons and Probation Ombudsman (PPO), 2017). This once insignificant section of the prison population now stands at approximately 13,433, with 3,366 between 60 and 69—the largest increase of any age group compared to the previous year (+7%) (MOJ 2022a).

The beginning of the marked increase in the aging prison population can be traced back to New Labour's thirteen-year reign (1997–2010) which saw the implementation of a number of legislative changes which served to widen the carceral net and inflate sentence lengths. Such changes included the introduction of the mandatory life sentence for those convicted of a second serious sexual assault under the Crime Sentences Act 1997 (Maguire et al., 1997), and the introduction of indeterminate sentences for public protection (IPP) in 2003 (Matravers and Hughes, 2003, 53–54). IPP was investigated in 2011 and later abolished in 2012 due to problems stemming from its use beyond intended purpose. Minimum sentences of IPP were replaced by more punitive sentences for violent and sexual offenders as well as extended supervision on license. In the wake of revelations of extensive sexual abuse by the media personality Jimmy Savile in 2012, there was an increase in the investigation and prosecution of historical sexual abuse. In subsequent years, such trends have continued to characterise the criminal justice system in England and Wales, resulting in rapid growth in the older prisoner population.

The Prison Service in England and Wales was poorly prepared for their new role as the largest providers of residential care for frail and elderly men in England and Wales (PPO, 2017). The increased presence of aging individuals with complex and heterogeneous needs within prison establishments originally designed for able-bodied young men has resulted in an extremely complex and costly management challenge for the Prison Service, in a time of record high populations and significant cuts to their budget (Prison Reform Trust, 2017). Many of the prisons in England and Wales were built in the Victorian era and as such, present an extremely challenging environment for aging prisoners to live in, something acknowledged by Crawley and Sparks' (2005) notion of "institutional thoughtlessness." They state,

> Their [prisons] very fabric (the stairs and steps and walkways, the distances, the gates, the football pitches and gymnasia; the serveries and queues; the communal showers; the incessant background noise) is, in general, constructed in blithe unconsciousness of the needs and sensibilities of the old (2005).

The suitability of the prison estate for older offenders is something which has long concerned both academics and third sector organisations, however, in 2004 the Prison Service acknowledged the need for specialised facilities, and HMP Norwich opened the first purpose built older offender unit which took the form of a care home style facility providing beds for fifteen aging prisoners who required assistance with daily living (Mann, 2012; Moll, 2013). This pioneering facility was welcomed as a sign of progress for the less mobile and more infirm older prisoners, but at a cost of £1.5 million, it was a clear demonstration of the financial implications of an aging prison population.

16.2.1 Trends in crimes committed by elderly offenders

Whilst there is no defined age category for 'older prisoners' in England and Wales (Justice Select Committee, 2013; MOJ, 2014; PPO, 2017), the older prison population can be divided into four main categories; those who have committed a crime for the first time in old age; those who were sentenced to lengthy periods of custody and have grown old in prison; those who have been sentenced in old age for historical crimes; and those who are repeat offenders (Moll, 2013; MOJ, 2014). Despite serving sentences for a range of crimes including property, violence, drugs, and fraud, along with more serious offences such as murder and manslaughter, the older prison population in England and Wales is disproportionately made up of those serving a sentence for a sexual offence (Mann, 2012; Justice Select Committee, 2013; Moll, 2013; MOJ, 2014; PPO, 2017). For prisoners aged 60 and over, 59% are currently serving a custodial sentence for sexual offences (MOJ, 2014), whilst for 50- to 59 years olds, this figure decreases slightly to approximately 34% (Centre for Policy on Ageing, 2016). Such high numbers of sexual offenders in the system, has led to the development of eight specialist prisons across England and Wales, which exclusively house sexual offenders (The Telegraph, 2014).

16.2.2 Trends in conditions in prison

16.2.2.1 Health

The health complaints of the older prison population unsurprisingly reflects the morbidity of the older and aging population in general society and includes heart disease, diabetes, cancer, hypertension, and mental health problems, such as depression and anxiety disorders (Fazel et al., 2001; Hayes et al., 2012; Justice Select Committee, 2013). These specific health issues, coupled with the psychological strains of prison life and the relative inactivity of older prisoners, further accelerates the aging process and places even greater demand on prison healthcare. However, despite such high incidences of age-related problems, and the legal entitlement to have access to the same level of care in prison as they would in general society (PPO, 2017), provisions and standards of health care for older people in prison vary and very often fall short of that delivered in the community (Senior et al., 2013).

Experiences of healthcare are all too often characterised by poor access, delays in treatment, poor quality of care, and delayed diagnoses or misdiagnoses (Mann, 2012; Justice Select Committee, 2013; PPO, 2017). Healthcare for older prisoners can cost up to three times more than that of younger prisoners (Mann, 2012), and this, coupled with the ongoing cut-backs which have affected prisons in England and Wales, means that the Prison Service has neither the funding nor the resources to employ the preventative model of healthcare which currently exists in general society.

16.2.2.2 Dementia

There is no official figure on the rate of dementia amongst the aging prison population, but it has been estimated that approximately 5% of prisoners aged 55 years and older would have the condition (PPO, 2016). This figure is in fact likely to be an underestimation of the actual numbers because many of the signs of dementia are masked by the predictability and regimented nature of the prison regime (Moll, 2013), and cognitive screening and regular assessment is uneven across institutions (Brooke et al., 2020).

Prison Officers still receive just one hour of training on older prisoners, and as such, they often lack awareness and understanding of issues such as dementia and incontinence (Moll, 2013). Those who "care" for aging prisoners are less likely to notice the subtle changes which can take place at the onset of dementia, and thus it is likely that those prisoners demonstrating symptoms of memory loss, confusion, and withdrawal would simply be considered old and infirm (PPO, 2016), rather than suffering from dementia.

The prison environment itself has a substantial impact on the issue of dementia. Firstly, the poor physical and mental health of older prisoners, created by the stresses and strains of the prison environment and a lack of appropriate healthcare, puts individuals at a much greater risk of developing dementia initially (Maschi et al., 2012). Second, many of the common characteristics of the prison environment sit in stark contrast to those promoted by the Alzheimer's Society's "Dementia Friendly Communities" (2014). The bare walls, the poorly lit corridors and landings, multiple stairs, and undifferentiated floor surfaces are all likely to create significant difficulties for prisoners suffering from dementia.

Small changes such as "…proper lighting, use of different colors for walls, such as the bathrooms, use of large lettered signs and pictures, handrails, wheelchairs, and accessible showers…" (Maschi et al., 2012) can greatly enhance the experiences of prisoners with dementia, but if prison is to accommodate the needs of the fastest growing population in prison (Mann, 2012; Justice Select Committee, 2013), there needs to be systemic change in the training of prison staff, the allocation of resources, and the value placed on the human rights of a prisoner.

16.2.2.3 *Palliative and end of life care*

The "End of life Care Strategy" was published by the Government in 2008, but the Prison Service still has no formal guidance on expectations. As Turner et al. (2011) found in their study, the continual conflict of care versus custody often sees the potential security risks of the prisoner as a major barrier to accessing the quality of service delivered in outside hospices.

This is something noted by PPO (2017), who discusses how prisons tend to assess their prisoners based on the risk they posed when healthy; this can lead to prisoners being denied compassionate leave, denied access to external hospices, and even being physically restrained at the end of life (PPO, 2017). This issue of prisoner security, coupled with the fact that much of our prison estate is noisy, decrepit, and wholly insufficient as a place for palliative care delivery, means that prisons are failing to provide a much-needed service and failing to adapt to the changing demographics of their incarcerated population.

The lack of a general national strategy on the care and management of aging prisoners has resulted in grave differences in service and delivery across the prison estate, and, as is the case with so much of the aging prisoner experience, pockets of good practice are largely due to the dedication and innovation of staff working with this age group.

Palliative and end of life care in prison are also characterised by some very good experiences (Turner et al., 2011; Papadopoulos and Lay, 2016; PPO, 2017), such as the development of palliative care suites, the recognition of the importance of family and fellow prisoner involvement in the dying process, and the development of excellent working relationships with local hospices. These pockets of good practice highlight how successful end of life care can be delivered within the prison setting, providing there is funding for equipment, training, and delivery.

16.2.2.4 *Education and employment*

The reality of prison life for many aging prisoners is boredom, isolation, and loneliness (Mann, 2012). Older prisoners often find themselves engaged in monotonous activity, or simply left to "stagnate" in their cell (Aday, 1994; Mann, 2012). Over two decades ago, the Prison Reform Trust noted a grave lack of age-appropriateness and differentiation in prison activities, particularly within the area of education and training (PRT, 2003), a finding supported by the Justice Select Committee (2013). Sadly, this lack of differentiation still exists today, and whilst some prisons have utilised the services of non-profit organisations such as Age UK or RECOOP, in order to run "age tailored" programmes, nostalgia groups, and specialised gym sessions (Mann, 2012; Justice Select Committee, 2013), the continued austerity measures which have seen HM Prison and Probation Service's budget reduced by nearly a quarter since 2011 (Prison Reform Trust, 2017), mean even these piecemeal offerings are at risk.

The current penal crisis, which has seen a continual rise in the prison population, an increase in incidences of violence, escalating drug addiction, and increasing rates of suicide (HMIP, 2017), has resulted in a dire situation where keeping prisons safe and well-ordered on a daily basis is as much as staff can hope to achieve. Within such a climate, there are still many aging prisoners who remain unemployed and unengaged.

16.3 Re-entry/resettlement of elderly prisoners

Release On Temporary License orders (ROTL), whereby a prisoner is released for a day or longer, may be used with long term prisoners to gradually assist them to re-establish themselves in outside communities prior to release from prison (Cornish et al., 2016; Pedder, 2017). However, there is no specific policy on older prisoner resettlement. Furthermore, dedicated resettlement support in and out of prison is very patchy and fragmented (Cornish et al., 2016).

A significant proportion of older prisoners leave prison with no appropriate accommodation arranged and so are classified as no fixed abode (NFA) (Justice Select Committee, 2013). This is particularly challenging for older prisoners as they may have requirements related to their health, frailty, or disabilities which make many forms of accommodation unsuitable, exacerbated by older prisoners often experiencing social isolation stemming from the loss of contact with family, peers, and work networks (being of pensionable age), as well as their health and social care needs (Cornish et al., 2016; Cadet, 2021). Furthermore, as such a significant proportion has committed sexual offences, this again limits the community accommodation assessed as suitable for them. As a result, many older prisoners are required to reside in Probation Approved Premises (PAP) on release. These provide semi-secure hostel type accommodation within which residents are observed and undertake offence-related work to reduce their risks of reoffending as well as to support resettlement (Reeves and Cowe, 2012, 2013; Reeves, 2016).

As PAP only house higher risk offenders whilst they are subject to their prison release license, those assessed as lower risk or have reached their sentence end-date may be released into emergency accommodation such as homeless hostels, shelters, or Bed and Breakfast Guest Houses. There are strict criteria to qualify for longer term housing support, which includes prisoners' homeless status not being the fault of the prisoner, and being classed as 'vulnerable'.

Even where a released prisoner qualifies for this support, suitable accommodation can be difficult to find in practice, especially due to the complex needs of many older ex-prisoners. This situation is exacerbated by local authorities and private housing agencies often refusing to accommodate sex offenders, and even where they can, such housing may be unsuitable for the needs of older people. Mills et al. (2013) found that even dedicated third sector organisations found it extremely challenging to place older ex-prisoners in suitable housing in a context of social stigma, high demand, stock shortage, budget cuts, and strict risk assessments. To mitigate these difficulties the authors called for housing providers to be more willing to take released prisoners and work closely with local authorities in developing supportive housing strategies.

16.4 Reasons for re-offending

In the last full year data are provided (2019/20), official proven reoffending statistics show that 24.1% of all adult offenders released from custody or court orders reoffend within one year (MOJ, 2022b). As has been consistently reported in life-course research on criminality and desistance (see Rocque et al., 2016 for an overview), age is consistently correlated with reductions in re-offending across cultures, crimes, social and criminal justice contexts. For 2014/15, therefore, offenders over 50 years had a proven reoffending rate of 12%. This rate gradually reduced across prisoner age categories, with 18–20 years being the most likely to reoffend within the adult age categories (MOJ, 2014). Thus, Brunton-Smith et al. (2013) reported that each year of prisoner age was associated with a two percent reduction in the likelihood of reoffending. This is coupled with those serving longer sentences (over one year, as older offenders are often) also having lower reoffending rates (MOJ, 2014).

There is a dearth of research exploring why older prisoners reoffend (Forsyth et al., 2015). However, research into prisoner reoffending in general indicates that many of the issues experienced by older prisoners both in prison and on release are risk factors for reoffending. For example, Brunton-Smith and Hopkins (2013) conducted longitudinal studies of proven reoffending by ex-prisoners across three waves of cohorts between 2005 and 2010, finding that reoffending is associated with post-release drug use, stability of accommodation, employment (or similar positive social engagement), prior offending records (particularly associated with acquisitive crime), backgrounds, and in-prison behaviours and attitudes. This has led to calls for work with older prisoners to focus on the establishment of pro-social and familial networks on release from prison, not only to support the integration and well-being of the released older prisoners, but to support desistance out of crime. McCarthy and Brunton-Smith (2017), for example, demonstrated for a general prison population that positive prisoner-family relationships are significantly associated with lower rates of reoffending, commenting that maintaining such ties is particularly challenging for older prisoners due to their likelihood of having long prison histories or of family breakdown or death.

16.5 Conclusion

While it is beyond the scope of this chapter to suggest specific practical policy measures to reduce the numbers of older adults committing crimes or serving sentences in prison, we do hope that the volume as a whole will generate greater attention to the effects of contemporary systems of crime and incarceration in aging societies. Such considerations can serve to highlight trends in attitudes toward crime and punishment, the institutional challenges of building and maintaining barrier-free environments, and training for staff, as well as gaps in the adequate provision of care for ex-offenders resettling in the community.

However, we also want to emphasise the importance of viewing culture and society as dynamic and complex. The lifeworlds of older adult offenders cannot be captured by the very rough general outlines of the systems provided here, we also need to pay attention to older adult offenders' first-hand experiences as well. Furthermore, we keep in mind that these experiences are not bound within the temporal and spatial confines of direct encounter with criminal and penal institutions. Therefore, any account of why crimes are committed, how older offenders cope with time in prison, and how they rebuild their lives after re-entry must be undertaken with consideration of individual cases and local conditions. That said, even in these individual accounts, valuable points of exploration are still likely to arise. Here are a few potential areas that we believe might generate useful consideration:

1 Types of crimes contributing to the aging prison population: Looking at the case of England and Wales, as well as other countries, indicates that changing laws and public attitudes regarding sexual offenses could have a profound effect on the incarcerated older adult population.
2 Dementia and cognitive impairment: England and Wales have already acknowledged the high rates of disability, chronic health needs, and mental illness (including addictions) that affect the majority of older adult offenders. Trends in the aging prison population suggest that additional provision may also be important for prisoners with dementia. This includes not only screening and treatment, but also remodelling facilities and training of staff as well as employing dedicated staff specialists to conduct regular reassessments as prisoners age.
3 The role of voluntary organisations: While the 2014 Care Act has set out a clear agenda for providing care for older and disabled prisoners and ex-offenders, continuity of care still depends on cooperation between prisons, probation, and various non-governmental or volunteer organisations such as RECOOP and Restore Support Network. However, with very high re-offending rates persisting, there may be a greater need to expand cooperation with the voluntary sector.

These three areas are not exhaustive by any means, but each area can only be addressed through a further analysis of both policy trends and practices, as well as through research that explores the lifeworlds of older adults.

Note

1 Although Scotland and Northern Ireland are part of the United Kingdom, their judiciary and prison systems are separate. In 2017, Scotland held 7,500 offenders in prisons, while Northern Ireland held about 1,600, so the prison population of England and Wales accounts for the vast majority of the overall population of the UK.

References

Aday, R. (1994) 'Golden Years Behind Bars', *Federal Probation*, 58(2), pp. 47–54.

Alzheimer's Society. (2014) *Foundation Criteria for the Dementia Friendly Communities Recognition Process*. Available at https://www.alzheimers.org.uk/download/downloads/id/2886/foundation_criteria_for_the_recognition_process.pdf. (Accessed 16th January 2018)

Brooke, J., Diaz-Gil, A., and Jackson, D. (2020) 'The Impact of Dementia in the Prison Setting: A Systematic Review', *Dementia*, 19(5), pp. 1509–1531.

Brunton-Smith, I., and Hopkins, K. (2013) 'The Factors Associated with Proven Re-Offending Following Release from Prison: Findings from Waves 1 To 3 Of SPCR', *Results from the Surveying Prisoner Crime Reduction (SPCR) Longitudinal Cohort Study of Prisoners*.

Cadet, N. (2021) 'An Ageing Client Base: How Can Probation Deliver Support for Older Service Users?', *British Journal of Community Justice*, 17(2), pp. 119–133.

Centre for Policy on Ageing. (2016) *Diversity in Older Age: Older Offenders*. Available at http://www.cpa.org.uk/information/reviews/CPA-Rapid-Review-Diversity-in-Older-Age-Older-Offenders.pdf. (Accessed 19th January 2018)

Cornish, N., Edgar, K., Hewson, A., and Ware, S. (2016) 'Social Care or Systematic Neglect? Older People on Release from Prison', *Prison Reform Trust and Restore Support Network*.

Council of Europe. (2017) *Annual Penal Statistics (Statistiques Pénales Annuelles du Conseil de l'Europe)*. Available at http://wp.unil.ch/space/space-i/prison-stock-on-1st-january/prison-stock-on-01-jan-2015-2016/ (Accessed 28 February 2018).

Crawley, E., and Sparks, R. (2005) 'Hidden Injuries? Researching the Experiences of Older Men in English Prisons', *The Howard Journal of Criminal Justice*, 44(4), pp. 345–356.

Fassin, D. (2017) *Prison Worlds: An Ethnography of the Carceral Condition*. Malden, MA: Polity Press.

Fazel, S., Hope, T., and O'Donnell, I., et al. (2001) 'Health of Elderly Male Prisoners: Worse than the General Population, Worse than Younger Prisoners', *Age and Ageing*, 30(5), pp. 403–407.

Forsyth, K., Senior, J., and Stevenson, C., et al. (2015) "They Just Throw You Out': Release Planning for Older Prisoners', *Ageing and Society*, 35(9), pp. 2011–2025.

Foucault, M. ([1975]1995) *Discipline and Punish: The Birth of the Prison*. New York: Vintage Books.

Hayes, A.J., Burns, A., Turnbull, P., and Shaw, J.J. (2012) 'The Health and Social Needs of Older Male Prisoners', *International Journal of Geriatric Psychiatry*, 27, pp. 1155–1162.

HCJC (House of Commons Justice Committee). (2019) 'Prison Governance: First Report of Session 2019 HC191', *House of Commons*. https://publications.parliament.uk/pa/cm201919/cmselect/cmjust/191/191.pdf (accessed 11th February, 2022).

HMIP. (2017) *Life in Prison: Living Conditions.* Available at https://www.justiceinspectorates.gov.uk/hmiprisons/wp-content/uploads/sites/4/2017/10/Findings-paper-Living-conditions-FINAL-.pdf. (Accessed 12th January, 2018)

Justice Select Committee. (2013) *Older Prisoners.* Available at http://www.parliament.uk/documents/commons-committees/Justice/Older-prisoners.pdf. (Accessed 23rd January 2015)

Maguire, M., Morgan, R., and Reiner, R. (1997) *The Oxford Handbook of Criminology* (2nd edition), Oxford, UK: Clarendon Press.

Mann, N. (2012) *Doing Harder Time? The Experiences of an Ageing Male Prison Population in England and Wales.* Aldershot, UK: Ashgate Publishing.

Maschi, T., Kwak, J., Ko, E., and Morrissey, M.B. (2012) 'Forget Me Not: Dementia in Prison', *The Gerontologist*, 52(4), pp. 441–451.

Matravers, A., and Hughes, G.V. (2003) 'Unprincipled Sentencing? The Policy Approach to Dangerous Sex Offenders'. In Tonry, M. (ed.) *Confronting Crime: Crime Control Policy under New Labour*, Devon, UK, Willan Publishing.

McCarthy, D., and Brunton-Smith, I. (2017) 'Prisoner-Family Ties during Imprisonment: Reassessing Resettlement Outcomes and The Role of Visitation', *Prison Services Journal*, 233, pp. 23–33.

Mills, A., Gojkovic, D., Meek, R., & Mullins, D. (2013). Housing ex-prisoners: The role of the third sector, *Safer Communities, 12*(1), 38–49.

Ministry of Justice (MOJ). (2014) *The Needs and Characteristics of Older Prisoners.* Available at https://www.gov.uk/government/uploads/system/uploads/attachment_data/file/368177/needs-older-prisoners-spcr-survey.pdf. (Accessed 16th January 2018)

Ministry of Justice (MOJ). (2022a) *Offender Management Statistics Quarterly: July-September 2021.* London: Ministry of Justice.

Ministry of Justice (MOJ). (2022b) *Proven Reoffending Statistics: January-March 2020.* London: Ministry of Justice.

Moll, A., (2013) 'Losing Track of Time' Dementia and The Ageing Prison Population: Treatment Challenges and Examples of Good Practice'. London: The Mental Health Foundation

Papadopoulos, I., and Lay, M. (2016) 'Current and Emerging Practice of End-of-Life Care in British Prisons: Findings from an Online Survey of Prison Nurses', *BMJ Supportive & Palliative Care*, 6(1), pp. 101–104.

Pedder, K. (2017) *Out for Good: Lessons for The Future.* London: Prison Reform Trust.

Pratt, J. (2007) *Penal Populism.* London: Routledge.

Prison Reform Trust (2017) 'Prison: The Facts', *Bromley Briefings, Summer 2017.* Available at http://www.prisonreformtrust.org.uk/Portals/0/Documents/Bromley%20Briefings/Summer%202017%20factfile.pdf. (Accessed 12th January 2018)

Prisons and Probation Ombudsman (PPO) (2016) 'Dementia'. *Learning Lessons Bulletin Fatal Incidents Investigations Issue.* Available at http://www.ppo.gov.uk/app/uploads/2016/07/PPO-Learning-Lessons-Bulletins_fatal-incident-investigations_issue-11_Dementia_WEB_Final.pdf. Accessed (16th January, 2018).

Prisons and Probation Ombudsman (PPO) (2017) *Older Prisoners.* Available from https://s3-eu-west-2.amazonaws.com/ppo-prod-storage-1g9rkhjhkjmgw/uploads/2017/06/6-3460_PPO_Older-Prisoners_WEB.pdf. (Accessed 10th January 2018)

Reeves, C. (2013) '"The Others": Sex Offenders' Social Identities in Probation Approved Premises', *Howard Journal of Criminal Justice*, 52(4), pp. 383–398.

Reeves, C. (2016) *Experiencing Imprisonment: Research on the Experience of Living and Working in Carceral Institutions.* London: Routledge.

Reeves, C., and Cowe, F. (2012) 'Residential Work with Sex Offenders - Places of Collusion and Segregation or Preparation for Resettlement and Reintegration'. In *Sex Offenders: Punish, Help, Change or Control? Theory, Policy and Practice Explored.* London: Taylor and Francis.

Rocque, M., Posick, C., and Hoyle, J. (2016). 'Age and Crime'. In Jennings, W.G. (ed.) *Encyclopedia of Crime and Punishment*, Hoboken, NJ: Wiley-Blackwell, p. 275.

Senior, J., Forsyth, K., and Walsh, E., et al. (2013) 'Health and Social Care Services for Older Male Adults in Prison: The Identification of Current Service Provision and Piloting of an Assessment and Care Planning Model', *Health Services Delivery Research*, 1 (5).

Sturge, G. (2021) 'UK Prison Population Statistics', *House of Commons Library Research Briefing 04334.*

The Telegraph (2014) *Eight Prisons Now Hold Only Sex Offenders, Says Chris Grayling.* Available at http://www.telegraph.co.uk/news/uknews/crime/11001309/Eight-jails-now-hold-only-sex-offenders-says-Chris-Grayling.html. (Accessed 19th January 2018)

Turner, M., Payne, S., and Barbarachild, Z. (2011) 'Care or Custody? An Evaluation of Palliative Care in Prisons in North West England', *Palliative Medicine*, 25(4), pp. 370–377.

Wacquant, L. (2009) *Punishing the Poor: The Neoliberal Government of Social Insecurity.* Durham NC: Duke University Press Books.

Section IV

A Comparative Cultural Study on Elderly Crime

Results of a Joint Questionnaire Survey in Four Countries (New Zealand, Hong Kong, Australia, and Japan)

17 Comparison between New Zealand and Japan

Yoko Hosoi

Toyo University, Japan

As a study group, we planned and proceeded to conduct an international comparison of elderly inmates. In doing so, we received a research grant in 2012 to conduct a questionnaire survey and interview surveys of elderly inmates in Japan and New Zealand.

17.1 A comparison between characteristics of elderly convicts from Japan and New Zealand

First, we will describe the outline and results of "the 2012 survey" conducted in Japan and New Zealand, and we will introduce the results of the cluster analysis performed on the overall data obtained from the two countries at the end. The results obtained from Japanese convicts are described in Section 2, and here we compare their characteristics to the convicts from New Zealand.

1 The subjects were 62 New Zealanders (recovery rate 35.0%) and 635 Japanese (90.7%). Most were male aged between 65 to 69. The average sentence was 7.34 years in New Zealand and 2.37 years in Japan. New Zealanders and the Japanese had an average of 2.53 and 4.57 years of prison experience, respectively. Sex crimes account for 77.4%[1] of the crimes in New Zealand, while theft accounts for 49.1% in Japan.
2 Background of elderly convicts
    a Older adults account for 3-5% of all the convicts in many western countries, including New Zealand. On the other hand, in Japan, 18.4% are over 60 years old (Annual Report of Correction Statistics 2014).
    b In New Zealand, 77.4% of the crimes are sexual offenses, while in Japan, 49.1% are larceny with very few sexual offenses.
    c For victims, 37.1% of prisoners in New Zealand consider it important to "know more about them," "apologize," and "get forgiveness," while only 3.2% of the Japanese convicts think so.
    d In New Zealand, 47% of the crimes are against acquaintances such as family, friends, and acquaintances, compared to 12% in Japan.
    e The average age of elderly convicts in Japan is 66.73 years while that of the convicts from New Zealand is 56.87 years; approximately ten years

DOI: 10.4324/9781032669519-22

younger than that in Japan. Given that life expectancy is about the same in both the countries, it may be closely related to the types of crimes in both countries (theft and sex crimes).

f Regarding employment, 27.4% and 19% of convicts in New Zealand and Japan, respectively, are employed full-time.
g The main reason for unemployment is "health" in New Zealand, but "no job" in Japan.
h In terms of housing, about half of New Zealanders have a "home" and live with a "family," whereas in Japan, they live alone in a "rental apartment."
i In marital relations, most subjects in both countries have undergone "divorce" and are now "unmarried" (71% vs. 65%).
j The pension recipients are 48.4% in New Zealand and 30.9% in Japan.

3 Concerns after being released that they thought about while they were in prison.

In New Zealand, "health anxiety" was 61.3% (Japan 44.9%), "family relations" 32.8% (Japan 15.1%), and "debt" 27.4% (Japan 6.6%). On the other hand, in Japan, "anxiety about livelihood" is high at 19.8% (New Zealand, 6.5%). As for "hope," 87.3% in New Zealand and most want to live on a "pension," while in Japan, it is 40.6%, which is less than half of that in New Zealand. In Japan, 37.9% want "unemployment insurance," while only 8.1% of the convicts seek so in New Zealand.

4 The self-conception of elderly convicts

What kind of a person did the convicts think they were before they went to prison? In New Zealand, compared to in Japan, more people said they were "isolated from others" and "felt alone"; however, 69.4% of the respondents also answered that people "depended on them." However, many Japanese convicts answered "often had to do something for family" and "depended on people," and many of them were self-determined that they were not dependent on people (Table 17.1).

Life after release (hopes): In both countries, many convicts answered, "do not commit crimes again," "do not bother others," "want to live brightly," and "want to live leisurely." The significant differences between the two countries are "want to believe in God" (43.5%, 2.4%, New Zealand to Japan, respectively) and "want to live without embarrassing the person in charge (prison officer, social worker, staff, etc.)" (71.0%, 11.0%, respectively), and "want to respect the moral obligations and humane feelings" (61.3%, 13.5%, respectively). It was surprising to know that New Zealanders are cautious so as to not embarrass themselves or those who supported them. Furthermore, they also felt morally and legally obliged to respect and treat those around them humanely. Did the Japanese culture of caring for others become a mere ghost, or did the convicts lose that culture significantly? I would like to take up this issue in the future.

Table 17.1 Personality profile of an elderly inmate: Comparison between Japan and New Zealand

Q. Do you think the following applied to you when you committed the crime? Circle the number of an option that most accurately describes you. (You can select as many items as you like)

	Japan		*New Zealand*	
	N = 635	*%*	*N = 62*	*%*
1. I had a lot I had to do for my family	136	21.4	10	16.1
2. I was frequently ostracized by others	22	3.5	15	24.2
3. I frequently got away from others	106	16.7	16	25.8
4. I was alone	169	26.6	23	37.1
5. I tended to have trust in others	295	46.5	30	48.4
6. I tended to gain the trust of others	202	31.8	34	54.8
7. I consulted with my family about anything	91	14.3	16	25.8
8. I frequently talked with my colleagues	132	20.8	23	37.1
9. I was worried that I was harmed by others	36	5.7	15	24.2
10. I tended to rely on others	119	18.7	6	9.7
11. I tended to being relied on by others	232	36.5	43	69.4
12. I frequently got funny looks from others	41	6.5	11	17.7
13. I tended to watch out for others	70	11.0	25	40.3
14. I lived a thrilling life	97	15.3	23	37.1
15. I lived a livable life	111	17.5	18	29.0
16. I lived an orderly life	100	15.7	28	45.2
17. I had an incentive to work	306	48.2	33	53.2
18. I was interested in politics	116	18.3	11	17.7
19. I was dissatisfied with current politics and social system	129	20.3	12	19.4
20. I was careful about my health	351	55.3	40	64.5
21. I had no willingness about anything	48	7.6		
22. I tended to see things positively	316	49.8	38	61.3
23. I tended to see things negatively	75	11.8	5	8.1

The direct cause of this crime: Although it is impossible to make a simple comparison because of different types of crimes, "sexual desire" is the most common in New Zealand and "money" in Japan.

17.2 The image of elderly convicts: Comparison between New Zealand and Japan seen from interview surveys

17.2.1 Interview survey: New Zealand

<Case 1>

- Place (Wellington), Date (June 18, 2015), Interviewer (Dr. E. Mossman)
- Subject: Male, 71 years old, white New Zealander. Ended schooling at 15.5 years of age. No qualifications. Retired, living on NZ$288-a-week

pension. Forty-seven years of marriage with no dependents. Being in good health.

- Criminal record: Indecent assault of four adult women at 62. First-time imprisonment. Sentenced to nine years in prison. Released on parole after serving five years.
- Prison life and impressions: I never want to return to prison, but I think imprisonment prevented me from committing crimes. I could understand why I committed those crimes through introspection. The first year in prison was harsh. I was bullied by my cellmate (physically, mentally, and verbally). Although corrections officers and nurses did the bare minimum, doctors were conscientious. I spent every day just thinking about myself and mostly reading books. I sometimes took a walk nearby. After being transferred to another institution, I participated in the Sycamore program where an offender and a victim of a similar crime have a conversation to understand the influence and background factors of the crime. The program proved to be a major turning point for me. In the program, I learned "anger control," "daily life skills,, and "the way of thinking about things." Working hard to take care of my cellmate in its advanced course, I became aware of being an "elder" who is capable of aiding others. At the same time, I earned a Bachelor of Divinity degree to develop myself mentally.

  But I was not permitted to exercise the qualification at church as a condition for parole. After I moved to Unit 7 but before my release from prison, my wife and children, sometimes accompanied by my grandchildren, visited me once a week. My wife supported my family's livelihood. She sent in things for my life in prison, including paying the telephone bills and buying dairy products. That was a great help.
- Background of crime: I was bullied by a female teacher when I was a boy. It traumatized me, and deep-seated hatred and desire for revenge for women grew inside me with each passing day. Consequently, I committed these crimes. However, thanks to the Sycamore program that I took in prison, I came to realize that such an idea was wrong. Psychological services that I received concurrently with the program focused on real crimes and were not of much help to learn the root cause of the crime.
- Feelings for victims: I realized that I had great misconceptions.
- Thoughts on family: Thanks to the Christian faith, my love for my family was deepened. My wife also forgave me for my past conduct and accepted me for who I am today. I became intensely aware with each day that a powerful God always exists above us. That was something I could learn in Unit 7.
- Determination not to re-offend: It all comes down to "support." Although I could firmly prepare for it by knowing the existence of God, different approaches are needed for those who are not like me.
- Assistance after release: Liaison officers play a major role. They provided consultation for the things needed after release from prison and referred me to a medical institution. They also arranged a residence for those who

do not have a house. Work in prison comprised physical labor. Because of my age, if I had acquired computer skills a little more, I would have found a place to work after release.

- Present life (after release) and comments: I did not know when a decision to grant parole would be made until just before it happened. So, I could not prepare a plan for my life after release (including mental preparedness) in advance. If I could have experienced life outside the prison to know the situation of the town and how to get on a train, let's say, once every two weeks for several months before release, my life after release would have been less worrisome. Spending time with my wife is my only pleasure currently. However, since she works during the day, I grow vegetables during the time in a field that I have rented nearby. Our current house is a temporary residence arranged by the Salvation Army, and we have to move out soon. Unfortunately, I may no longer be able to continue fieldwork. Given a place to live and people to consult with by the church's support, I manage to live my life. Besides, I had a good probation officer. I am glad the officer took me to small community meetings and convinced people that I am not a "great demon."

<Case 2>

- Place (Wellington), Date (July 6, 2015)
- Subject: Male, 70 years old, white New Zealander. Graduated from school at 15. No qualifications. Retired, living on a pension. Married with no dependents. Being in good health.
- Criminal record: First-time imprisonment. Forty-four crimes related to child sexual abuse in the past. The suspicion of crimes 30 years ago. Sentenced at 63. Served a two-year sentence. Released at 65.
- Prison life and impressions: The prison sentence was for "sex offenses in the past." I felt relieved in a sense. I had concealed those offenses deep in my heart for a long time, but they were discovered and ruled as crimes. Getting a sentence was a big opportunity for me. I searched for the causes of the crimes I committed in the past through the programs provided in prison and expressed them to my cellmate. During confession, I could confront myself honestly, which made me see my life afterward positively. Churches play a major role in getting convicts back on the truck. My wife and friends visited me in prison at least once a month. I made phone calls and wrote letters to tell them how things were going. I had no health problems. Also, I was often asked for advice by my cellmate because of having worked as a counselor assistant at a local hospital for 17 years. I think I was of some help to others.
- Background of crime: I think multiple factors are entwined. In my childhood, I was sexually abused and was left with my grandparents away from my parents. As the second of seven siblings, I was ordered to do manual labor rather than study. I could not find a place to stay because of bullying

at school and delay in studying. I felt alienated both at home and at school. Without realizing it, attacking people weaker than me became a compensatory behavior, and I think sexually abusing children had become a kind of a routine for me.

- Feelings for victims: I did not think about those victims at the time. However, now I believe that my crimes did affect their lives later.
- Thoughts on family: My wife knew my offenses. However, as my prison sentence was longer than expected, rumors spread across our community, which exhausted my wife. Thanks to faith, our relationship did not break down. My relationship with my children became threatened once and was close to breaking down. However, now I manage to maintain our relationship.
- Determination not to re-offend: I have been taken care of by church officials. Those people have made an arrangement that keeps me from being involved with little children. As long as I have people around me, I think I can prevent myself from pulling the trigger (committing a crime).
- Assistance after release: A place to live, support networks, bank accounts, etc.
- Present life and comments: My parole was decided at the first parole board hearing, so I was released before I could even prepare. It was in the middle of the Christmas holidays, and no one was there to meet me. It was a lonely return to home. I want to live with my wife quietly for a while. However, since being told that spending time doing nothing was not good for my health, I was referred to work by church officials. Using the skills of carpentry work that I practiced in the past, I repair church facilities. I also grow seasonal vegetables in an allotment and share them with my acquaintances. When walking around the town, I encounter my old acquaintances. I am not sure those people know about my case, but they greet me. I appreciate that.

<Case 3>

- Place (Wellington), Date (July 28, 2015), Interviewer (Dr. E. Mossman)
- Subject: Male, 83 years old, white New Zealander. Ended schooling at 15 and worked as a carpenter and civil engineer afterward. Retired, living on a pension. Married but separated after he was accused of the crime. No dependents. Heart diseases, hearing loss in one ear, etc.
- Criminal record: Sexual abuse of a minor (his grandchild) in the past. Sentenced to four years and six months. Started serving the sentence at 78. Released at 82.
- Prison life and impressions: I was extremely shocked when I entered prison because it was my first experience of imprisonment. One chair in a room for two. One person sat on the toilet seat. Leaving meals unattended on the floor, we moved to another facility. The shower was a shared shower, but the rest was ordinary. A year later, I was transferred to a unit for the aged and handicapped, fully equipped with medical systems. It was an open ward. I helped with laundry work. Spending pleasant time together with the cellmate of my generation. Unfortunately, programs in prison were of

little help. Instead, I often taught English to my uneducated fellows. They wanted to learn much about IT, but there was no program for that.
- Assistance for release: I was helped by the Salvation Army. They arranged a residence, transportation, money, a driver's license, and a hospital appointment before release. However, my probation officer was strict and did not allow me to enter the places where young women went out (pools, sports grounds, etc.).
- Goal: I want to get out of my temporary residence as soon as possible to move to the warm northern region where my wife lives and live my life quietly there.

<Case 4>

- Place (Wellington), Date (July 28, 2015), Interviewer (Dr. E. Mossman)
- Subject: Male, 87 years old, white New Zealander. Graduated from a state secondary school in Britain at 17. He entered a school of architecture, which was interrupted by war. Served in the army for three years. After that, he was qualified as a surveying inspector in New Zealand. Retired, living on NZ$347-a-week pension. Divorced at 25 and had a de facto marriage three times after that. Living alone for 18 years. No dependents. Being in good health.
- Criminal record: A lewd act on a 13-year-old-boy with whom he had been close. A four-year-and-nine-month sentence. First-time imprisonment at 83. Released at 87. Two months after release.
- Prison life and impressions: The first prison I was sent to be the worst. I was placed in a solitary cell, which were lonely days. Although I was released, my parole was canceled because I did not obey the compliance rule that I must not go to see my children. I was imprisoned again in a strict facility. However, my body became weak, and consequently, I was sent to a hospital. It was comfortable there.
- Assistance after release: The Salvation Army helped me when I was released. Because my parole conditions include not approaching children under the age of 16, I cannot interact with my grandchildren, which is the toughest thing for me. I asked the parole board to withdraw the condition, but they did not listen to my request. Board members told me that if I could not adhere to the condition, I had no choice but to return to prison. Nobody asked about my feelings. I want to express my sincerity to my wife, children, and grandchildren, sell my house to provide compensation to them legally, and find another place to live by myself.

17.2.2 Interview survey: Japan

<Case 1>

- Place (Tokyo), Date (December 27, 2014), Interviewers (HOSOI and WATANABE)

- Subject: An ex-convict, male, 70 years old, Japanese, university dropout, unemployed, on public assistance of 135,000 yen/month, married and divorced, no dependents, regularly seeing a doctor for back pain and hernia.
- Criminal record: a year of imprisonment for physical injury with a three-year suspended execution, life imprisonment for robbery causing death, on parole since 2012 after serving 35 years.
- Prison life and impressions: It took me only a few years in jail to realize how severe life imprisonment was. Even after my release from prison, I must report to the probation officer twice a month. I also must report whenever I go on a trip for a week or longer, when getting married, or moving to another place. Thinking that I need to live as a sinner for the rest of my life, I felt great regret for what I have done. Previously an inmate became eligible for parole after serving 15 years of the sentence. However, with the amendment of the law in 2004, the maximum definite term of imprisonment was raised from 20 years to 30 years, and the parole review committee is now held only after 30 years of service. 30-year imprisonment required me to be cooperative. The prison staff only says something that sounds superficially good to the Ministry of Justice and the public, but I think the reality was quite different. Something good in society was not acceptable inside the prison. Those who gave or received food from others were eligible for punishment. At the time of recreational activities, we all had to keep our eyes closed silently with our hands behind our backs until the start of the show to prevent us from making eye contact with the visitors. In prison life, my personality collapsed in terms of human will and responsibility, but I was able to train myself to maintain an amicable relationship with others. Also, I had the time to read books, pursue my hobbies, and study.
- Background of crime: Regarding a robbery-murder, I cannot explain why I did it even now because it all happened at once. I was 33 years old at that time. Having gotten married and divorced again, I was desperate. As for my work, I tried various jobs as a driver, a nightclub staff, and a sales representative. I had no one to trust. I was short-tempered and always ready to fight with anyone. I lived in a company dormitory but was short of money all the time because I spent all my money on alcohol and horse racing. I did not have a high tolerance for alcohol but always drank. Looking back, I would not have committed such a serious crime if I had a normal life with my family.
- Feelings for victims: The victim had a son in high school at the time. When I was in prison, I sent a letter to the temple every year in Bon Festival with money for flowers and incense sticks. I visited his grave in Zoshigaya a few times after the release. If I am given a chance to see his bereaved family, I would like to apologize to them. They might not want to see me, but I think it could make me feel better.
- Thoughts on family: Since the trial was held in my hometown, everyone knew what I did. My father passed away four to five years after the incident. I guess his death had something to do with my crime. After that, my

mother continued to send me money but died before I was released. My brothers now answer me if I call. However, they lost their jobs at that time and could not live with their heads held high. I do not contact my ex-wife at all. I have a daughter, but I never met her.

- Life history: I joined a baseball club in high school and aimed for the national championship at the Koshien Stadium, although we could not achieve it. I was also thinking of becoming a baseball coach in the future. I went to a technical high school. After graduating from high school, I moved to Tokyo and worked at a furniture store. Then I quit the job to aim for Waseda University. I entered the department of English studies, the school of humanities and social sciences, in 1964 when the Tokyo Olympic Games were held. I did not study much and always played Mahjong. While receiving all the credits required, I technically dropped out as the graduation process was not completed. I listened to the speech of Robert Francis Kennedy in the Okuma Auditorium twice. When Zengakuren, the All-Japan Federation of Students' Self-Governing Associations, was very active, I also joined their activities. I enjoyed everything I did, and my life was crime-free. After that, I worked as a sales representative and field assistant in real estate but quit after two years. Then, I got a job as a receptionist in the tourism industry and married. Later, we were divorced due to her affair. We had a daughter. I think it was a turning point in my life.
- Determination not to re-offend: I am so old that I would not pick a fight with others. However, if somebody picks one with me, I might fight back without being tolerant. However, feelings toward those who have helped me would hold me back.
- Assistance after release: I received a phone call from my volunteer probation officer two weeks before being released on parole and then went on a field trip. I had no one to consult with about my life after the release. After I stayed in an offenders' rehabilitation center, my friend introduced me to the chief director of Mother House.
- Current life after the release: My way of thinking was, of course, changed when I was released on parole at the age of 70 after going to prison at the age of 33. It took me a year and a half to two years to get used to it. The speed was different. I think I have become a calmer person than before. Now I take a walk in the morning and watch TV during the day. I sometimes participate in volunteer work at the church. Usually, I cook for myself.

<Case 2>

- Place (Maebashi, Gunma), Date of the interview (February 19, 2015), Interviewer (HOSOI)
- Subject: Male, 70 years old, high school graduate, married, living by himself, unemployed, renting an apartment, on public assistance of 135,000 yen/month.

- Criminal record: a year of imprisonment with a three-year suspended execution for possessing obscene electromagnetic recording media with the objective of paid distribution at the age of 50 for the first time, a year and two months of imprisonment for the same offense in his 60s, 10 months of stay in prison.
- Prison life and impressions: The level of prison officers was low. They were childish and inflexible. It would be fine if they understood what they were doing; however, I believe they simply obeyed their superior's order without thinking. In prison, I read books and worked in a woodworking factory. I had pain in my knee and so was grateful to receive medicine.
- Background of the crimes: Since I was young, I have trusted people, and people have also gotten to trust me. My life was worthwhile with purpose and reason. I was somewhat optimistic. I knew I was always at a risk of committing a crime but lost myself in providing what customers wanted. I was defiant, thinking that no one was troubled by my business, unlike fraud. Many of my customers were lawyers, police officers, and judges, and I was doing the business based on a tacit agreement. I thought it was unfair that only the people who sell are punished, not those who purchase. At the bottom of my heart, I wanted money. I was always afraid of being caught, and I even set up surveillance cameras as a precautionary means to stay alerted. At the last moment, I fired the entire staff, about seven or eight of them, to protect them, so I do not believe that I caused any trouble to anyone.
- Current life after the release: I have gained many experiences compared with others. I got everything that I wanted but lost them all with the incident. I have no regrets, however, because I did my best. Whatever happens, we should live positively. There is nothing that I want now. This would be the state of mind that MIYAMOTO Musashi attained. I have a daughter in Saitama with a grandchild. I meet them sometimes. I have a son but lost contact with him. I want to reach him somehow. He is a child with my ex-wife, which is uncomfortable and does not have good feelings about me as I have been doing whatever I want.

<Case 3>

- Place (Tokyo), Date of the interview (May 2, 2015), Interviewers (HOSOI, NISHIMURA, IGARASHI)
- Subject: An ex-convict, male, 69 years old, high school graduate, married and divorced twice, living by himself, high blood pressure and backache, unemployed due to illness, on public assistance of 130,000 yen.
- Criminal record: guilty of assault in his 20s with punishment unknown, a year and six months of imprisonment for theft at the age of 63, on parole after a year and three months of serving. I borrowed 2.5 million yen from a moneylender to hold a funeral for my mother. Nevertheless, they forced me to write a receipt of 4 million yen and eventually took my house. I went broke and stole 10,000 yen from a parked car.

- Prison life and impressions: Life in prison was tougher than I thought. The food there was not good. I watched TV with relative freedom. I requested medicine for high blood pressure but was not given.
- Life history: My father passed away when I was a child, so I lived alone with my mother. I worked as a part-time employee at a construction company when I was in high school, but the company went out of business in a year or so. I got bullied by my friends but I never retaliated. After graduating from high school, I worked as a fisherman and built a house, which was quite fulfilling. My turning point toward evil was when my mother died seven years ago, and I borrowed money from my friends. After that, I lived alone with no friends to trust and talk with. I was always lonely.
- Determination not to re-offend: I am not a vain person, nor am I violent. Therefore, I do not think I would re-offend in the future. However, I might risk committing theft if I cannot receive public assistance due to financial hardship. Nevertheless, I believe I can hold on to myself because I never want to go back to prison. If possible, I want to go to a nursing home. I do not want to rely on God.
- Assistance after release: I had no one to consult to when I was released. I entered Saishukai, an offenders' rehabilitation organization, in Edogawa on parole three months before completing my service. I stayed there when the term of the sentence was completed and subsequently decided to rent an apartment. I went to a real estate agent with 100,000 yen in my hand and rented a room at a cheap price. After that, I visited a welfare office to apply for public assistance and could receive it immediately after the application. I pay 55,000 yen for my rent from the public assistance of 133,000 yen, and only 50,000 yen remains in my hand. Thus, I find it difficult to make ends meet.

17.3 Discussions

This study consisted of the following three original investigations (refer to Chapter 1) except for several official statistics: "questionnaire survey" (quantitative data), "interview survey" (qualitative data), and "free-answer survey" (quantitative/qualitative data). In that sense, this study could be considered an "evidence-based empirical study" based on first-hand data. The authors examined the life histories of elderly convicts (male and female) in Japan and the transitions of their life consciousness by associating the results obtained from each investigation.

1 From a standpoint of comparative sociology, interesting properties of elderly convicts in both countries were revealed.

   As shown by the results of the "questionnaire survey", elderly convicts in New Zealand could be stated to be more "other-oriented" and "positive" than convicts in Japan. In response to "How would you like to live after release from prison?" the comments provided by the convicts in New Zealand included "I want to live so as not to bring any shame" upon "persons who supported me (such as caseworker, nurse, prison officer, and probation officer)" and "I feel my obligation" to them, which showed that the convicts in New Zealand had a much higher tendency toward the other-oriented property than the convicts in Japan. Their backgrounds could not be read in the "questionnaire survey" but were shown by the "interview survey." In New Zealand, convicts more often talk about their worries and hopes with each other as well as persons in charge of them on a daily basis. Convicts seem to proactively make suggestions to persons in charge of them and expect suggestions from them. The rate of answering "I want to live a cheerful life" after release from prison in the convicts in New Zealand was 1.5 times that of the convicts in Japan, and the rate of answering "I want to live a life that makes the most of my hobbies" was 2.5 times. The rate of answering that they would live on a "pension" after release was 90% of the convicts in New Zealand with different economic contexts and 37.8% of the convicts in Japan, and 40.2% of the convicts in Japan answered that they expected "public assistance," which was the most common answer. Japanese societies are stated to be familial and community-based. However, in response to "Why do you want to be released from prison early?" the rate of answering "because I have a place to go back to and my family is waiting for me" was 73.4% of the convicts in New Zealand and 34.7% of the convicts in Japan, which showed that the rate in the convicts in Japan was half than that among the convicts in New Zealand. Additionally, in response to "Why do you want to be released from prison early?" the rate of answering "because I want to live proudly in society" was 77.1% of the convicts in New Zealand, which meant that they faced society. In contrast, the comments provided by the convicts in Japan included "I feel gradually deteriorated while in prison," and "I feel like I am becoming another person while in prison," which meant that they could be considered to be "inward-looking" and "negative." Meanwhile, 56.5% of the convicts in New Zealand commented that "it is very important" "to suffer for the crime I committed," which showed the rate in the convicts in New Zealand was 2.5 times that of the convicts in Japan. The rate of convicts in Japan was only 21.1%. It could be stated that the convicts in Japan did not consider the crime they had committed as their own significant problem.

2 In response to "What is important for me in the future," many of the female elderly convicts in Japan answered that all items were "important" compared to the male elderly convicts, which might show that the female convicts made efforts to face the crime they had committed. They placed particular importance on "supported by my family," "getting people around me to understand my remorse," and "compensating the victim." It has been pointed out that more female elderly convicts have recently tended to re-offend. If their efforts to face the crime they committed do not help prevent their recommitment, the authors will reveal what makes them re-offend.

Note

1 New Zealand has a high rate of sex crimes due to the recent prosecution of "historical offending," which means "crimes committed in the past." There is no law or ordinance that provides a specific definition for such crimes, and in this sense, they can charge you for a crime committed 50 years ago. These crimes have been appealed for many years, usually by the victims of sexual crimes. When the crime is revealed by the victim's complaint, and if sufficient evidence is presented or the accused admits the crime, it is then that they can establish it as a criminal case. The length of the sentence depends on the age of the accused, as well as on the accused's social position and social responsibility (e.g., parent, teacher, community club leader). Sentences are usually for 5 or 6 years, or longer if the victim is a child. Most of the convicts in New Zealand in this study were convicted of sexual crimes, and this "past crime" is thought to be a major factor in the significant difference between the charges of convicts in New Zealand and those in Japan.

18 Comparison of Prisoners in New Zealand, Hong Kong, Australia, and Japan

Bunri Tatsuno

Kokushikan University, Japan

With the aim of comparing older prisoners, the study group conducted a survey of male prisoners aged 65 years and older in Japan, New Zealand, Australia, and Hong Kong. The survey was conducted in several countries and regions with the cooperation of local researchers, based on the survey items used in Japan in the 2012 survey.

18.1 Survey methodology

The survey method and other details are described below (Table 18.1). In the following sections, we will compare the results of several common items from the questionnaire survey of male inmates aged 65 years and older.

18.2 Living conditions

In this section, we compare the living expenses before entering prison and the planned living expenses after release.

In Japan, before entering prison, 39.4% of the respondents were "working," 27.7% on "pension," and 27.3% on "welfare," while after release, 42.6% were on "welfare, etc.," 36.0% on "pension," and 30.5% "working." In New Zealand, before release, "pension" applied to 53.8% of the respondents, and "work" to 32.7%, but after release, "pension" changed significantly to 90.4%. In Australia, 66.2% of the respondents reported being on "pension," 23.4% "working," and 23.4% on "savings" before their release from prison, while 84.4% cited "pension" and 23.4% "savings" after their release.

In all countries, even those who were earning their living expenses through work before release are expected to shift to other sources after release. In New Zealand and Australia, the number of those who use pensions as a source of income will increase significantly. In Hong Kong, a high percentage of the respondents rely on welfare-like state support both before and after release from prison.

In terms of employment status, prior to admission, 49.1% of the respondents in Japan, 55.8% in New Zealand, 62.3% in Australia, and 65.3% in Hong Kong stated that they were not working, while 47.9% in Japan stated that

DOI: 10.4324/9781032669519-23

Table 18.1 Survey methods

	Japan	*New Zealand*	*Australia*	*Hong Kong*
Survey period	December 2012—	2013—	November 2018	May–July 2015
Survey subject	Inmates in 56 facilities	Prisoners and former prisoners	Inmates in the facility	Inmates in 3 facilities
Survey method	Self-completion of survey form	Questionnaires/ interviews	Self-completed survey form	Filling out survey form
Collection method	Collected at facilities	Direct collection	Mailed from inmates	Collected at the facility
Effective collection rate	90.7	—	—	Directly administered and collected from those who requested it

they looked for work but could not find any. Conversely, in New Zealand, the reason for this was that they (65.5%) were receiving a pension, and (44.8%) were unable to work due to illness, while in Australia, 75.0% were receiving a pension. In Hong Kong, the 56.3% figure is likely to include social security beneficiaries who were not included in the response items.

When asked about whether they had financial difficulties prior to admission, 64.4% of the respondents in Japan answered that they "sometimes" and "always" had financial difficulties, compared to 17.3% in New Zealand, 5.2% in Australia, and slightly more than 38.3% in Hong Kong. However, 68.7% of the respondents in Japan answered that they had some income before entering prison, implying that their income was not enough to sustain their livelihoods.

Note that a higher percentage of respondents in New Zealand (32.7%), Australia (36.4%), and Hong Kong (48.7%) were in poor health compared to 16.0% in Japan and 36.4% in Australia, respectively, who stated that they were in trouble due to illness regarding their current health status.

18.3 Life after release

Next, we consider attitudes toward life after release from prison. The following is a comparison of how the respondents would like to live after their release from prison. In both countries, the most common response was "not to commit crimes again," but the other most common response in Japan was "not to cause trouble for others" (62.8%). In contrast, in New Zealand, "want to live up to the expectations of my supporters" (75.0%) and "want to be happy" (71.2%) were high, while in Australia, "want to be happy" (61.0%) was high, and the same trend was seen in Hong Kong.

In all countries, "health" and "daily living expenses" were the most common concerns after leaving prison, followed by "work worries" at 22.2% in Japan. In contrast, in New Zealand, "relationships with family" and "relationships with friends" were high at 38.5% and 32.7%, respectively, while in Australia, "nothing in particular" and "relationships with family" were high at 28.6% and 28.6%, respectively.

Next, a comparison is made regarding "things that are important to me."

In Japan, "being accepted by society," "being treated fairly and equitably," and "receiving help to get back on my feet" were high; in New Zealand, "being accepted by society," "receiving help to get back on my feet," and "having family support" were high; in Australia, it was "having family support," "being accepted by society," and "being treated fairly and justly"; and in Hong Kong, "being treated fairly and equitably" and "having family support" were valued highly.

18.4 Summary

In this section, we compared the results of a questionnaire survey of male inmates aged 65 years and older in Japan, New Zealand, Australia, and Hong Kong. Although it is difficult to make general comparisons due to the variation in the names of the offenses, generally, the respondents were concerned about "health" and "daily living expenses" in their post-release lives. Respondents in Japan were more concerned about earning an income from work, while those in New Zealand and Australia were more concerned about their relationships with family and friends. A characteristic of Japan that can be seen from the four-country comparison is that older prisoners are concerned about living expenses and rely on their work income for living expenses after release from prison.

Summary and Conclusions

What We Learn and Pass on from Research on Elderly Crimes

Yoko Hosoi

Toyo University, Japan

Discussing crimes from international viewpoints is, in a sense, an act of projecting distortions on the subjected society. In this book, we focused on elderly people and tried to grasp various social aspects in light of their issues. Since the late 1990s, Asian nations, including Japan, and many nations in the Western world have witnessed an increase in the aging population as never experienced before. Along with this wave, elderly crimes have also increased at a rate even higher than the elderly population increase. Our research endeavor, spanning more than ten years, regarding crimes committed by the elderly revealed that the crimes committed by the elderly in Asian countries, including Japan, had similar characteristics, while the crimes committed by the elderly in English-speaking nations, such as New Zealand, Australia, and the United Kingdom, differed in several aspects. For Hong Kong, the relevant data indicated that these exhibited partial characteristics of other Asian nations, nevertheless, reflecting the factors observed in English-speaking nations' types of crimes and social structure. Thus, the cases in Hong Kong can be described as a combination of those in other Asian and English-speaking nations. Although the studies discussed in this book provide only partial knowledge in terms of comparisons, we believe that they provide a significant foundation for future research. Below, we summarize our discussion thus far.

Crimes by the elderly, which have increased since the late 1990s in Japan, mainly constituted minor offenses, such as property crimes like theft. Moreover, these crimes were committed repeatedly; they would re-offend shortly after being released from prison. The questions remain, what factors lie behind this behavior? and is a crime, for them, not a one-time deal but a menace that lurks in their everyday lives? In contrast, crimes committed by the elderly in the English-speaking nations of New Zealand, Australia, and the United Kingdom are primarily sexual crimes. Here, we attempted to explore the differences in the structural factors of society between Japan and other Asian nations and the Western world.

1. Social background for the increase of theft and its repetition in Japan

How do we explain the increase of elderly criminals in an aging society being faster than the increase in the elderly population? The aging of society has

DOI: 10.4324/9781032669519-24

been progressing at an unexpectedly rapid pace. Corresponding social systems and awareness of people have been unable to catch up with the aging progress, creating a temporary "aging anomie" that has caused various "social issues." Elderly crime is one such representative phenomenon, which is more evidently observed in Japan than in other Asian societies. While omitted from the English edition for editorial reasons, the Japanese edition includes studies conducted in South Korea and Taiwan, both of which exhibit a similar trend, though slightly late compared to Japan. Changes in society in the past two decades have been observed in four areas: demographic structure (declining birthrate and increasing aging population), shrinking households as a living unit (from two to three generation households to couple or single person households), introduction and revision of social security systems (long-term care insurance system and pension system), and establishment of Japanese-style employment systems and practices (shrinking of family or self-owned businesses and shift of employment style to non-regular employment). Although various systems, ordinances, and agreements have been actively implemented, none of these measures were sufficient. In addition, due to the adverse effects of the vertically-divided administration, these measures did not suffice to support the lives of the elderly, resulting in significant dysfunction and shortfalls. Structural issues in society observed here are not unique to Japanese society; a similar trend can be seen in South Korea and Taiwan.

Over the past half-century, with the wave of society's aging population, the elderly have been pushed from the center of society to the periphery, isolated from the infrastructure network such as family and community, and divided within and outside the "pension system" in social security. The aging anomie did not affect the elderly evenly but affected specific segments of the elderly more strongly than others. In Japan, despite its inception and repeated revisions since its introduction, the pension system has left many issues unresolved. The result has been a bifurcation of the elderly into two groups: those who have been fortunate to be included in the social system and those who have been excluded. According to the 2019 government statistics, more than 570,000 "non-pensioners," aged 65 and above, were excluded from the public pension system. Although their numbers are small, the main option left to them is to avail of public assistance in the form of welfare payments. The number of elderly people applying for public assistance is increasing every year, and there are many reported cases where they do not receive it, depending on the local government's circumstances that decide their eligibility. Moving from being pensionless to welfare recipients is the only option for the elderly living at the bottom of society. Many of them have families and relatives who split households or have left their hometowns for work or study, making it difficult for the elderly to receive local community benefits. Thus, one of the routes they take to is crime, evident in the "National Survey of Prisoners," which forms the foundation of this book. They choose to commit crimes for their well-being. However, it was never their intention to do so and, due to circumstances, they were forced to believe that "no other choice was available" to them. At this level of severity, it is futile to demand "self-responsibility" from them because there is no "human ability" left in them to consider this concept. Meanwhile, in the neighboring country of South Korea, the "economic distress" of the elderly has been pointed out as the reason for the recent increase in crime among the elderly. In Taiwan, although economic distress is not as severe as in Japan and South Korea, the elderly are unable to keep up with the rapid pace of social transformation and unwillingly and carelessly violate the "rules" of financial transactions and treaties. As a result, they become "victims" and "perpetrators" (parties) of crimes. "Theft due to poverty" and "fraud due to alienation from social rules" are the result of failure to survive the economic wave and the precise structural anomie that represents the crimes committed by the elderly in Asia.

2. The background of the high rate of sexual crimes among the elderly in English-speaking countries: Situations in New Zealand, Australia, and the United Kingdom

In the English-speaking country of New Zealand, survey results showed that approximately 20% of the respondents were in financial difficulties, while more than 80% had an income. The source of income was either work or pension, with nearly 90% of the respondents indicating that pension was their source of income even after release from prison. Pensions are, in principle, guaranteed to all citizens in New Zealand, Australia, and the UK; therefore, there are marked differences in social security systems compared to Japan. Economic crimes, such as those seen in Japan and South Korea, are absent in New Zealand.

However, the relationship between the two is reversed when looking at sexual crimes. How can we explain the fact that sexual crimes are representative of crimes committed by the elderly in English-speaking countries? Three points became apparent in this series of studies that may assist in understanding the reason. First is the problem in the legal system surrounding sexual crimes related to "penal populism." This is the result of tracking past sex offenders who had not been tried. In New Zealand, the legislative policy of not setting a statute of limitations on the prosecution of most sexual crimes has existed for quite some time. Nevertheless, it is noteworthy that the 2011 Criminal Procedure Act came to fruition, encouraged by the movement for harsher punishment and a strong civil rights advocacy movement for "women and children." The government recently focused on the detection of "historical offending." Although victims of sexual crimes have long been complaining to the police, little progress has been made over the years. However, what was once difficult to do has now been done in one fell swoop. Sexual crimes come to light upon victims' complaints and, if any evidence is confirmed or the perpetrator(s) confesses, the case is established. Since the government can prosecute even if the crime was committed 50 years ago, the perpetrators are sentenced at an advanced age for past crimes that they had not been tried and incarcerated for. The elderly have borne the brunt of this, leading to the recent increase in the number of elderly inmates.

Although the second reason for the high rate of sex offenses will have to await future research, much of this may be concerned with ethnicity, race, and age. In New Zealand, more than 90% of the elderly sentenced for sex offenses are white. In general, inmates in prison, both juvenile and adult, are mostly the indigenous Maori. This is largely the same in Australia. In the UK, age is an issue. The proportion of sex offenders differs between those under and over the age of 50, being more prevalent among the elderly. It can be assumed that the number of older sex offenders is rising in proportion to the increase in the elderly population.

The third reason, as seen through several case studies, is the issue of "the state of the family." The perception of family differs in the West and Asia. In the West, the individual comes first, and multiple individuals form a collective unit of family through marriage; however, in Asia, a family is formed by integrating individuals into legal frameworks, such as a family register. In the West, several individuals go through divorce and remarriage during the course of their lifetime, creating new "extended families." Since the family is an aggregation of individuals, there are family members who become the object of sex. In contrast, in Japan and other Asian countries, a family member has little presence as an individual because a family is not a collective unit of individuals, but rather a framework in which an individual participates as a member. We learned during the joint research discussed in this book that many victims of sexual crimes in English-speaking nations are children, especially those of remarried parents. In Japan, however, the number of singles among the elderly is noticeably large, and those excluded from the family framework have probably few opportunities to establish a new connection with new individuals, thus leading to fewer risks of committing sexual crimes. At the same time, sexual crimes may be latent in Japan and become a new problem through triggers such as public opinion, politicians' proposals, and experts' statements in a different form than in Europe and the U.S. Whether it will be a new problem for the elderly is as yet unknown.

3. The lifeworld of elderly criminals: A joint survey of Japan and New Zealand

In the 1990s, the rate of aging was faster than expected, leading to aging anomie. In these circumstances, the elderly kept running on the rails laid out by the government and society and took a break in their 60s. While looking back on their past, many elderly criminals, whom we studied, looked confused, unable to understand why things turned this way for them. In the long run, they may be healed by the waves of time or feel alive with family support; nevertheless, they have become criminals and are facing the consequences in prison. In this study, we sought to hear their perspective to understand them better. One of the questions we asked was about self-conception. The results are discussed in detail in this book; therefore, we briefly summarize them. In the "2012 survey," we conducted several statistical processes of survey results, focusing on the results of "self-conception" (Q19). We extracted two axes ("strength of relationships" and "trust in people and society"), established four groups through cluster analysis, and created four categories by applying each individual's data, namely, "Stable," "Self-reliant," "Dependent on others," and "Unstable." The "Stable" type was relatively stable in terms of the spouse, family, work, finances, and housing and was similar to the general elderly population. The "Self-reliant" type was relatively similar to the "Stable" type but faced more challenging situations than the "Stable" type. The "Dependent on others" type was more common among women and those overly dependent on family members. Compared to the other types, the life of the "Unstable" type was the most challenging. They mostly received social welfare assistance, such as public assistance, and were expected to receive public support after release from prison. The "Stable" and "Unstable" types were contrasted in their attributes and regarding "What is important for me in the future?" (Q10). As shown in Figure C.1, the "Stable" type considered "to be supported by the family" important, while the "Unstable" type considered "receiving support to rehabilitate" important. In New Zealand, in contrast, the analysis revealed that the former type was further divided into the "Stable" and "Lonely" types, with the former considering "relationships with people, including family" as "important to me" and the latter not considering relationships with people as important.

The above analysis was drawn out based on the questionnaire survey from which clues to the "process of rehabilitation and the nature of support" were found for each type (subgroup) extracted from the survey. Next, we would like to focus on the social factors driving the individual subjects, based on the answers written by the inmates for the "free-answer questions" and the interviews conducted by the researchers with the subjects. In other words,

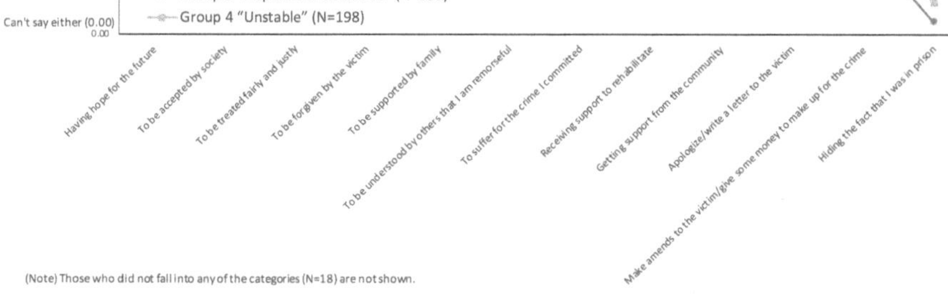

Figure C.1 What is important for me in the future? (By type.)

we attempted to pay attention to the social and structural conditions that forced the inmates to "choose the unwilling act" of "committing a crime." As a result, we could draw out the following three types. In the three decades since the late 1990s, social changes (e.g., demographic structure, employment status, family structure, social security system) have progressed rapidly. The first type was those who could not catch up with the change, and their plans for the latter half of their lives collapsed. They occasionally encountered unexpected events, became disappointed and desperate, and amid this loss of self-confidence, became tempted to deviate. The path to crime was the consequence of longstanding "life struggles and resentments." Their "release" from their suffering in the future will determine whether they can move forward on the path to rehabilitation.

The second type were those who could not escape the dominant values of the past and repeated deviant behavior because they could not bear the gap between the present and the past. This type mainly comprised the elderly who lived before and after World War II, in particular, some of those who achieved success during the post-war recovery period. However, circumstances changed since the peak of that period as they entered the middle age of downfall and were unable to fully awaken from their past dreams. They repeatedly engaged in unscrupulous behavior, from distrust of others to aiming to make an easy fortune.

The third type, which had the maximum number of people, were those who had a high probability of downfall due to the negative influence of bad company based on their life history and few opportunities to think for themselves. They learned to live in dependence in the face of adversity since their childhood. Men mostly became involved in local gang groups early in life and repeatedly left and re-joined one group or another, walking the border between legal and illegal communities. The nature of "support for rehabilitation" requires long-term care and, at the same time, a detailed program, tailored to the diverse needs of the individuals involved.

4. Crimes by elderly women: Women's unique life course and awakening of the "self"

The number of elderly convicts is constantly increasing and remains high. In this situation, the increase of female criminals is particularly significant in Japan. Most of their crimes are thefts, often shoplifting, and repeated offenses. There are few countries in the world where the overpopulation of elderly female inmates has become a social problem. While there are few empirical studies on female criminals, the results of the "2012 Survey," discussed in this book, indicated that female criminals had a more significant family presence both in "the process of committing crimes" and "the process of rehabilitation from crimes." It must be understood that female inmates were more pronouncedly "dependent on others" for their "sense of self" than their male counterparts, both in the "range" and "strength" of their social relationships. This can be seen both in macro and micro aspects from the remarks in the free-answer questions of the "2017 and 2019 Surveys" that followed the above-mentioned survey. In relation to the social structure viewpoints, changes over the past three decades, including the increase in life expectancy, shrinking family sizes, economic deprivation of the younger generation, and the functional weakening of local communities due to long-term care insurance systems have had a more significant impact than expected on female criminals. The life course of elderly women forms a linear track compared to that of men. Many women choose "marriage." However, the problem is what comes after marriage. "Separation (bereavement or death)" makes a significant difference in their lives. When asked "What is the happiest thing in your life so far?" several female criminals answered, "Marriage and childbirth." The same was true for non-prisoners (general and underclass women). In contrast, "physical abuse by husband/partner," "separation from children (bereavement/separation)," "disability of children," and "physical and mental abuse by parents" stand out as the "most painful experiences." However, an exact comparison is not possible since the same question was not asked of the non-prisoners. Nearly half of the elderly inmates lived with their children, received a fixed, though not large, pension, and earned through "part-time or irregular work" before imprisonment. Although the underclass of elderly inmates is small, I believe this is the root of the characteristics of elderly offenders. Most of them are "shoplifters" and are not involved in other crimes; however, they are extremely positive about their sense of self. They took care of their health, were devoted to their family, and worked hard at their jobs. However, they were distant from those around them, spent little time with friends, and rarely discussed their problems with others. They tried their best to cope in everyday life and lived with their children (only half of them). They felt "satisfied" in their ways and tried to break free from a sense of "lower-class feeling." Thus, they lived a reasonably fulfilling life before imprisonment. However, it is significant that they did not feel "happiness" in their lives since "satisfaction with life" and "happiness" can be two different things. Thus, it is important to consider the true nature of the state commonly referred to as "loneliness."

5. Cooperation and distance between justice and welfare for elderly criminals: Focusing on entrance and exit supports

In Japan, there has been a noticeable movement in the criminal justice process concerning the elderly over the past decade. The increase in the number of crimes committed by the elderly and the fact that most of them are recidivists have become major social problems. In response, a significant change in society's attitude became the driving force to make several improvements in the judicial process. In this study, however, we focused mainly on hearing the story of the elderly criminals and did not investigate the overall situation of the criminal justice process. Thus, let us review the situation in Japan from the limited data available and overview the relevant situations in other countries.

The most dominant crime among the elderly inmates in 2019 was theft, followed by illicit drug use. These elderly inmates can be broadly divided into three categories: "recidivists" who continue to repeat crimes, the "late offenders" who have committed crimes in their old age, and the "long-term type" who have become old during their long-term imprisonment. Each of these categories has its characteristics. In this study, we focused on the "recidivists." They repeatedly commit relatively minor crimes and repeat the cycle of arrest, trial, short-term imprisonment, and release. Several re-offend within a few months of release and are sentenced repeatedly. They do not care much about being sent to prison, and imprisonment constitutes a significant part of their lives. Many elderly "recidivists" have a mental disorder as the foundation; however, some have weak economic foundations, poor health, and family discord, among other factors. The analysis of a survey of prisoners discussed in this book revealed that their motivations for crime were complexly intertwined with social structural factors, which were the major forces working against the elderly to stand their ground.

In Japan, the elderly have not been treated differently from suspects and defendants of other age groups in the criminal justice system. In response to the increase in crimes committed by the elderly and elderly criminals who would re-offend in a relatively short period from their release from prison, a need for measures to deal with recidivists and first-time offenders has become a pressing issue, though this trend is relatively recent. Moreover, in the course of recidivism prevention, emphasis has been placed on supporting them after release (**exit support**), as seen in the government program for recidivism prevention, rather than on preventing them from re-offending. However, as the reality of these offenders becomes more evident, the need for unique consideration for them during the criminal justice process has been pointed out; namely, the process between their arrest, trial, and imprisonment and a supportive measure, introduced as the **entrance support** before their admittance to correctional facilities. Cooperation between the judiciary and welfare was called for and specific efforts were introduced in practice. It is clear that these elderly criminals would re-offend because of the underlying, complexly intertwined, social structural factors that have led them to their situation. It has also become clear that, in the process of their arrest, trial, and prosecution, appropriate support for their situation will significantly impact their rehabilitation. In other words, the role of supportive measures in the process of seeking support at an early stage has come to attract attention. In a sense, the role of a companion, in place of the family, is more crucial. Although this system has just started, I am involved in it as a supporter to observe how the offenders give themselves a fresh start.

6. Rehabilitation process of elderly criminals: How to expand "self-reliance"

In this book, we have focused our discussion on "elderly criminals" who have been committed to criminal justice institutions (prisons) through the criminal justice processes in various countries. Not all who commit "criminal acts" go to prison. Although there are differences according to the national laws, most go through the police, prosecution, and trial process and only those who fulfil certain conditions are incarcerated. How do incarcerated people perceive prisons?

Many of the countries that participated in this joint study have taken up the prison issue to varying degrees, and some countries have begun to take steps to reform their prisons, mainly from a humanitarian point of view, in response to the concerns voiced regarding the inadequacy of the penal institutions, especially for the elderly. The UK and Japan, concerned about the increasing number of elderly people, have shown a willingness to establish facilities to help the elderly recover from long-term health problems and return to society. Nevertheless, many challenges remain. In Japan, the financial issues of those released from prison weigh heavily, and the extent to which social workers and other professionals can support the self-reliance of the elderly beyond the judicial system remains a major question. In contrast, elderly people in Europe and the U.S. who have been sentenced for sexual crimes are not allowed to visit the hubs of social life (e.g., places where families and children gather, public facilities frequently visited by women) for a certain period after leaving the justice system due to the nature of their crimes. The challenges presented here indicate that a certain amount of determination and patience is required to get one's social life back on track. To free themselves from criminal activities and to live "happily as decent human beings," the elderly need, above all, a "strong will and determination toward oneself" and "forgiveness and consideration from society." Nevertheless, we noticed, during the limited scope of our joint research project, that the presence of an "intermediate group" positioned between the family and others is indispensable to support the determination of the elderly and society. While listening to these elderly criminals, we realized that a specific new form of "family-like companionship" could be pursued as a short- or middle-term prospect, considering the feelings (awareness) of the elderly criminals, the financial source to support the social security system in the economic status where a rapid economic growth should no longer be expected, and above all, the decline of birthrate and aging of society at a pace considered the fastest in the world. Is it possible to seek a new, family-like relationship, different from the old-fashioned family group but something that has been the foundation of the Japanese-style welfare system and respects "freedom and human rights of the individual"? This vision of Japanese society differs from its Western counterparts. A series of investigations in this research project has taught us that seeking "family-like companionship" would be the solution to stop the increasing number of elderly crimes in Japan.

Request for questionnaire

This questionnaire is intended to survey the lives of prisoners at age 40 or over.

Japan is facing an aging society. Because of this, it is important for Japan to understand what measures should be taken to help ensure the health and happiness of elderly people, why elderly people commit crimes, and what support is required for their smooth social rehabilitation.

Researchers from various universities, receiving national scientific research funds, decided to conduct this survey as an academic study of these issues. Please answer the questions for this survey.

You may choose whether or not to complete this survey. This is not compulsory. If you do not want to answer the questionnaire, please submit it to an official without answering it. Not cooperating with this survey does not affect your performance in prison nor bring disadvantages.

However, if it is convenient for you, you understand the intent of this survey, and you are willing to cooperate, answer the questionnaire, and submit it in an envelope to an official. We will not use your questionnaire for purposes other than this survey, and your personal information is not disclosed. Please answer it at your convenience.

Though the results of this survey will be released as a report, we will not connect the results to individual respondents.

First, please show your willingness to participate (Mark ✓ in the appropriate □).

□ I will cooperate with this survey. → Fill in the survey slip.
□ I will not cooperate with this survey. → Submit it to an official without answering it.

XXX XX, XXXX Yoko Hosoi (Professor Emeritus at Toyo University)
Bunri Tatsuno (Professor of the Faculty of Law of Kokushikan University)

Read the following questions and circle the number of an option that most accurately describes you.

[Job and family]

Question1 **Were you working when you committed the crime?**

Circle the number of an option that most accurately describes you. (You can select several answers.)

1. I was in regular work
2. I was working as a contracted worker for a definite term
3. I was working as a dispatched worker/part-time worker/day worker)
4. I was helping my family's business
5. Other (Please tell us exactly:)
6. I was not working

→ **Circle the number of an option that most accurately describes the reasons why you were not working.**

(You can select several answers.)

1. I could not work due to illness
2. I was engaged in housework, childcare, nursing care, or assistance
3. I tried to find a job, but I could not
4. I was unwilling to work
5. I was not distressed about money
6. I was on welfare
7. Other (Please tell us exactly:)

Question 2 **Additional question: How many years have you worked?**

Approx. ( ) year(s)

Among the year(s) you worked

(1) How many were in regular work Approx. ( ) year(s)
(2) How many years were you working as a contracted worker for a definite term Approx. ( ) year(s)
(3) How many years were you working as a dispatched worker/part-time worker/day worker Approx. ( ) year(s)
(4) How many years were you helping your family business Approx. ( ) year(s)

(No problem if any period overlaps among these four work patterns.)

Question 3 **Where did you live when you committed the crime?**

Question 4 **Did you have a spouse (including common-law marriage and living-together arrangement) or partner when you committed the crime?**

1. Yes
2. No

Question 5 **We would like to ask you about your housemate when you committed the crime.**

1. I had a housemate → (person(s) other than myself)
2. I lived alone → (Go to Question 6)

→**Additional question: Who was your housemate? Circle the number of an option that most accurately describes you.**

Also answer the number of your housemates in (   ).

1. Husband or partner
2. Child (   )
3. Parent of husband or partner (   )
4. My parent (   )
5. My brother or sister (   )
6. Husband's brother or sister (   )
7. Husband's grandparent (   )
8. My grandparent (   )
9. Grandchild (   )
10. Other relatives (   )
11. Other (Please tell us exactly:)

Question 6 **Did you have a family member you associated with, but did not live together with when you committed the crime?**

1. Yes
2. No (→ Go to Question 7)

→**Additional question: Circle the number of an option that most accurately describes the family member you are associated with, but did not live with.**

1. Husband or partner
2. Child
3. Parent of husband or partner
4. My parents
5. My brother or sister
6. Husband's brother or sister
7. Husband's grandparent

8. My grandparent
9. Grandchild
10. Other relatives
11. Other (Please tell us exactly:)

Question 7 **Have you been married, divorced, or lived together?**

Circle the number of an option that most accurately describes you and answer the number of times.

1. Marriage (time(s))
2. Divorce (time(s))
3. Common-law marriage such as living together or getting separated (time(s))
4. No experience

Question 8 **Circle the number of the item you have experienced.**

1. Pregnancy
2. Childbirth
3. Miscarriage
4. Abortion
5. Sexual intercourse with people other than husband or partner
6. Sexual assault
7. Victimized by bullying
8. DV (Domestic violence)
9. Patronage dating
10. Marriage fraud (1) Committing, (2) Victimized, (3) Both)

Question 9 **Do you have a family member, relative, or person other than your family with whom you have lived?**

Circle the number of an option that most accurately describes you.

1. Husband or partner
2. Child
3. Parent of husband or partner
4. My parent
5. My brother or sister
6. Husband's brother or sister
7. Husband's grandparent
8. My grandparent
9. Grandchild
10. Other relatives
11. Person who belongs to antisocial groups other than 1-10
12. Other (Please tell us exactly:)

Question 10 **Have you lived alone?**

1. Yes
2. No (→ **Go to Question 11**)

→**How long? (Answer the total period)**

1. Under 1 year
2. Under 3 years
3. Under 5 years
4. Under 10 years
5. 10 years or longer

[Life and behavior when you committed the crime]

Question 11 **Did you have anything you felt bad or worried about when you committed the crime?**

1. Yes
2. No (→ **Go to Question 12**)

→**What was it concerning? Circle the number of an option that most accurately describes you.**

(You can select as many items as you like.)

1. My health
2. Family member's health
3. Relationship with a family member
4. Relationship with a relative
5. Relationship with a neighbor or workplace
6. Relationship with a friend
7. Daily living expense
8. Debt repayment
9. Problem in business
10. Heterosexual relationship
11. My character
12. Dependence on alcohol
13. Dependence on gambling
14. Recommitment of shoplifting and theft
15. Dependence on drugs
16. Tendency to shop
17. Husband's or partner's character and behavior
18. Child's character and behavior
19. Loneliness
20. No reliable person to consult
21. Losing my vigor
22. No tomb

23. Other if any (Please tell us exactly:)
24. Nothing special

Question 12 **How was your financial life when you committed the crime?**

1. Very poor
2. Slightly poor
3. Neither
4. Slightly easy
5. Very easy

Additional question 1: Then, how was it compared to five years ago?

1. **Much poorer**
2. **Slightly poorer**
3. **Same**
4. **Slightly easier**
5. **Much easier**

Additional question 2: Why did your life change?

Please tell us exactly:

Question 13 **How was your mental health and physical health when you committed the crime?**

1. I felt very anxious and worried
2. I felt slightly anxious and worried
3. Neither
4. I did not feel very anxious and worried
5. I did not feel anxious and worried at all

Additional question 1: Then, how was it compared to five years ago?

1. I felt much more anxious and worried
2. I felt slightly more anxious and worried
3. Same
4. I felt slightly less anxious and worried
5. I felt much less anxious and worried

Additional question 2: What caused your increased anxiety and worry?

1. Myself ( )
2. Family ( )
3. Other ( )

Question 14 **What was your monthly income and how much money was at your command when you committed the crime?**

(1) **Income** 1. About ( ) yen on average 2. No income
(2) **My pocket money (money at my command excluding house rent for my family, fuel and light expenses, communications expenses, educational expenses, savings, food expenses, and living expenses) was (**) yen on average

Question 15 **How did you pay living expenses when you committed the crime?**

Circle the number of an option that most accurately describes you. (You can select as many items as you like.)

1. Income from job
2. Annual pension
3. Deposits and savings
4. Property
5. Debt
6. Spouse's or partner's income
7. Aid from family or relative
8. Welfare
9. Aid from friend
10. Aid from supporter
11. Other if any (Please tell us exactly:)

Additional question: What was the monthly income of your whole family?

About ( ) yen **on average**

Question 16 **Do you think the following applied to you when you committed the crime?**

Circle the number of an option that most accurately describes you. (You can select as many items as you like.)

1. I had a lot I had to do for my family
2. I was frequently ostracized by others
3. I deliberately avoided interacting with others
4. I was alone
5. I tended to have trust in others
6. I tended to gain the trust of others
7. I consulted with my family about anything

8. I frequently talked with my colleagues
9. I was worried that I was being harmed by others
10. I tended to rely on others
11. Others tended to rely on me.
12. I frequently got funny looks from others
13. I tended to watch out for others
14. I lived a thrilling life
15. I lived a livable life
16. I lived an orderly life
17. I had an incentive to work
18. I was interested in politics
19. I was dissatisfied with current politics and social systems
20. I was careful about my health
21. The person have not been feeling like doing anything
22. I tended to see things positively
23. I tended to see things negatively
24. None of the above
25. Select any other options that are applicable to your character and impression Other (Please tell us exactly:)
26. I do not know

Question 17 **What do you think caused the crime?**

Circle the number of an option that most accurately describes you. (You can select as many items as you like.)

1. I wanted money
2. I had little patience for myself
3. I was attacked by the other party
4. I wanted goods
5. I was hungry
6. I wanted to take drugs
7. I did not work due to illness
8. I had a relationship with a bad friend
9. I had a quarrel with my family
10. I envied rich people
11. I envied happy-looking people
12. I thought it was good for my family
13. I wanted to protect my honor
14. I thought it was good for people other than my family
15. I was forced to do it by order of another person
16. I could not refuse invitations by my fellows
17. Other if any (Please tell us exactly:)
18. I do not know

Question 18 **What do you think influenced you, your family, and others the most when you committed the crime?**

(1) Answer what influenced you the most exactly.

Please tell us exactly:

(2) What do you think influenced your family the most, who was influenced, and how was he/she influenced?
Please tell us exactly.

Please tell us exactly:

(3) What do you think influenced others (when you have a victim, include him/her) the most, who was influenced and how he/she was influenced? Please tell us specifically.:

Please tell us exactly:

Question 19 **We would like to ask about living expenses after being released from prison.**

Circle the number of an option that most accurately describes you. (You can select several answers.)

1. Income from job
2. Annual pension
3. Deposits and savings
4. Property
5. Debt
6. Husband's or partner's income
7. Aid from family or relative
8. Welfare
9. Aid from friend
10. Aid from supporter
11. Other if any (Please tell us exactly:)

Question 20 **How do you want to live after being released from prison?**

Circle the number of an option that most accurately describes you. (You can select several answers.)

1. I want to live a work-centered life
2. I want to live a relaxed life
3. I want to live a life I can take advantage of my hobby
4. I want to avoid bothering others
5. I want to live with my family
6. I want to live alone
7. I want to try not to reoffend
8. I want to be admitted to a welfare facility such as a nursing home
9. I want to go to a hospital for dependence treatment
10. I want to go to a hospital for other diseases
11. I want to get married again
12. I want to live a cheerful life
13. I want to live an easy life free from dictates
14. I want to ask God for help
15. I want to live without bringing shame on my officer
16. I want to respect duty and obligations
17. I want to believe in luck rather than plugging away
18. Other if any (Please tell us exactly:)
19. I have no particular wishes
20. I have not thought about it

Question 21 **Do you have anxiety and worry after being released from prison?**

Circle the number of an option that most accurately describes you. (You can select several answers.)

Do you have anxiety and worry after being released from prison?

1. My health
2. Family member's health
3. Relationship with a family member
4. Relationship with a relative
5. Relationship with a neighbor or workplace
6. Relationship with a friend
7. Daily living expense
8. Debt repayment
9. Problem in business
10. Heterosexual relationship
11. My character
12. Dependence on alcohol
13. Dependence on gambling

14. Recommitment of shoplifting and theft
15. Dependence on drugs
16. Tendency to shop
17. Husband's or partner's character and behavior
18. Child's character and behavior
19. Loneliness
20. No reliable person to consult
21. Age-related absentmindedness
22. No tomb
23. Undesired guarantor appears
24. Guarantor is undetermined
25. Other)
26. Nothing special

Question 22 **How important are the following items for you now?**

Circle one number for each.

		Very important	***Important***	***Not sure which***	***Not important***	***Not important at all***	***I do not know***
Example taking a bath			*2*	*3*	*4*	*5*	*6*
(1)	Being accepted by society and community	1	2	3	4	5	6
(2)	Being supported by my family	1	2	3	4	5	6
(3)	Being treated equally and fairly by the world	1	2	3	4	5	6
(4)	Being supported for recovery	1	2	3	4	5	6
(5)	Being pardoned by the victim	1	2	3	4	5	6
(6)	Being supported by local people	1	2	3	4	5	6
(7)	Suffering from a guilt feeling	1	2	3	4	5	6
(8)	Feeling hopeful about the future	1	2	3	4	5	6
(9)	Apologizing and writing a letter of apology to the victim	1	2	3	4	5	6
(10)	Winning other's recognition that I truly repent my crime	1	2	3	4	5	6
(11)	Voluntarily paying compensation to the victim if possible and offering restitution to him/her as much as possible	1	2	3	4	5	6
(12)	Hiding serving prison time	1	2	3	4	5	6
(13)	Changing myself	1	2	3	4	5	6
(14)	Becoming self-reliant and getting a job	1	2	3	4	5	6

Question 23 **What do you think about prison? Circle one of five options.**

If you selected 1-3, select the reason in the field shown by the arrow.

1. I want to be in prison all my life and to hold a funeral in prison
2. I want to return to prison temporarily without committing a crime if necessary
3. I want to be released from prison as soon as possible
4. I think the prison is just a place to serve my sentence given by the judge → **(Go to the next page)**
5. It is hard to say → **(Go to the next page)**

►<Circle the number of an item that most accurately describes the reason in 1. (You can select as many items as you like.)>

1. Being afraid of going out into the world
2. Being unable to live even if I return
3. I feel comfortable in prison
4. My official is good to me
5. I feel free living while being in prison
6. I can live in ease in prison
7. The person thinks it as a room with three meals and iron bars
8. I have trust in prison
9. I have lost the desire to live
10. For no specific reason

►<Circle the number of an item that most accurately describes the reason in 2. (You can select as many items as you like.)>

1. I feel comfortable in prison
2. My official is good to me
3. I feel free living while being in prison
4. I can live in ease in prison
5. I have trust in prison
6. I am afraid of public eye
7. I have nowhere to go even if I become unable to continue by myself
8. I am afraid of getting exposed as an ex-convict sooner or later
9. None of the above

►<Circle the number of an item that most accurately describes the reason in 3. (You can select as many items as you like.)>

1. I have no freedom in various ways
2. I did not get along with officials
3. I did not get along with my mates
4. I have a place to go back to and family waiting for me
5. I want to break off with prison
6. I want to learn a skill and make good use of it in society

7. I want to live magnificently
8. There are many interesting things in society
9. I want to apologize to the victim if possible
10. I gradually feel I am wrong when I am in prison
11. I feel I am not myself when I am in prison
12. For some other reason

Question 24 **Have you gone through the following?**

Circle the number of items that most accurately describes you in chronological order.

(Items are to be considered)			*10s*	*20s*	*30s*	*40s*	*50s*	*60s*	*70s*
Mental and medical	(1)	Nail-biting, skin-peeling, crust-peeling	1	2	3	4	5	6	7
	(2)	Atopic dermatitis	1	2	3	4	5	6	7
	(3)	Intense fear of strangers	1	2	3	4	5	6	7
	(4)	Obsessive-compulsive disorder	1	2	3	4	5	6	7
	(5)	Chronic pain	1	2	3	4	5	6	7
	(6)	Anger attack	1	2	3	4	5	6	7
	(7)	Menstrual cramps, irregular menses, premenstrual syndrome	1	2	3	4	5	6	7
	(8)	Excessive strain, hyperpnoea	1	2	3	4	5	6	7
	(9)	Eating disorder (bulimia)	1	2	3	4	5	6	7
	(10)	Eating disorder (anorexia)	1	2	3	4	5	6	7
Social behavior	(11)	Violence and verbal abuse (standpoint of victimizer)	1	2	3	4	5	6	7
	(12)	Violence and verbal abuse (standpoint of victim)	1	2	3	4	5	6	7
	(13)	Bullying (standpoint of victimizer/ victim)	1	2	3	4	5	6	7
	(14)	Idleness	1	2	3	4	5	6	7
	(15)	Runaway	1	2	3	4	5	6	7
	(16)	Delinquency	1	2	3	4	5	6	7
	(17)	Shoplifting	1	2	3	4	5	6	7
	(18)	Stealing other than shoplifting	1	2	3	4	5	6	7
	(19)	Smoking (120 or more cigarettes/ day since reaching manhood)	1	2	3	4	5	6	7
	(20)	Tendency to shop	1	2	3	4	5	6	7
	(21)	Bed-hopping	1	2	3	4	5	6	7
	(22)	Sexual addiction	1	2	3	4	5	6	7
	(23)	Alcohol and drug dependence	1	2	3	4	5	6	7

(*Continued*)

Question 24 (Continued)

	(24)	Dependence on gambling such as Japanese pinball, mah-jongg and horseracing	1	2	3	4	5	6	7
	(25)	Dependence on games	1	2	3	4	5	6	7
	(26)	Provision of sex business	1	2	3	4	5	6	7
	(27)	Patronage dating (prostituted)	1	2	3	4	5	6	7
	(28)	Patronage dating (prostituting)	1	2	3	4	5	6	7

Question 25 **Did you have the following behaviors and symptoms?**

Circle the numbers of items that most accurately describe you in chronological order.

Items under consideration			*10s*	*20s*	*30s*	*40s*	*50s*	*60s*	*70s*
Symptom and behavior	(1)	Unbalanced diet	1	2	3	4	5	6	7
	(2)	Not eating	1	2	3	4	5	6	7
	(3)	Excessive eating (eating food of my family and eating more than one needs)	1	2	3	4	5	6	7
	(4)	Adhering to how to eat (time and order are determined)	1	2	3	4	5	6	7
	(5)	Forcing my family to eat (making them eat)	1	2	3	4	5	6	7
	(6)	Making my family conform to my life	1	2	3	4	5	6	7
	(7)	Being hyperactive and moving all day	1	2	3	4	5	6	7
	(8)	Going to far places (shopping and walking)	1	2	3	4	5	6	7
	(9)	Being resistant to disrupting my life pattern	1	2	3	4	5	6	7
	(10)	Communal life with my family becomes inconvenient	1	2	3	4	5	6	7
	(11)	Being unable to go out alone	1	2	3	4	5	6	7
	(12)	Being unable to take a job (go to school)	1	2	3	4	5	6	7
	(13)	Showing hints of self-harm and suicide	1	2	3	4	5	6	7
	(14)	Stress disorder such as PTSD resulting from experience of victimization	1	2	3	4	5	6	7
	(15)	Bipolar disorder (alternating depression and mania)	1	2	3	4	5	6	7

(*Continued*)

Question 25 (Continued)

Solutions	(16)	Consulting with my family	1	2	3	4	5	6	7
	(17)	Consulting with specialist	1	2	3	4	5	6	7
	(18)	Experience of admission	1	2	3	4	5	6	7
	(19)	Experience of discharge	1	2	3	4	5	6	7

Question 26 **Have you experienced the following?**

Circle the number of items that most accurately describe you in chronological order.

(Items are to be considered)		*10s*	*20s*	*30s*	*40s*	*50s*	*60s*	*70s*
(1)	I stole what I wanted	1	2	3	4	5	6	7
(2)	I stole to save money	1	2	3	4	5	6	7
(3)	I wanted money for playing	1	2	3	4	5	6	7
(4)	I wanted money for gambling such as Japanese pinball, mah-jongg and horseracing	1	2	3	4	5	6	7
(5)	I wanted money to buy illegal drugs	1	2	3	4	5	6	7
(6)	I had a strong urge to steal	1	2	3	4	5	6	7
(7)	I could not stop stealing though I wanted to	1	2	3	4	5	6	7
(8)	I stole deliberately	1	2	3	4	5	6	7
(9)	I felt my tension rising before stealing	1	2	3	4	5	6	7
(10)	I had a sense of satisfaction and achievement after stealing	1	2	3	4	5	6	7
(11)	I stole for anger and retaliation	1	2	3	4	5	6	7
(12)	I had a sense of guilt after stealing	1	2	3	4	5	6	7
(13)	I predetermined a target shop and item	1	2	3	4	5	6	7
(14)	I stole even though it was highly possible I'd be arrested because a policeman was nearby	1	2	3	4	5	6	7
(15)	I was aware that it is possible to be arrested if stealing was revealed	1	2	3	4	5	6	7
(16)	I was ordered or forced to steal	1	2	3	4	5	6	7

Question 27 **Have you consulted a professional medical organization and received treatment about symptoms that are difficult to treat, not about common injuries or illnesses?**

1. Yes
2. No → **(Go to Question 28 on the next page)**

Additional question: 1 We would like to ask respondents with the experience above.

(1) What was your illness?

(________ ____________, ______________ ______________)

(2) Please answer specific aspects of your illness, such as specific symptoms, the influence on your life, treatment you underwent, and the results.

[Awareness of a woman when committing the crime]

Question 28 **Did you have anyone from whom you expected the following types of support when you committed the crime?**

If you had, circle all appropriate people.

Double-circle people who supported you.

You can select as many items as you like.

Content of support		*Circle people from whom you expected support* *Double-circle people who supported you*			
		Husband Partner	*Family*	*Friend*	*Other Specialist, etc.*
(1)	Listening to me				
(2)	Giving advice				
(3)	Economically reliable				
(4)	Temporarily lending money				
(5)	Asking personal care such as nursing				
(6)	Asking help for moving, etc.				
(7)	Helping me with housework and childcare				
(8)	Emotionally supporting				
(9)	Giving necessary information				

Question 29 **Did you feel the following awareness and symptoms common in middle age women when you committed the crime?**

Circle the number of the degree that most accurately describes you.

		Applicable	*Slightly applicable*	*Yes and no*	*Slightly inapplicable*	*Totally inapplicable*
(1)	I feel myself getting out of shape more than people of the same age	1	2	3	4	5
(2)	I want to achieve more success ins my life	1	2	3	4	5
(3)	I feel worried about the death of myself and my partner (husband or boyfriend)	1	2	3	4	5
(4)	I suffer from my weight and changes in weight due to my fat belly	1	2	3	4	5
(5)	I get exhausted when doing housework (work) for a long time	1	2	3	4	5
(6)	I want to find a true life as my life is not so	1	2	3	4	5
(7)	I am nervous about spots and wrinkles on my face	1	2	3	4	5
(8)	I get tired when doing even small housework (work)	1	2	3	4	5
(9)	I want to show my ability in my work and hobby as I have not done so yet	1	2	3	4	5
(10)	I imagine how my family and relatives will behave when I die	1	2	3	4	5
(11)	I feel I am shorter on physical strength than when I was young	1	2	3	4	5
(12)	I feel sad I do not look good in clothes, shoes, and accessories I want to wear	1	2	3	4	5
(13)	I feel bad when thinking I am preceded in death by my partner (husband or boyfriend)	1	2	3	4	5
(14)	I will find a true way of living after raising my child	1	2	3	4	5
(15)	I feel my looks deteriorated compared to when I was young	1	2	3	4	5
(16)	I imagine how I will die	1	2	3	4	5
(17)	I want to take care of my work and hobby in the future as I cannot find true happiness while I am enslaved to living with my partner (husband or boyfriend)	1	2	3	4	5

Question 30 **We have the following opinions. Do you think these opinions are applicable to you when you committed the crime?**

Circle the number of the degree that most accurately describes you.

		Applicable	*Slightly applicable*	*Yes and no*	*Slightly inapplicable*	*Totally inapplicable*
(1)	I am confident in doing a plan I draw up well	1	2	3	4	5
(2)	I am slow at doing even what I have to do	1	2	3	4	5
(3)	I continue to do what I am not at first good at	1	2	3	4	5
(4)	I am not good at making friends	1	2	3	4	5
(5)	I rarely succeed in achieving an important goal I set	1	2	3	4	5
(6)	I give up doing anything before completing it	1	2	3	4	5
(7)	I visit a person I want to see before he/she comes to me	1	2	3	4	5
(8)	Avoiding encountering difficulties	1	2	3	4	5
(9)	Avoiding very perplexing problems	1	2	3	4	5
(10)	Immediately stopping becoming friends even if I want to	1	2	3	4	5
(11)	I keep on doing something uninteresting until I complete it	1	2	3	4	5
(12)	I start immediately to do anything I want to do	1	2	3	4	5
(13)	I get off on the wrong foot even if I decide to start doing something new	1	2	3	4	5
(14)	I try to become friends with someone I do not want to at first	1	2	3	4	5
(15)	I cannot cope effectively with an unexpected problem	1	2	3	4	5
(16)	I do not want to learn something that seems difficult	1	2	3	4	5
(17)	I try to do my best even when I fail	1	2	3	4	5
(18)	I cannot do well in a group	1	2	3	4	5
(19)	I become anxious about doing anything	1	2	3	4	5
(20)	I do not tend to rely on others	1	2	3	4	5
(21)	I am good at making friends by initiating conversations from my side	1	2	3	4	5
(22)	I tend to give up quickly	1	2	3	4	5
(23)	I do not think I can address many problems that occur in my life	1	2	3	4	5

[We ask you about yourself and your crime]

Circle the number of an option that most accurately describes you or put a corresponding number in ( ).

Question 1 **Birthday:** Year ( ) Month ( )

Question 2 **Date when you committed the crime:** Year ( ) Month ( )

Question 3 **Age at which you committed the crime:** Age ( )

Question 4 **Age at which you entered the prison:** Age ( )

Question 5 **Date when you entered the prison:** Month ( ), Year ( )

Question 6 **Guarantor when you came out of prison:**

1. Husband or partner
2. Brother or sister
3. Child
4. Parent
5. Employer
6. Relief and rehabilitation facility
7. Person who belongs to antisocial groups other than 1-5
8. Other ( )
9. Not decided yet
10. None

Question 7 **This time's charged offense (Circle the number of an option that most accurately describes you.)**

If you have two criminal sentences, put the second in the section labeled Two Criminal Sentences below.

1. Stealing
2. Fraud
3. Robbery
4. Violence and injury
5. Murder
6. Professional negligence (including violation of the Road Traffic Law)
7. Drug
8. Other ( )

1. Stealing
2. Fraud
3. Robbery
4. Violence and injury
5. Murder
6. Professional negligence (including violation of the Road Traffic Law)
7. Drug
8. Other ( )

1. Stealing
2. Fraud
3. Robbery
4. Violence and injury
5. Murder
6. Professional negligence (including violation of the Road Traffic Law)
7. Drug
8. Other (   )

Two criminal sentences (Select an applicable number):

______________ , ______________ , ______________ , ______________

Question 8 **Modus operandi and victim of your crime (Circle an applicable number)**

Stealing 1. Shoplifting
Stealing 2. Household burglary
Stealing 3. Stealing from car
Stealing 4. Snatching
Stealing 5. Other theft
Fraud 6. Dine and dash
Fraud 7. Other frauds
Violence and injury 8. Unknown person
Violence and injury 9. Known person
Murder 10. My child
Murder 11. Husband or partner
Murder 12. Relative
Murder 13. Other
Drug 14. Using for myself
Drug 15. Other drugs
Other

exactly:)

Question 9 **Prison term**

1. Indefinite prison term
2. (   ) year(s) and (   ) month(s) of imprisonment

If you have two criminal sentences, answer the term for the second sentence:

1. Indefinite prison term
2. (   ) year(s) and (   ) month(s) of imprisonment

Question 10 **Number of times of being thrown into prison:**

(_____) times (Write 1 if this is the first time)

Twice or more

***Additional question 1*: Charged offense when you were sent to prison the last time (one major case)** (Charged offense:)

***Additional question 2*: Last time's prison term, year of release, circumstances of release**

(1) **Prison term:** ( ) year(s) and ( ) month(s) **(2) Year of release** Year ( )
(2) **Circumstances of release**
 1. Parole
 2. Release on expiration of prison term
 3. Other

Question 11 **Age at which you committed a crime for the first time:** ( )

Question 12 **Age at which you committed a crime with which you faced imprisonment for the first time:** ( )

Question 13 **How many years have you lived in prison? If you got into prison one time, give that term. If you got into prison several times, give the total term.** ( ) year(s) and ( ) month(s) of imprisonment

Question 14 **Do you have illness?** 1. No 2. Yes (Please tell us exactly:)

Question 15 **Are you healthy now? Circle only one.**

1. Yes
2. Not so healthy, but I have no illness
3. I am prone to illness
4. I am in trouble with illness
5. I frequently receive assistance and nursing care

Question 16 **Are you prescribed any medicines?:**

1. Yes
2. No

Question 17 **Past crimes (We would like to ask what your crimes were)**

1. Stealing
2. Fraud
3. Robbery
4. Violence and injury
5. Murder
6. Professional negligence (including violation of the Road Traffic Law)
7. Drugs
8. Other (Please tell us exactly:)
9. None (This is the first time)

Question 18 **Education background:**

1. Elementary school dropout
2. Graduated from elementary school
3. Middle school dropout
4. Graduated from middle school
5. High school dropout
6. Graduated from high school
7. Two-year college and university dropout
8. Graduated from university or higher

Thank you for answering the questions.
These are the last questions.
(1) What is the most painful for you in your entire life?

When:

Please tell us exactly:

(2) What is the happiest for you in your entire life as a woman?

When:

Please tell us exactly:

(3) What is the unhappiest for you in your entire life as a woman?

When:

Please tell us exactly:

These are our questions.
Thank you for your cooperation.

- **This is not a question.**

If you have anything to tell young people as one with more experience, please feel free to write it.

Anything is okay.

Afterword

Bunri Tatsuno

Kokushikan University

While the compilation of this publication is in progress, the crime situation in Japan is still moving.

The number of senior citizens in Japan aged 65 and above is now 36.21 million, or 28.9% of the total population. The number of people aged 70 and above is 28.35 million, or 22.6% of the population, whereas the proportion of those aged 50 and above is only 0.1%. Regarding crimes, the percentage of arrests for criminal offenses by persons aged 65 and above rose to 23.6%. The percentage is particularly high among women, at 33.5%. The main crime among the elderly is theft (69.9%), mostly shoplifting (51.0%). For females, theft accounts for 89.0%, and shoplifting for 72.3%. (Statistics for 2021)

As a response to the situation surrounding these older offenders, the government has formulated the "Plan for the Promotion of Recidivism Prevention," which outlines steps to lower the rate of recurrent criminal activities through preventing recidivism. Among these measures, those aimed at reducing recidivism among older persons are thought to be focused on how to connect them with welfare support. Specifically, these measures include coordinating the admission to welfare facilities after release while the offender is still in a correctional facility and bridging the offender to welfare services at the stage of indictment deferral. There are limits to what criminal justice agencies alone can do in dealing with elderly offenders: strengthening cooperation among local governments, community life settlement support centers, the Ministry of Health, Labor and Welfare, welfare specialists, lawyers, and other relevant parties that are considered essential.

This book focuses on the situation of and efforts for elderly offenders in Japan and refers to other countries' situations from a comparative social theoretical perspective. In this analysis, we have not only considered the trends and responses of each country from a macro perspective at the national and governmental levels but also paid attention to the personal perspectives and feelings of individual offenders as human beings and their views on life. In other words, as they looked at themselves and traced the recovery process from crime, we also looked at the social, cultural, and political events behind it.

The series of studies on which this book is based includes a report by Hosoi and Pratt on a Japan-New Zealand bilateral collaboration entitled "Prisoners beyond Law and Welfare System" presented at the XV111 ISA World Congress of Sociology: Facing an Unequal World-Challenges for Global Sociology, held in Yokohama, Japan, in June 2014.

Since then, we have communicated and discussed with scientists from several countries, including Japan, Australia, the United Kingdom, Hong Kong, and others. The results were first published in Japan as "A Comprehensive Study of Crime against the Elderly" (2021, Kazama Shobo), funded by the Japan Society for the Promotion of Science (2020) to promote the publication of research results. The same book was subsequently reviewed, edited, compacted, and compiled into an English version.

We salute Ms. Keiko Kazama, President of Kazama Shobo, for all her assistance with the Japanese version. We thank Mr. Ryosuke Sasaki of CRL Inc. for the English version and his expert advice. With their help, we were able to publish this book. In addition, we are extremely grateful to Ms. Katie Peace of Routledge Publishing for her assistance. Thank you again for your cooperation.

Index

Note: **Bold** page numbers refer to tables, *italic* page numbers refer to figures and page numbers followed by "n" refer to end notes.

FSC
www.fsc.org
MIX
Papier | Fördert gute Waldnutzung
FSC® C083411

Kolibri 360 GmbH
Ferdinand-Jühlke-Straße 7
99095 Erfurt, Deutschland
produktsicherheit@kolibri360.de